THE AMERICAN

GUIDE TO

CONSUMER
LAW

Other Books by the American Bar Association

The American Bar Association Family Legal Guide
The American Bar Association Guide to Home Ownership
The American Bar Association Guide to Wills and Estates
The American Bar Association Guide to Family Law

THE AMERICAN BAR ASSOCIATION

GUIDE TO

CONSUMER LAW

Everything You Need to Know
About Buying, Selling, Contracts,
and Guarantees

TIMES BOOKS

RANDOM HOUSE

Points of view or opinions in this publication do not necessarily represent the official policies or positions of the American Bar Association.

This book is not a substitute for an attorney, nor does it attempt to answer all questions about all situations you may encounter.

Copyright © 1997 by the American Bar Association

All rights reserved under International and Pan-American Copyright Conventions. Published in the United States by Times Books, a division of Random House, Inc., New York, and simultaneously in Canada by Random House of Canada, Limited, Toronto.

Library of Congress Cataloging-in-Publication Data

The American Bar Association guide to consumer law : everything you need to know about buying, selling, contracts, and guarantees.—1st ed.
   p.   cm.
  Includes index.
  ISBN 0-8129-2347-2 (pbk.)
  1. Consumer protection—Law and legislation—United States—Popular works. 2. Contracts—United States—Popular works. 3. Warranty—United States—Popular works. I. American Bar Association.
KF1610.A468 1997
343.73'071—dc20
[347.30371]   96-21617

Random House website address: http://www.randomhouse.com/

Printed in the United States of America on acid-free paper

2 4 6 8 9 7 5 3

First Edition

CONTENTS

FOREWORD

Howard H. Vogel, *Chair*
ABA *Standing Committee on Public Education*

CONSUMER LAW AFFECTS YOU every time you buy a ticket
for the movies, pick out a cantaloupe at the grocery store, make
an airline reservation, or purchase computer software. Each of these
consumer transactions is governed and shaped by the law. Sometimes these transactions involve large sums of money—as, for example, when you buy a car, a home, or stocks and bonds. Sometimes
the initial cost may not be high, as, for example, when you buy insurance, but the stakes could be huge if you have to make a claim.
You're at a big disadvantage if you don't understand how the law
can protect you as a consumer, and how you can protect yourself,
but this book can help.

In simple, easy-to-read language, we give you guidance on how to
negotiate the best possible contract, what special contract terms to
watch out for, and how to make sure that your contract is valid. We
also discuss how you might be able to cancel contracts under certain
circumstances, and what to do if the other side is not keeping its end
of the bargain.

This book looks at all the key consumer areas, from specific laws
protecting consumers to form contracts (and what you can do about
them), buying by mail, warranties, advertising and the law, and pit-
falls to avoid as a savvy consumer. We also focus on many important types of consumer transactions: buying (or renting) a home,
buying or leasing a car, getting a credit card, purchasing insurance,
and even buying computers and software. The final section of the
book gives you contact information about dozens of organizations
that can provide free or inexpensive help to consumers.

To make this book as helpful as possible, we define all the key terms in everyday language, use plenty of examples drawn from ordinary life, and accompany the text with short articles highlighting additional points of interest.

Sometimes a problem is so complex, or so much is at stake, that you'll want to seek legal advice from someone who knows the facts of your particular case and can give you advice tailored to your situation. But this book will give you a solid grounding in consumer protection that will help you in big transactions and little ones. Armed with the information in this book, you can be sure that the actions you take will be in your best interest.

Howard H. Vogel is the managing partner of a Knoxville, Tennessee, law firm. He is a former member of the ABA Board of Governors, and he served as president of the Tennessee Bar Association from 1995 through 1996.

FOREWORD

PREFACE

■

Robert A. Stein, *Executive Director*
American Bar Association

THE AMERICAN BAR ASSOCIATION legal guides are designed to provide guidance for people on important legal questions they encounter in everyday life. When American families are asked to describe their legal needs, the topics that come up repeatedly are housing, personal finance, family and domestic concerns (usually in conjunction with divorce and child support), wills and estates, and employment-related issues. In addition, more and more Americans have questions about operating a business, often out of the home.

These are the topics that *The American Bar Association Legal Guides* cover in plain, direct language. We have made a special effort to make the books practical, by using situations and problems you are likely to encounter. The goal of these books is to give helpful information on a range of options that can be used in solving everyday legal problems, so that you can make informed decisions on how best to handle your particular question.

The American Bar Association wants Americans to be aware of the full range of options available when they are confronted with a problem that might have a "legal" solution. The Association has supported programs to eliminate delay in the courts, and has worked to promote fast, affordable alternatives to lawsuits, such as mediation, arbitration, conciliation, and small claims court. Through ABA support for lawyer referral programs and pro bono services (where lawyers donate their time), people have been able to find the best lawyer for their particular case and have received quality legal help within their budget.

The American Bar Association Legal Guides discuss all these alternatives, suggesting the wide range of options open to you. We hope that they will help you feel more comfortable with the law and will remove much of the mystery from the legal system.

Several hundred members of the Association have contributed to *The American Bar Association Legal Guides*—as authors and as reviewers who have guaranteed the guides' accuracy. To them—and to the ABA's Standing Committee on Public Education, which was the primary force behind the publications—I express my thanks and gratitude, and that of the Association and of lawyers everywhere.

Robert A. Stein is executive director of the American Bar Association. He was formerly dean of the University of Minnesota Law School.

PREFACE

THE AMERICAN BAR ASSOCIATION

GUIDE TO

CONSUMER LAW

■

CHAPTER ONE

Who, What, When, and How

How Consumer Law Fits into the Big Picture

WHO IS A CONSUMER AND WHEN?

"PROGRESS THROUGH APPLIANCES" might be a tongue-in-cheek way to describe the idea of consumer satisfaction as a national aspiration. But while it's great to be able to enjoy the fruits of your labor, you probably want more out of life than guaranteed low prices, extended warranties, and a compact disc player in every room. Consumer goods, after all, are just things, and although most Americans are privileged to enjoy a lot of things, they aren't the be-all and end-all of existence. Consumerism isn't what this book is about.

This book *is* about helping you understand the everyday transactions that make up economic life and setting out the basic rights and obligations of people playing the free-enterprise game. When you're better informed, your choices will be greater, and you'll get the most for your money. And the more able you are to protect what you earn—by spending or investing it wisely—the more opportunity you'll have to enjoy the rewards of your hard work.

Consumer law, then, is the law of everyday contracts and transactions involving individual consumers. By consumers, we mean real people acting on their own behalf, as opposed to those same real people when they are working for a business or company. Consumer law usually deals with smaller amounts of money than business law, but sometimes hundreds of thousands are at stake, considering that home buying and even investing can be categorized as consumer transactions.

HOW LAW AFFECTS CONSUMERS

What does "the law" have to do with everyday economic dealings? There is always some underlying set of rules that governs the way people deal with each other, especially when value (usually money, goods, and services) is changing hands. When you buy bread at the grocery store, you and the grocer operate under a set of unspoken expectations, based on legal principles you may never have thought about: that the bread is really bread, it's fresh, it's tasty, and it's sanitary. The person behind the counter has a set of expectations, too—mostly that the means of payment will prove to be valid (the check will clear, the credit card is authorized, the cash is real—not something you ran off on your color copier that morning).

Assuming that, like most purchases of bread, nothing goes wrong on either end, it's unlikely either of you will have to call on the law to set out whose expectations have been wrongly frustrated. But you depend on the law to guide the relationship of dealings like this and to settle any disputes. The more complex the transaction, the more law is involved.

ALTERNATIVES TO LAW

Many social groups don't rely on the kind of law we talk about here to settle disputes. In some countries, such as Japan, social pressure is the main way disputes are resolved, rather than by police, lawyers, and courts. Some social or ethnic groups have their own legal system parallel to the one we will talk about, such as religious courts.

When both parties agree to it, they are usually free to have their disputes settled by any private system. The vast majority of disputes are settled by negotiation rather than a formal court finding. **Mediation**, perhaps through a neighborhood justice center, is a process in which a third-party mediator helps the disputants reach a voluntary negotiated settlement. There are other forms of **alternative dispute resolution**, such as **arbitration**, which we will discuss later.

Contract law is the main concern of this book, but consumers' rights and obligations may also be affected by other areas of law.

- **Statutory and regulatory consumer protection.** This is the main area of noncontract law addressed in this book. Many consumer transactions and relationships are the subjects of special government laws and regulations. An important one is the **Federal Trade Commission Act,** which created (not surprisingly) the Federal Trade Commission (FTC). This government agency regulates a wide variety of consumer transactions, focusing on deceptive practices such as false advertising, phony investment schemes, and bogus health claims. (The FTC also regulates the practices of many industries, although most of these regulations are concerned with business-to-business relations.) FTC trade regulation rules come about when FTC staff find evidence of unfair or deceptive practices in an entire industry and recommend that the commission begin a rule-making proceeding, which involves hearings and written comments. FTC rules include, among many others, the **Funeral Rule,** which requires funeral directors to disclose price and other information about

---

Small claims court is a simplified civil court that exists in almost every state to resolve disputes under a certain dollar amount set by law. Strictly speaking, it's not an alternative to law, because it is governed by applicable laws and legal practices, but it is far more informal than regular court, as well as faster and less expensive.

There are two exceptions to informal settlements: **illegal contracts** (see below) are unlawful, regardless of what body tries to enforce them, and **family-law disputes,** such as divorces and child custody, are reserved for final decision by the state (although many jurisdictions encourage the parties to propose a settlement subject to court approval). Another exception is disputes "settled" by violence—even if both sides agree to it. Dueling has been illegal in all fifty states for quite some time!

---

goods and services; the **Cooling-off Rule**, which gives consumers three days to cancel sales of $25 or more made away from the seller's place of business; and the **Used Car Rule**, which requires dealers to post on each used car a "Buyers Guide," which must disclose warranty and other important information. FTC regulators have the power to take court action to stop a deceptive practice, and can also use various administrative remedies to correct a problem.

Besides the FTC Act, there are federal laws such as the **Consumer Credit Protection Act**, which includes the Truth-in-Lending Act, the Fair Debt Collection Practices Act, the Consumer Leasing Act, the Equal Credit Opportunity Act, the Electronic Funds Transfer Act, and the Fair Credit Reporting Act. You can tell what areas these laws regulate by their titles.

Many states have analogous laws, such as the "little FTC acts," by which many states have created their own versions of the FTC. One of the notable aspects of the little FTC acts, or the consumer fraud laws, is that private citizens are often authorized to recover **extra damages** (that is, more than they lost) and attorneys' fees if they show that a deceptive practice by a merchant caused them a loss. We will discuss this more in the "Remedies" section of chapter 15.

While federal law may set the standard by which businesses are expected to operate, it is often the state and local agencies that enforce state and local laws that provide relief for individuals. Because these agencies are smaller, they may be more responsive to the "little person." Moreover, the remedies provided by state and local law are often stronger and apply to more merchant practices than those under federal law.

Other areas of law, although not aimed at protecting consumers, do affect them, such as regulation of industries such as insurance, banking, and securities. We will address many of these issues as we come to them.

• **Tort law.** A **tort** is a legal wrong done by one person to another, which is not based on a contractual relationship. A common example is an auto accident in which someone is injured as a result of a driver's negligence. There is no contract between the driver and injured party but there is a legally imposed duty of care. You could conceivably be damaged beyond the scope of your contractual relationship with a seller if, for example, you tripped on a pothole in the store parking lot. In this example, though, the consumer-seller relationship is incidental to the accident. It is a general principle of contract law that the **contract**—the terms of the transaction between two parties—defines the whole relationship between them, and any dispute actually related to that contract (as opposed to out in the parking lot) will be decided under contract law only.

On the other hand, a consumer could have a tort claim if a merchant's actions are so outrageous that they go beyond any behavior that could possibly have been anticipated in the contractual relationship. Suppose the day before he was due to paint your house, and after he'd scraped off all the old paint, the housepainter cancels your contract with him, saying he can make more money on another job. You're having a graduation party at home next week and you want the house to be painted quickly, so you end up paying a higher amount to get the work done fast. As outrageous as the painter's

---

LAW IN "ACTION"

There are a number of ways to describe a court suit, a topic we will discuss in the "Remedies" section of chapter 15. One term is **lawsuit** and another is **action**, which has spawned such terms as **legal action** and **court action**. For all practical purposes, these terms mean the same thing: When you sue someone, you have begun an **adversary proceeding**—a hearing pitting one party against another—presided over by a judge, who decides all legal issues, and a "fact-finder"—a judge or jury who decides all fact issues. The relatively few lawsuits that are not settled reach their ultimate conclusion at a trial, but technical proceedings (often many) must take place before a case is tried. In noncriminal (**civil**) cases, if the parties involved go through the whole trial, the party being sued is found **liable** or not liable. The terms **guilty** and **not guilty** do not apply in civil cases.

---

actions sound, your damages would be limited to your additional cost for the second painter. If, however, the first painter not only cancelled your contract but glued all the paint he had scraped off back onto the house—gluing all your windows shut in the process—you probably would have a tort action against the painter for damaging your house. Besides extreme examples such as these, which involve personal injuries or physical damage to property, tort law is not usually a source of relief for aggrieved consumers.

• **Criminal law.** Some behavior involving consumer transactions can be **criminal**—that is, the person who does them is subject to serious fines or prison. Fraud is a crime, although it is rarely prosecuted unless it affects many people or is very large in scope. There are also specialized areas of government regulation of concern to consumers, which can give rise to criminal liability, such as the sale of securities and insurance. A criminal prosecution might not benefit the consumer who was defrauded. Sometimes a person convicted of a crime is ordered by a court to make **restitution**, that is, to pay back the people who were harmed by his or her crimes, but often the money is long gone by then. Criminal law is beyond the scope of this book.

• **Property law.** There are two kinds of property law. What lawyers generally mean when they use the term is the law regarding **real property**, or real estate—land and buildings. There are many specialties within property law, such as zoning and land use. But to the extent property law is relevant to consumers, property law is merely a form of contract law. This kind of property law is discussed in chapter 7 on home buying and chapter 11 on residential leases.

The second kind of property law deals with **personal property** (any tangible thing a person can own besides real estate). Much contract law, of course, is about transactions involving personal property.

• **Business and corporation law.** Business and corporation law is highly technical and usually is not concerned with consumers' rights. Its main concern is the formation of different kinds of business entities, the transactions they engage in, and finance. Corporations and some other forms of businesses are fictional **persons** created by the law precisely to allow their owners (stockholders, limited partners, etc.) to avoid personal liability or legal responsibility for the business's debts and actions. Each state has strict laws concerning corporations, limited liability companies, real estate trusts, limited liability partnerships, and other business entities, including rules about how and when out-of-state entities may do business in that state. Your ability to get relief against an entity that has injured you or your rights may depend on its form, its place of business, and, in a contract, what the contract says about when and how you may sue the entity. We will discuss these issues as we come to them.

• **Constitutional and civil rights law.** Many legal doctrines protect people from unlawful discrimination, even in consumer transactions. Gone are the days when public places such as eateries, buses, and trains were segregated by race. In consumer transactions, you have the right not to be discriminated against on the basis of sex, marital status, race, or national origin. The same goes for equal opportunity in employment. But this highly technical area is beyond the scope of consumer law and is best handled by a lawyer.

Now that we have a sense of what "kind" of law consumer law is, we will spend a couple of chapters on the main part of it, contract law, and learn some of the basics.

■

CHAPTER TWO

Fundamentals of Contract Law

How to Know When You've "Got a Deal"

WHAT IS A CONTRACT?

Having an appreciation for the fundamental principles of contract law will enable you to answer many of your own questions about everyday consumer transactions and enhance your ability to use other parts of this book.

A **contract** consists of voluntary promises, enforceable by the law, between competent parties to do, or not to do, something. These binding promises may be oral or written. Depending on the situation, a contract could obligate someone even if he or she wants to call the deal off before receiving anything from the other side. The details of the contract—who, what, how, how much, how many, when, etc.—are called its **provisions** or **terms**.

You don't need a lawyer to form a contract. If you satisfy the maturity and mental capacity requirements discussed below, you don't need anyone else (besides the other party). But it's probably a good idea to see a lawyer before you sign complex contracts such as business deals or contracts involving large amounts of money.

For a promise to qualify as a contract, it must be supported by the exchange of something of value between the participants, or parties. This something is called **consideration**. Consideration is most often money given in exchange for property or services, but it can be some other bargained-for benefit or detriment (as explained below). The final qualification for a contract is that the subject of the promise (including the consideration) may not be illegal.

For example: Suppose a friend agrees to buy your car, an Edsel in less-than-mint condition, for $1,000. That is the promise. The money is the consideration for the sale. You benefit by getting the cash. Your friend benefits by getting the Edsel. Because it is your car, the sale is legal, and you and your friend have a contract.

CAPACITY

Not just anyone can enter into a contract. For the contract to be enforceable, the parties involved must be able to understand what they're doing. That requires both **maturity** and **mental capacity**. Without both of these, one party could be at a disadvantage in the bargaining process, which could invalidate the contract.

In this sense maturity is defined as a certain age a person reaches, regardless of whether he or she is in fact "mature." State laws permit persons to make contracts if they have reached the **age of majority** (the end of being a minor), which is usually eighteen.

That doesn't mean minors can't make contracts, by the way. But courts may choose not to enforce them. The law presumes that minors need to be protected from their lack of maturity and won't

---

CONTRACT LANGUAGE

A valid contract does not have to be a printed, legalistic-looking document. Nor does it have to be called a contract. A typed or even handwritten "agreement," "letter of agreement," or "letter of understanding" signed by the parties will be valid if it meets the legal requirements of a contract. Don't sign something assuming it's not a contract and therefore not important.

It is also common for the word "contract" to be used as a verb meaning "to enter into a contract." And we speak of **contractual relationships** to refer to the whole of sometimes complex relationships or transactions that may comprise one or many contracts.

---

allow, for example, a Porsche salesperson to exploit a minor's naiveté by enforcing a signed sales contract whose real implications a young person is unlikely to have comprehended. Sometimes this results in minors receiving benefits (such as goods or services) and not having to pay for them, although they would have to return any goods still in their possession. This applies even to minors who are **emancipated**—living entirely on their own—who become involved in contractual relationships as well as minors who live at home but are unsupervised long enough to get into a contractual fix.

A court may require a minor or his or her parents to pay the fair market value (not necessarily the contract price) for what courts call **necessaries** (what you and I would likely call "necessities"). The definition of a "necessary" depends entirely on the person and the situation. It will probably always include food and will probably never include CDs, Nintendo cartridges, or Porsches. Minors who reach full age and do not disavow their contracts may then have to

---

CAPACITY

We've discussed the fundamental requirements for competence to make a contract—maturity and mental capacity. Of course it should go without saying that there's an even more fundamental requirement: that both parties be people. In the case of a corporation or other legal entity, which the law considers a "person," this could be an issue. A problem in the formation or status of the entity could cause it to cease to exist legally, thus making it impossible to enter into a contract. In that case, however, the individuals who signed the contract on behalf of the legally nonexistent entity could be personally liable for fulfilling the contract.

Historically the law has had other criteria for capacity. Slaves, married women, and convicts were at one time not considered capable of entering into contracts in most states. Even today, certain American Indians are regarded as **wards** of the U.S. government for many purposes, and their contract-law status is similar to that of minors.

---

comply with all the contract terms, and in some states courts may require a minor to pay the fair value of goods or services purchased and received under a contract that the minor has disavowed.

There are other people besides minors who may not be able to form enforceable contracts. While the age test for legal maturity is easy to determine, the standards for determining mental capacity are remarkably complex and differ widely from one state to another. One common test is whether someone had the capacity to understand what he or she was doing and to appreciate its effects when the deal was made. Another approach is evaluating whether someone has self-control, regardless of his or her understanding.

That brings up the question of whether an intoxicated person can be held to a contract. Very often someone who is "under the influence" can get out of a contract. The courts don't like to let a voluntarily intoxicated person revoke a contract with innocent parties this way, but if the evidence shows that someone acted drunk when making a contract, a court may well assume that the other party probably was trying to take advantage. On the other hand, if someone doesn't appear to be intoxicated he or she probably will have to follow the terms of the contract. (In this area the key may be a person's medical history. Someone who can show a history of alcohol abuse, blackouts, and the like may be able to void the contract, regardless of his or her appearance when the contract is made. This is true especially if the other party involved knew about the prior medical history.)

WRITTEN AND ORAL CONTRACTS

Some people mistakenly believe that an oral contract "isn't worth the paper it's printed on." But many types of contracts don't have to be written to be enforceable. An example is purchasing an item in a retail store. You pay money in exchange for an item that the store warrants (by implication, as discussed later) will perform a certain function. Your receipt is proof of the contract.

As with a written contract, the existence of an oral contract must be proved before the courts will enforce it. But as you can imagine, an oral contract can be very hard to prove—you seldom have it on video. An oral contract is usually proved by showing that outside circumstances would lead a reasonable observer to conclude that a contract most likely existed. Even then, there is always the problem of what the terms of the oral contract were.

Although most states recognize and enforce oral contracts, the safest practice is to put substantial agreements in writing. Get any promise from a salesperson or an agent in writing, especially if there already is a written document that might arguably be a contract covering any part of the same deal. If the court concludes that the parties intended the written document—a handwritten "letter of agreement" or "understanding," or even an order form—to contain all its terms and be a complete statement of all understandings between the parties, then the court will be very hesitant to add words or terms to the document. This is the important **parol evidence rule**, under which courts typically look only to **unrefuted** (uncontested) testimony to help them "fill in the blanks" of a contract. Anything not in that written contract would be deemed not to be part of the deal.

Writing down the terms of a good-faith agreement is the best way to ensure that all parties are aware of their rights and duties—even if no party intends to lie about the provisions of the agreement.

Having said that, know that there are some contracts that are completely unenforceable if they're not in writing. This requirement, which exists in varying forms in nearly all the states, had its origins in the famous **statute of frauds**, an English law dating from 1677. It refers to "frauds" because it attempts to prevent fraudulent testimony in support of nonexistent agreements. In most states, the courts will enforce certain contracts only if they are in writing and are signed by the parties who are going to be obligated to fulfill them. These contracts often include:

- any promise to be responsible for someone else's debts—often called a **surety contract** or a **guaranty** (for example, an agreement by parents to guarantee payment of a loan made by a bank to their child);

- any promise, made with consideration, to marry (although this rule has been eliminated in many states);

- any promise that the parties cannot possibly fulfill within one year from when they made the promise;

- any promise involving the change in ownership of or interests in land, such as leases;

- any promise to pay a broker a commission for the sale of real estate;

- any promise for the sale of goods worth more than $500 or lease of goods worth more than $1,000 (amounts may vary from state to state);

- any promise to **bequeath** property (give it after death);

- any promise to sell stocks and bonds (this provision is eliminated in some states).

Some states have additional requirements for written contracts. These statutes are designed to prevent fraudulent claims in areas in which it is uniquely difficult to prove that oral contracts have been made or where important policies are at stake, such as the dependability of real estate ownership rights. Promises to extend credit are often in this category. One typical area of state regulation is automobile repairs; many states require that estimates for repair work be given in writing. If they aren't, and the repair is done anyway, the contract may not be enforceable. The repair shop may not be able to get its money if the customer disputes authorizing the repairs.

When a written contract is required, a signature by the **party to be charged**—that is, the person whom the other party wants to hold to the contract—is also necessary. A signature can be handwritten, but a stamped, photocopied, or engraved signature is often valid as well, as are signatures written by electronic pens. Even a simple mark or other indication of a name may be enough. What matters is whether the signature is authorized and intended to authenticate a writing, that is, indicate the signer's **execution** (completion and acceptance) of it. That means that you can authorize someone else to sign for you as well. But the least risky and most persuasive evidence of assent is your own handwritten signature.

Incidentally, hardly any contracts require notarization today. Notary publics or notaries, once important officials who were specially authorized to draw up contracts and transcribe official proceedings, now act mostly to administer oaths and authenticate documents by attesting or certifying that a signature is genuine. Many commercial contracts, such as promissory notes or loan contracts, are routinely notarized with the notary's signature and seal to ensure that they are authentic, even when this is not strictly required. Many technical documents required by law, such as certificates of incorporation and real property deeds, must be notarized if they are to be recorded in a local or state filing office.

OFFER AND ACCEPTANCE

Offer and acceptance are the fundamental parts of a contract, once capacity is established. An **offer** is a communication by an offeror of a present intention to enter a contract. (The **offeror** is the person making the offer.) It is not simply an invitation to bargain or negotiate. For the communication to be effective, the **offeree** (the one who is receiving the offer) must receive it. In a contract to buy and sell, for an offer to be valid all of the following must be clear:

- Who is making the offer?
- What is the subject matter of the offer?
- How many/much of the subject matter does the offer involve (quantity)?
- How much is offered (price)?

Let's say you told your friend, "I'll sell you my mauve-colored Edsel for $1,000." You're making the offer, your friend is receiving it, and the car is the subject matter. Describing the car as a mauve Edsel makes your friend reasonably sure that both of you are talking about the same car (and only one of them). Finally, the price is $1,000. It's a perfectly good offer.

Advertisements are not offers, much as they may seem like it.

Instead, courts usually consider advertisements an "expression of intent to sell" or an invitation to bargain. We will discuss this further in chapter 5.

An offer doesn't stay open indefinitely, unless the offeree has an **option**, which is an irrevocable offer (discussed below). Otherwise, an offer ends when:

- the time to accept is up—either a "reasonable" amount of time or the deadline stated in the offer;
- the offeror cancels (revokes) the offer;
- the offeree rejects the offer; or
- the offeree dies or is incapacitated.

An offer is also closed, even if the offeree has an option, if:

- a change in the law makes the contract illegal; or
- the subject matter of the contract is destroyed (see below).

Note that there are special kinds of contracts called **option contracts**. An option contract is an agreement, made for consideration, to keep an offer open for a certain period. For example, in return for $50 today, you might agree to give your friend until next Friday to accept your offer to sell her your Edsel for $1,000. Now you have an option contract. The money is not a down payment or a deposit but the price of the option. Selling an option puts a limit on your ability to revoke an offer, a limit that the **optionee** (the option-holder) bargains for with you in return for the $50.

GIVE AND TAKE

A contract can only come about through the bargaining process, which may take many forms. This chapter discusses the definitions of consideration, offer, and acceptance. All the principles discussed here will have to be present, in some form, in any contract.

ACCEPTANCE

A contract is not complete unless an offer is accepted. But what exactly constitutes the acceptance of an offer? **Acceptance** is the offeree's voluntary, communicated agreement or assent to the terms and conditions of the offer. **Assent** is an act or promise of agreement. An easy example of an assent might be your friend saying, "I agree to buy your mauve Edsel for $1,000."

Generally, a valid acceptance requires that every material term agreed on be the same as in the offer. In addition, if the offer requires acceptance by mail, you must accept by mail for the offer to be effective. Be aware that under the **mailbox rule**, an offer accepted by mail is usually effective when you put the letter in the mailbox, *not* when it is received, unless the terms for acceptance state otherwise. If there is no such requirement, you must communicate your acceptance by some reasonable means (not by carrier pigeon, smoke signals, or channeling but by telephone, mail, or facsimile). On the other hand, an assent that is not quite so specific but crystal-clear in its meaning would also suffice, such as in the Edsel example, saying, "It's a deal. I'll pick it up tomorrow." The standard is whether a reasonable observer would think there was an assent.

In most cases silence does not constitute acceptance of an offer. It isn't fair to allow someone to impose a contract on you unless you go out of your way to stop it. Hence your cable TV company cannot force a contract for additional services on you simply because you failed to reject its offer. Yet there are circumstances in which failure to respond may have a contractual effect. Past dealings between the parties, for example, can create a situation in which silence constitutes acceptance. Suppose a fire insurance company, according to past practice to which you have assented, sends you a renewal policy (which is in effect a new contract for insurance) and bills you for the premium. If you kept the policy but later refused to pay the premium, you would be liable for the premium. This works to everyone's benefit: If your house burned down after the original insurance policy had expired but before you had paid the renewal premium, you obviously would want the policy still to be effective. And the insurer is protected from your deciding to pay the premium only when you know you have sustained a casualty loss.

On the other hand, speechless acts *can* constitute an acceptance. Any conduct that would lead a reasonable observer to believe that the offeree had accepted the offer qualifies as an acceptance. Suppose you say, "Ed, I will pay you $50 to clean my garage on Sunday at nine A.M." If Ed shows up at nine A.M. on Sunday and begins cleaning, he adequately shows acceptance (assuming you're home or you otherwise would know he showed up).

As another example, you don't normally have to pay for goods shipped to you that you didn't order (a subsequent section discusses

---

THE REASONABLE PERSON

Throughout this and any other law book, the word "reasonable" will appear many times. Very often you'll see references to the **reasonable man** or the **reasonable person**. Why is the law so preoccupied with this mythical being?

The answer is that no contract can possibly predict the infinite number of disputes that might arise under it. Similarly, no set of laws regulating liability for personal or property injury can possibly foresee the countless ways human beings and their property can harm other people or property. Because the law can't provide for every possibility, it has developed the standard of the "reasonable person" to furnish some uniform standards and guide the courts.

Through the fiction of the "reasonable person," the law creates a standard that the judge or jury may apply to each set of circumstances. It is a standard that reflects community values rather than the judgment of the people involved in the actual case. Thus, a court might decide whether an oral contract was formed by asking whether a "reasonable person" would conclude from people's actions that one did exist. Or the court might decide an automobile accident case by asking what a "reasonable person" might have done in a particular traffic or hazard situation.

---

this in more detail). You otherwise would only have to allow them to be taken back at no cost. But if you owned a shop and you put them on display in your store and sold them, you would have accepted the offer to buy them from the wholesaler and you would be obligated to pay the invoice. Sometimes this is called an **implied** (as opposed to an **express**) contract. Either one is a genuine contract.

A contract usually is "in effect" as soon as the offeree transmits or communicates the acceptance—unless the offer has expired or the offeror has specified that the acceptance must be *received* before it is effective or before an option expires (as discussed previously). In these situations there's no contract until the offeror receives the answer and in the way specified, if any.

CONDITIONS

Most contracts have conditions. People often use the word "condition" to mean one of the terms of a contract. But a more precise definition is that a **condition** is an event that must occur before one or both parties must perform.

NONACCEPTANCE

An **agreement to agree** is seldom a contract, because it suggests that important terms are still missing. Rarely will a court supply those terms itself. An agreement to agree is another way of saying that there has not yet been a meeting of the minds, although the parties would like there to be.

Another common question people have, funny as it sounds, is whether a joke can be an offer. That depends on whether a reasonable observer would know it's a joke and on whether the acceptance was adequate. In our Edsel example, you probably couldn't get out of the contract by saying, "How could you think I'd sell this for $1,000? I meant it as a joke!" On the other hand, if someone sued you because you "backed out" on your "promise" to sell her France for $15, the joke would be on her—no one could have reasonably thought you were serious.

A condition can be a promise. For example, if your friend from our earlier case had said, "I'll buy your mauve Edsel only if you deliver it to me by midnight," and you accept that condition, you have both promised delivery by midnight and made that a condition of the contract.

On the other hand, many conditions involve uncertain events not under the direct control of the parties to the contract. Thus, neither of them can promise anything about the condition, but the conditions must still be fulfilled for the contract to go forward. Examples are conditioning a home purchase on obtaining financing, the sale of the buyer's present home, or an acceptable home inspection report.

CONSIDERATION

For a contract to exist, both sides must give some consideration. A crucial principle in contract law is **mutuality of obligations**. This means that both sides must be committed to giving up something or doing something. If either party reserves an unqualified right to bail out, that person's promise is illusory: it is no promise at all.

IN CONSIDERATION

The doctrine that consideration is critical to formation of a contract came about in the last few centuries. Until then elaborate formality rather than consideration was the chief requirement. The necessary formalities were a sufficient signed writing, a seal or other attestation of authenticity, and delivery to whomever would have the rights under the contract. A seal could be an impression on wax or some other surface, bearing the mark (often found on a signet ring) of the person making the promise. The vestiges of the seal remain in some contracts, where the initials "L.S." (for the Latin *locus sigilli,* "place of the seal") or simply the word "seal," is printed to represent symbolically the authentication of the contract's execution. Even today, traditional Jewish wedding contracts are made on these formal bases: a writing by the groom, an attestation by witnesses, then delivery (also witnessed) to the bride.

No minimum amount of consideration is required to effect a contract. A price is only how people agree to value something, so there's no absolute standard of whether a price is fair or reasonable. The courts presume that people will only make deals that they consider worthwhile. So if you make a contract to sell your car for $1, a court will probably enforce it. (But don't sell it for $1,000 and report only a one-dollar sale to the state to avoid paying the full sales tax. It's unethical, illegal, and dangerous: many states have systems in place to check for just such abuses.) The exception is something that would "shock the conscience of the court." The idea of unconscionability will be discussed later in this book on page 37.

Consideration is any promise, act, or transfer of value that induces a party to enter a contract. Consideration is a bargained-for benefit or advantage or a bargained-for detriment or disadvantage. A benefit might be receiving $10. An advantage might be getting first dibs on Super Bowl tickets. A disadvantage may involve promising not to do something, such as a promise not to sue someone. For these purposes, even quitting smoking, done with the reasonable expectation of some reward or benefit from someone else, is regarded as a detriment: even though it's good for your health, quitting smoking cost you effort that you otherwise would not have made. Even if it were effortless, your commitment to forbear from engaging in lawful conduct would still constitute consideration.

For example, you could agree to give your car to your friend in exchange for her promise that she'll stop letting her schnauzer out late at night. Your friend is giving up what is presumably her right to let her dog out any time she wants. In return you are giving up that Edsel. Other types of consideration include a promise to compromise in an existing dispute.

Consideration has to be a *new* obligation, because someone who promises to do what he or she is already obligated to do hasn't suffered any detriment or bestowed anything the other party wasn't already entitled to.

For example, suppose you agree to have a contractor paint your house this Thursday for $500. Before starting, though, his workers demand higher wages. On Wednesday night he tells you that he settled the strike, but now the job will cost $650. You need the house painted before you leave town on Friday and there's no time to hire another contractor, so you agree to the new price.

But the new "agreement" (the new price) is not enforceable by him. Under the original contract, he already was required to paint your house for $500. He should have figured the possible increased costs into the original price. You didn't get anything of benefit from the modified contract, because you already had his promise to paint the house. There is no new contract because there is no new consideration. Therefore, you only owe $500—the old agreement remains in effect. Along the same lines, police officers are never entitled to receive reward money posted for catching fugitives or turning in information leading to someone's conviction. That's their job.

Just because consideration has to be new doesn't mean a contract can never be voluntarily renegotiated. It only means that no one can force another party to renegotiate by taking advantage of an existing agreement. In the housepainting example, you may agree to a renegotiation even though it would technically not be enforceable. Perhaps you think the painter "deserved" more than he had agreed to take, or you want to maintain a good relationship with him. (Considerations like these are what motivate many sports teams to renegotiate their stars' salaries. Although they have no legal obligation to do so, they nonetheless may decide to keep their stars "happy.")

While it's true that you can go to the other party and ask for more money, keep in mind that whenever you become involved in a deal, you are taking a risk that it might be less beneficial for you than you planned when you agreed to the contract terms. The other party doesn't have to ensure your profit unless the two of you included that in your bargain.

Based on the rule of consideration, a promise to make a gift is not usually enforceable if it truly is only a promise to make a gift, because a gift lacks the two-sided obligation discussed above. But if the person promising the gift is asking for anything in return, even by implication, a contract may be formed. The key, again, is consideration.

RELIANCE

We said earlier that consideration is a two-way street, and that both parties must get something for a contract to be formed. There is an exception to that rule. Sometimes a contract will be formed by the reliance of one party on another person's promise, even if the one making the promise hasn't gained anything. The concept of **reliance** is that a contract may be formed if one party reasonably relies on the other's promise. That means that he or she does more than expect to receive what was promised. He or she must do something that wouldn't have been done or fail to do something that would have been done but for the promise. If that reliance causes some loss, he or she may have an enforceable contract.

Suppose that rich Aunt Alice loves your kids. On previous occasions she has asked you to buy them expensive presents and has reimbursed you for them. This past summer she told you she would like you to build a swimming pool for the kids and send her the bill. You did so, but moody Aunt Alice changed her mind. Now she refuses to pay for the pool and claims you can't enforce a promise to make a gift. The pool, however, is no longer considered a gift. You acted to your detriment in reasonable reliance on her promise by taking on the duty to pay for a swimming pool you would not normally have built. Aunt Alice has to pay if you prove that she induced you to build the pool, especially if this understanding was consistent with many previous gifts. Remember, however, that you still have to live with your aunt Alice.

AGENTS

You can have someone enter into a contract on your behalf, but only with your permission. The law refers to such an agreement as **agency**. We couldn't do business without it. For example, when you buy a car, you bargain and finally cut a deal with the salesperson. But she doesn't own the car she's selling you. She might not even have a car. She is an **agent**, someone with the authority to bind someone else— in this case, the car dealership—by contract. The law refers to that someone else as the **principal**. Most salespeople you deal with are agents.

As long as agents do not exceed the authority granted them by their principals, the contracts they make bind their principals as if the principals had made the contracts themselves. If something went wrong with the contract, you would sue the principal—not the agent—if you couldn't resolve the dispute in a friendly manner. An agent normally does not have any personal obligation.

While acting on behalf of principals, agents are required to put their own interests after those of the principal. Therefore, they may not personally profit beyond what the principal and agent have agreed to in their agency contract. That means they cannot take advantage of any opportunity which, under the terms of the agency, should be exploited for the principal.

When an agent exceeds her authority, a number of factors determine whether the contract can be enforced against the principal. Under the doctrine of **apparent authority**, if the person she's dealing with doesn't reasonably understand that she's exceeding her authority, the principal may be bound by the contract negotiated by the agent. If the other person was not being reasonable in believing that the agent was acting within her authority, the contract will only be enforceable against the principal if the principal has knowingly permitted the agent to do this sort of thing in the past.

What is reasonable belief in the scope of the agent's authority? Suppose the teenage boy wearing a service-station uniform who fills your gas tank and checks your oil—and who appears to be an agent,

---

AGENTS WHO EXCEED THEIR AUTHORITY

On occasion, while making a contract an agent might exceed the authority granted by the principal. An example might involve an automobile salesperson who signs a contract on behalf of a car dealer, which, without the dealer's authority, gives the customer a warranty for an extra forty thousand miles. In that case the dealer might very well be bound by the contract.

---

to some limited degree, of the service station—offers to sell you the whole service station in return for the sleek mauve Edsel you're driving. It's not reasonable for you to assume he has that power when common sense tells you he can only sell you his boss's gasoline and oil for a fixed price.

In contrast, if an insurance agent wrote you an insurance policy from her company that exceeded the policy amount she was authorized to write but the insurer never told you this, you would be acting reasonably to assume she was authorized, and you probably would be entitled to collect on a claim above her limit.

DELEGATIONS AND ASSIGNMENTS

You can transfer your duties under a contract to someone else unless the contract specifically prohibits such a transfer. The law refers to a transfer of duties or responsibilities as a **delegation**. But if someone contracts with you because of a special skill or talent only you have, you may not be able to transfer your duty. Such cases are quite rare. There are arguably no car mechanics who are so good at tuning an engine that they may not delegate someone else to do it for them, unless they specifically promise to do it themselves. On the other hand, if you hire specific entertainers to perform at your wedding, they may not send other entertainers (no matter how talented) as substitutes without your permission.

A transfer of rights, called an **assignment**, is more flexible than a transfer of duties. For example, you may wish to transfer the right to receive money from a buyer for something you have sold. Generally, a contract right is yours to do as you wish with it, as long as you didn't agree in the contract not to assign the right. You can sell it or give it away, although most states require you to put an assignment in writing, especially if it is a gift.

There are exceptions to the rule that assignments may be made freely. If an assignment would substantially increase the risk or materially change the duty of the other party to the contract, the contract may not be assignable, even if its terms contain no explicit agreement to the contrary. Such an assignment would be regarded as unfairly upsetting the expectations the other party had when he or she entered the contract, so that party would no longer be obligated by the terms of the contract.

For example, suppose you made a contract for fire insurance on a garage for your Edsel. Then a notorious convicted arsonist and insurance cheat contacted you upon release from prison and asked you to sell him the garage and assign him your rights under the garage's fire insurance policy. You would probably both be in for a disappointment, even if the insurance policy didn't prohibit assignment. Because the insurer's decision to insure was made in part based on your solid citizenship, insuring the arsonist would greatly increase the insurer's burden by exposing the insurer to a risk it never anticipated.

We've discussed some very basic ideas in contracts. But this is only half the story. The next chapter deals with situations where a contract may be unenforceable even when the elements of capacity, offer, acceptance, and consideration are present, but something fundamentally unfair or illegal is going on.

◼

CHAPTER THREE

Bars to a Contract

How to Know When It's "No Deal"

W HEN IS A CONTRACT NOT A CONTRACT? In the last chapter we discussed what you need to make a contract. Now we'll consider what kinds of things could still prevent a legally enforceable contract from being formed. These are often described as **contract defenses**. You should understand them, because if one or more contract defenses is present and provable, you might be in much better shape if you're having trouble with the terms of a "deal" you thought you were stuck with.

ILLEGALITY

Illegal contracts—such as a "contract" on someone's life—are not enforceable. The courts will not help someone collect an illegal gambling debt or payment for illegal drugs or prostitution. The law treats these contracts as if they never existed—they are **unenforceable** or **void**. This is the contract defense of illegality.

Similarly, some contracts that are not specifically outlawed nonetheless will not be enforced if a court determines that enforcement would violate public policy. An example would be a contract to become a slave, which may not be prohibited by a specific statute but offends the law's view of what kinds of contracts society will permit.

In some situations a contract was legal when entered into, but the law changes before it is executed by all parties. Generally speaking, the Constitution forbids lawmakers from passing laws that would impair the rights people bargain for in contracts, but law books are filled with exceptions to this general rule. Therefore, a contract is usually considered by courts in light of the law that applied at the time the contract was made—*unless the change in the law involves a compelling public policy.*

The key, then, is whether the new law reflects an important public policy. Here's an example of a law that did not involve such a policy. A property owner leased a right-of-way to a railroad. A contract between the railroad and the owner provided that the railroad was not responsible for any fire damage to the property caused by locomotives. Later the state legislature required certain precautions against fire damaging an adjoining property. The court held that

---

IS IT OR ISN'T IT A CONTRACT?

You now know that a contract has to be made between willing, competent parties. Also, the contract must concern a legal subject matter. The preceding chapter discussed many aspects of consideration.

But applying these principles isn't always easy. Sometimes special protections in the law complicate matters. If successfully invoked, only one of these may be needed to provide a complete defense against someone claiming you owe him or her money or something else you supposedly promised. It would prompt a court to resolve the dispute as if there never were a contract. Because the contract is void, neither party may enforce its terms in court against the other.

Other contracts are **voidable** but not automatically **void**. What's the difference? A contract produced by fraud is not automatically void. People who are victimized by fraud may have the choice of asking a court to declare the contract void or to **reform** (rewrite) it. On the other hand, if they went along with the contract for a substantial period of time, they could lose their right to get out of it. This is called **ratification**, based on the idea that they have, by their actions, made it clear that they are able to live with the terms. A checklist of contract defenses appears in this chapter.

---

even if that law would have made the contract illegal (because it didn't include the newly required precautions), because it was passed after the contract was made, the law did not affect the contract.

Typically, however, courts say that because of a change in *public policy* as a result of the change in the law, they will not enforce the old contract. Obviously, a contract to sell someone a slave could not be enforced after slavery became illegal; neither could you enforce a contract to purchase a banned weapon that was made before the ban went into effect. This works both ways: a contract that was illegal when made usually will not be enforced, even though it would be legal if entered into today. After World War II one party wanted to enforce a contract entered into during the war that violated wartime price controls. The court ruled that a contract that was so damaging to the public good when made (and when no change in the law was anticipated) should never be enforced. To do so would have been to provide an incentive to enter into illegal contracts in the hope that they will someday be enforceable—a bad prescription for public policy.

Remember that an illegal contract is different from an immoral contract. The courts will only enforce a moral code that the law (or public policy) already reflects, such as laws against prostitution or stealing. You may feel that X-rated movies or fur coats are immoral, but as long as they're legal, they can be the subjects of enforceable contracts.

DURESS

You don't usually have to worry about being held to a contract that you "entered into" against your will. A contract that someone agrees to under duress is void. **Duress** is a threat or act that overcomes free will. The classic case of duress is a contract signed by someone "with a gun to his head." That means *literally*. Because this kind of duress is very rare—and often very hard to prove—the defense of duress is rarely successful.

Duress is more than persuasion or hard selling. Persuasion in bargaining is perfectly legal. It also isn't duress when your friend says, "I would never pay that much for an Edsel if I had a choice." She does have a choice: buy a nice Taurus instead. But if she wants that mauve Edsel, she "has to" pay what the owner demands. In contrast, duress involves actual coercion, such as a threat of violence or imprisonment.

Besides threats of physical violence, it may be duress to threaten to abuse the court system to coerce your agreement, i.e., to tell someone that "I'll tie you up in litigation for ten years." There is also economic duress. That was alluded to earlier when the contractor demanded more money after his workers went on strike and you needed your house painted before you left town. This isn't the same as "driving a hard bargain." Rather, the contractor had already made a deal. When the contractor threatened to withhold his part of the deal, he left you with no practical choice but to agree. The classic case is where the supplier of a necessary ingredient or material threatens, on short notice and at a critical time, not to deliver it—in violation of an existing contract—unless he or she gets more favorable terms. Courts have set aside contracts made under such economic duress.

A lawyer can tell you how to protect yourself, helping you determine whether you have assumed any obligation and what legal rights you might have besides disavowing the contract. With duress it's important to act quickly, because the courts are especially skeptical of a claim of duress made long after the danger has passed.

WHEN SOMEONE FORCES YOU TO SIGN

Between the defenses of duress and undue influence, you should never have to fear a court holding you liable for a contract that someone forces you to sign. Both concepts are hard to define, though, and people often use them interchangeably. Their limits also vary from one state to another. If you think either might apply to an agreement you want to get out of, see a lawyer.

UNDUE INFLUENCE

There are other uses of unfair pressure, less severe than duress, that void a contract. One contract defense is called **undue influence**, which doesn't involve a threat. Rather it's the unfair use of a relationship of trust to pressure someone into an unbalanced contract. Undue influence usually involves someone who starts out at a disadvantage, perhaps due to illness, age, or emotional vulnerability. The other person often has some duty to look out for the weaker one's interests.

An example would be an adult child who "persuades" his elderly, failing mother to sell him the family homestead for a pittance. The sale contract would be unenforceable because of undue influence, regardless of whether the mother otherwise had the capacity to make a contract.

FRAUD

A contract can also be canceled by a court because of fraud. **Fraud** is when one person knowingly makes a material misrepresentation that the other person reasonably relied on and that disadvantaged that other person. A **material misrepresentation** is an untrue statement that is important to the deal, meaning it would affect the terms you'd agree to if you knew the truth. In many states this misrepresentation doesn't have to be made intentionally to make the contract voidable.

Consider our earlier example involving a car sale. You offered to sell your Edsel to a friend. Suppose you knew it had no transmission, and you knew she wanted it for the usual purpose of driving it. You told her it was working fine, and she relied on your statement. Then the contract you made may be set aside on the grounds of fraud.

There is no issue of the statement being merely the seller's opinion or exaggerated "sales talk" or puffery that people know not to believe literally. You didn't merely say it was a great car when it really was a mediocre car. Saying it's "great" is just an opinion, whereas fraud requires an outright lie or a substantial failure to state a material fact about an important part of the contract. For that reason—and because dishonest people often know well the fine line between fraud and puffing—actual fraud that will invalidate a contract is a lot less common than people think.

MISTAKE

Sometimes it seems unfair to hold parties to a contract they entered into by mistake, but this is a slender reed indeed on which to seek to void a contract. The other party's fraud is very different from your mistake, assuming the other party didn't know about your mistake. The defense of **unilateral mistake** is almost impossible to prove, even if the mistake is about the most important terms of the contract. If allowed liberally, it would lead to a lot of abuse. People would claim they made a mistake to get out of a contract they didn't like, even though they had no valid legal defense. Therefore, courts seldom permit such a defense and even then, mostly in specialized business cases.

Courts have permitted a mistake defense most commonly if there has been an honest error in calculations. The calculations must be material to the contract, and the overall effect must be to make the contract unconscionable (discussed below), that is, unfairly burdensome. Such mistakes often happen when a unit of government puts public work out for bid. If a contractor mistakenly bids $5 million to construct a bridge and a road when the true cost to build the bridge alone was $5 million, he or she might be able to raise this defense. Even then, however, if several months have elapsed and the government has materially relied on the mistaken figures before the mistake is discovered (for example, by taking a number of steps to move the process forward), then it would be unfair to the government to cancel the deal, and the defense would probably fail. (But see the discussion of reformation in chapter 15.)

Of course, if you explicitly state your mistaken idea, the other party has a duty to correct you. Then the issue is no longer one of mistake but of fraud. In our car-sale example, suppose the car's heater worked, but not too well, and you, the seller, knew that. Under contract law, if you and your friend hadn't discussed it, you probably wouldn't have to tell your friend about it. But suppose your friend told you, "The best thing about this car is that it's so hard to find an Edsel with a perfect heater." Then you would be obliged to tell your friend that the heater was faulty. If you didn't, many states would permit your friend to set aside the contract or allow your friend to collect damages for repairs to the heater.

Having said this, the best defense is a good offense. Don't assume anything important or questionable about a contract. Ask questions now—before you sign.

On the other hand, if *both* sides make a mistake, they share an erroneous basic assumption. Then, to avoid injustice, the court will sometimes set aside the contract, under the theory of a **mutual mistake**.

The classic case of mutual mistake occurred when someone sold a supposedly infertile cow for $80. It turned out soon afterward that the cow was pregnant, which made her worth $800. The court ruled that because both parties thought they were dealing with a barren cow, the contract could be set aside.

This does not mean that contracts always have a built-in guarantee against mistakes. As you can imagine, this is a very tricky and unpredictable area. After all, many people make purchases on the understanding that the object is worth more to one person than the other. You wouldn't pay $80 for a cow if she were not worth at least $80.01 to you. That is, you figure you're somewhat better off with the cow than with the $80, given your circumstances and opportunities. (Economists call this amount the "marginal benefit.") Similarly, the seller would not sell her if she were worth more than $79.99 to the seller, given the seller's circumstances and opportunities. Both people have to get some benefit to agree to the sale. In the case of the cow, both buyer and seller understood clearly—but mistakenly—that the cow could not get pregnant. It's as if they made the contract for a subject that turned out not to exist.

How serious does a mutual mistake have to be before a court will set aside a contract for that reason? To take our example, various courts would draw the line on a mistake between $80.01 and $800 at different places, if they were willing to draw it at all. Competent legal advice about the law in your state is crucial if you are considering voiding a contract because of a mistake.

STATUTES OF LIMITATIONS

You should also be aware of **statutes of limitations**. These are laws setting time limits during which a lawsuit can be brought. The typical deadline for bringing a contract action is six years from the time the breach occurs. The idea of this policy is that everyone is entitled, at some point, to "close the book" on a transaction. It encourages people to move on and reduces the uncertainty that businesses would face if they could be sued for breaching contracts that no one alive in the organization remembers.

CHANGING SITUATIONS

Sometimes changing circumstances make a contract impossible to perform. Suppose that you hire a contractor on Tuesday to paint your house, and it burns down Wednesday night through no fault of your own. Then the contract may be set aside because there's no way to perform it. You won't have to pay the painter, under the doctrine of **impossibility of performance**. Both of you are out of luck. The same is true if the contract covers a specific kind of product that becomes unavailable because of an act of God, such as an earthquake or blizzard. Courts usually will not enforce such a contract.

For example, suppose you contract to deliver one hundred barrels of a specific grade of oil from a specific Arabian oil field by a certain date. Then an earthquake devastates the oil field, making recovery of the oil impossible. You're probably off the hook under these circumstances.

This doctrine is also known as **impracticability of performance**, which reflects the fact that it may apply even if performance is not literally impossible but is still seriously impractical.

Sometimes changed circumstances radically change the costs of performing a contract, without making it literally impossible to do so. Courts probably would enforce the contract on the grounds that the new circumstances were foreseeable and that the possibility of increased costs was or could have been built into the contract. For instance, suppose again that you contract to deliver one hundred barrels of Arabian oil. This time fighting breaks out in the Persian Gulf, interrupting shipping and greatly increasing the cost of the oil. When a court considers these facts, it's likely to say that you should have foreseen the possibility of fighting and built that risk into the price. The contract will stand.

On the other hand, sometimes a change in conditions doesn't make performance impossible or impractical, but it does make performance meaningless. The legal term for this is **frustration of purpose**. One famous case decided around the turn of the century involved a man who rented an apartment in London to view the processions to be held in connection with the coronation of the king of England. Because of the king's illness, the coronation was canceled. The court excused the renter from paying for the room. Through no fault of his own, the whole purpose of renting it—which the people who owned the room knew—had disappeared. Such cases, though, are rare indeed. More typically you take your chances when you make a contract in expectation of a third party's or outside force's action. Many contracts, however, have a term excusing the parties from performance if any of a number of specified events occur.

SHOULD THE BUYER STILL BEWARE?

The well-known Latin maxim caveat emptor—"let the buyer beware"—is a strict rule placing the risk in a transaction with the buyer. Under this rule each party is protected only by inspecting and analyzing a potential transaction, because there is no remedy if there is a hidden problem. In fact, this "ancient" law really predominated only in the nineteenth and early twentieth centuries, when the idea of the sanctity of the contract reigned. More common are the principles of just prices and fair dealing in transactions. They are part of rabbinic, medieval, and more recently statutory law— particularly consumer fraud acts prohibiting unfair or deceptive acts and practices. Having said that, every buyer should recognize that the first line of defense is common sense and not depend on an expensive lawsuit and a sympathetic judge to save him or her from a bad deal or sharp practice.

There are three important criteria for a contract to be set aside for frustration of purpose. First, the frustration must be substantial—nearly total and with almost no chance of benefit. Second, the change in circumstances must not be reasonably foreseeable. Third, the frustration must not have been your fault.

UNCONSCIONABILITY

On rare occasions a court may let a party out of a contract because the court deems it "unconscionable" (from the word "conscience"). **Unconscionability** means that the bargaining process or the contract's provisions "shock the conscience of the court." An example would be selling thousands of dollars of rhumba lessons to a ninety-five-year-old invalid on Social Security. An unconscionable contract is one that produces a result unfairly surprising due to hidden or obscure language, or, as in the example given above, is grossly unfair, perhaps due to a lack of bargaining power. Its terms suggest that one party took unfair advantage of the other when they negotiated it. The courts are reluctant to use this weapon, but consumers have a better chance with it than anyone else, especially in installment contracts.

The important thing to remember is that you shouldn't rely on unconscionability in making a contract. Although the courts will sometimes void contracts on these grounds, the application of unconscionability is uncommon, uneven, and unpredictable. Make the effort to understand all the terms of a contract, and don't enter into it if it seems too one-sided. After all, it's also unconscionable to let someone take advantage of you.

PRACTICAL CONTRACTS

Sometimes you look at a form contract, throw up your hands, and decide not to read it. There doesn't seem to be much room to negotiate with a form contract. Believe it or not, however, it pays to read a form contract. Failure to read a contract is virtually never a valid legal defense. In most states the courts have held that people are bound by

FILL IN THE BLANKS

There are many kinds of form contracts. One is the kind you have to sign if you want to get insurance or a loan or if you're financing a car. These are called **contracts of adhesion**—if you want the deal, you have to "adhere" or stick to the terms.

Another common kind of form contract is one with numerous blanks on it, which can be filled in with the names of the parties, the monetary terms, dates, etc. These are used commonly for the sale of homes and leases of real estate. There are three main points to be aware of regarding these forms, which can be purchased at stationery stores.

First, while they may appear to be standardized, there's no such thing as a "standard contract." Many innocuous-looking forms are available in several different versions, each fulfilling the same function—for example, an apartment lease—but each subtly different. One might be a "landlord's" contract, where the preprinted terms are more favorable to the landlord, while a nearly identical one is a "tenant's" contract. In any event, don't let anyone tell you it's standard. Insist on crossing out or changing any term you don't like. If the other party refuses to accept changes that are important to you, then don't sign the contract. In today's economy there's usually more than one source for the product or service you want.

Second, fill in all the blanks! A contract with your original signature but containing blank spaces can be like a blank check if altered unscrupulously. Be sure all the blanks are filled, either with specific terms or straight lines to indicate that nothing goes there. And insist on your own copy with the other side's original signature.

Third, if the contract involves a significant amount of money to you or your family, take it to a lawyer before you sign. This is especially important in real estate transactions, where there is typically plenty of room to bargain. There is no such thing as a "preliminary agreement." An agreement is just that—a contract.

all the terms in a contract, even if they didn't read the contract before signing it (unless the other party engaged in fraud or unconscionable conduct). Don't trust the other party to tell you what it means; even with good intentions, he or she could be mistaken. Also, be suspicious if the salesperson urges you to "never mind, it's not important." (Ask, "If it's not important, is it okay to cross out the whole paragraph?") When a substantial amount of money is at stake, take the time to sit down, go over the form, and underline parts you don't understand. Then find out what they mean from someone you trust.

At the same time, you must be realistic about exercising your right to read a form contract. At the car rental counter at the airport, you probably don't have time to read the contract and get an explanation of the terms you don't understand. Even if you did take the time,

---

GETTING OUT OF A CONTRACT

A contract may be set aside if competent parties have not made it voluntarily. It may also be set aside if there was grossly insufficient consideration. In addition, certain contracts must be in writing or they are unenforceable. The following other contract defenses are discussed in this chapter:

- illegality
- duress
- undue influence
- fraud
- mistake
- unconscionability
- impossibility and impracticability of performance
- frustration of purpose

If you can prove any of these, the contract will probably be deemed void or voidable. In either case it's practically as if the contract never existed. If either party paid money, it would have to be returned.

---

with whom would you negotiate? The sales clerk almost certainly doesn't have the authority to change the contract (but see the discussion on page 38 on contracts of adhesion).

Don't ever skip reading the contract and rush to sign on the dotted line because you're afraid to lose the bargain of a lifetime. Rarely will a truly great bargain not be there tomorrow. For all the great deals you rush into that work out fine, the one you will remember is the one that went sour—when they socked you with the fine print you didn't bother to read. A great bargain won't fall into your lap, anyway. It requires a lot of footwork, research, and comparison shopping. If you've done all that, it's unlikely that someone else who has done it also is right behind you.

People are often intimidated by fine print. It's a good idea to get over that, because often the fine print contains terms that could greatly affect your personal finances beyond what the actual deal would lead you to believe. It may contain details about credit terms, your right to sue, and your right to a jury in a lawsuit.

You don't need a law degree to at least try to read the fine print. Often if you go over it, sentence by sentence, you'll find that you can understand a lot more than you expect, especially in states that have passed "plain-English laws" requiring that consumer contracts use nontechnical, easy-to-understand words. You will at least, by expending the effort, identify which terms raise questions for you. The trick is not to be intimidated by the salesperson or the fine print in the contract.

While working out the terms of a written contract, you may sometimes see or hear reference to a contract **rider**. A rider is a sheet of paper (or several pages) reflecting an addition or **amendment** (change) to the main body of a contract. Often it's simpler to put changes in a rider, which supersedes any contradictory parts of the main contract, than to try to incorporate the changes in the original form.

Once you've divined the meaning of a contract, it's in your hands to decide whether the bargain is one you want to enter into. You never have to accept a contract. Every part of a contract is open for negotiation, at least in theory. Just because the salesperson gave you a form contract doesn't mean that you have to stick to the form. You can cross out parts you don't like. You can write in terms that the contract doesn't include, such as oral promises by a salesperson. (Make sure that all changes to the form appear on all copies that will have your signature; initial altered but unsigned pages, and have the other party do the same.)

That doesn't mean the other side has to agree to your changes. You have no more power to dictate terms than they do. But if you encounter a lot of resistance on what seem to be reasonable issues, take a hard look at the other party—especially if they resist your request to put oral promises in writing.

Having said all that, there will be times when a contract is just too inscrutable to understand. "Legalese" most often occurs in contracts that include some type of credit terms, such as when you buy something on installment payments. This kind of legalese could threaten your property rights in your house or other important property, so it pays to make sure you know what you're signing. The parts of this book on consumer credit and automobiles explain many of these terms. If you still have questions, ask someone you trust (not the salesperson) to explain the terms to you. That could be someone experienced with the kind of contract you are considering, a state or local consumer agency, or a lawyer.

Many states now require plain-English consumer contracts, with potentially confusing sections or clauses in precise, standard terms that nearly anyone can understand. Even if not legally required, more and more merchants are having contracts prepared this way

---

READ THE FINE PRINT

Perhaps the most unpleasant part of making contracts comes after negotiating your best deal. It occurs when a salesperson presents you with a form contract, which is often one or two pages of tiny print that you might not understand even if you could read it. But the law usually assumes that you read and, to a reasonable extent, understand any contract you sign.

for customer relations. Federal and state truth-in-lending laws require providers (or grantors) of credit to furnish specific information about credit contracts in clearly understandable form.

Finally, the legal doctrine regarding contracts of adhesion may protect you. As mentioned briefly earlier, in these contracts you have little or no bargaining power, as is often the case in many of the form contracts discussed above, such as loan documents, insurance contracts, and automobile leases. The consumer has some protection, however. Courts generally assume that such contracts have been drafted to provide maximum benefit to the lender, lessor, or insurance company. So when a dispute arises over terms or language, the courts usually interpret them in the way most favorable to the consumer.

In one case, for example, a woman tried to collect on an airline-trip insurance policy she had purchased. The insurance company held that the policy applied only to a trip on a "scheduled airline," and that technically, under some obscure regulations, the woman's flight was not "scheduled," even though she had every reason to

---

GET IT IN WRITING

When dealing with a written contract, a court will almost always treat the contract's terms as the final, complete contract. The court usually will not even consider oral promises that are not in the contract. The main exception to this is when oral promises are used fraudulently to induce one party into signing the contract in the first place. That is, the party is persuaded by the fraudulent oral promise to enter into a contract he or she otherwise would have avoided. The general rule prohibiting evidence of oral promises in all other cases protects both parties, because they know that once they sign the contract, they have clearly and finally set the terms.

Don't be swayed if the salesperson orally promises you an extended warranty or a full refund if you're not completely satisfied. Get it in writing. If the salesperson refuses to put it in writing, walk away from the deal.

---

believe that it was. The court held in favor of the woman, saying the ordinary insurance buyer's understanding should apply.

There is a further protection for consumers. Even contracts that are not contracts of adhesion are interpreted or construed to favor the party who didn't draft them. Like the doctrines of unconscionability and fraud discussed earlier, this rule isn't something to depend on before signing a contract. Rather it's a defense that you and your lawyer may raise if a problem arises and the situation warrants.

In the previous two chapters we've considered how you make a contract and how certain contract defenses can help you avoid being held to an unfair or illegal contract. These principles only scratch the surface of the topic of contract law and don't deal with the millions of transactions between merchants that take place every day or the more complex subjects in contract law that require the assistance of a lawyer.

CHAPTER FOUR

■

Special Contract Terms

Waivers, Forum-Selection Clauses, and Other Wrinkles

You've now learned the basics of consumer contract law. With this foundation, you should be able to appreciate this chapter's discussion of types of contract terms that are often part of consumer contracts but were put there for the seller's benefit. You may be able to bargain these terms away. But as often as not, you'll be given a "standard" (form) contract and little choice if you want the product or service being offered. However, if you understand these terms, you'll be better able to evaluate whether the deal really is worth it to you. And if you do go ahead, you'll know where some of the potential problems are.

As discussed earlier, because these terms are usually found in form contracts—which are often take-it-or-leave-it contracts of adhesion—there could be a chance of being excused from performing them if the terms in question are ambiguous. But that is a fall-back position. At the outset you must act as if you're going to be held to every word in every contract you sign, because you well might.

We will focus on a number of the most important terms, especially the various types of **waivers**. You have given a waiver when you have knowingly surrendered (waived) one of your rights. After reading this chapter, you should have a good idea of what these types of clauses are about when you see them.

ARBITRATION CLAUSES

Arbitration clauses are one kind of waiver. If they are binding, you surrender any legal right to sue the company you're contracting with. Instead, you agree to submit to **binding** (final) **arbitration**, the most common form of **alternative dispute resolution,** or ADR. Arbitration is especially common in brokerage contracts.

Arbitration is not a bad thing. Sometimes it can be to a consumer's advantage. It gets rid of a lot of the formalities and technicalities of court proceedings and is often much faster and less expensive. There are some areas, however, in which seemingly simple issues are really much more complex than they appear. Then arbitration might cause problems. And there is usually no appeal from binding arbitration, except perhaps for fraud.

Thus, using the securities industry as an example, let's say you have a dispute with a stockbroker over how he or she executed your instructions on a transaction, or you're dissatisfied with the general handling of your account (too many trades, for instance). Obviously you would begin by contacting the broker directly, and then, as necessary, go up the line through supervisors to try to get satisfaction. (You may be surprised at how willing reputable brokerages are to help customers who are dissatisfied with their service.) If all attempts at amicable settlement fail (this technique will be discussed more fully in chapter 15), you might finally decide that you want to sue to enforce your legal rights, and perhaps go as far as letting a jury see who is right.

But you cannot, because of the arbitration clause found in virtually all brokerage agreements. It probably reads something like this:

Subject to the limitations of federal or state law, any controversy arising out of or relating to my accounts, to transactions with you for me or to this agreement, or breach thereof, shall be settled by arbitration in accordance with the rules then in effect at the National Association of Securities Dealers, the New York Stock Exchange, or the American Stock Exchange.

You don't have much choice about this clause or one like it. It is in use by virtually every brokerage in every type of trading. Whether it's buried in an eight-page "New Account Agreement" full of dotted lines to sign or even if it's brought to your attention in bold type, there's no way out of it in most brokerage contracts.

The associations and boards that most brokerage contracts designate as arbitrators are not governmental. They are made up of members of industries that the government regulates, as a form of self-regulation. The rules in effect for arbitration at these various boards are not unfair. But arbitrations under these rules may not be as friendly for consumers as those of the best-recognized arbitration organization, the American Arbitration Association, or AAA.

Some arbitration clauses are more or less restrictive than the one quoted above, including other elements, such as a waiver of any right to punitive damages, which is discussed below. Others, such as the one used in the commodities trading industry, give customers a forty-five day "window"—forty-five days after a dispute arises to go to court before losing that right. That's better than nothing. But compared to the six years you may have under a statute of limitations for breach of contract, forty-five days is not much time.

The fact is that if you want to invest through brokerages, especially when you want the option of margin trading on credit provided by the brokerage, you must sign this agreement. Some brokerages say that cash account customers, who trade only with money deposited with the broker and not on margin, do not need to submit to arbitration. But few brokers will present this option to you. If, however, you know that you don't want margin trading—which offers investors unique opportunities, with corresponding risks—try to get a brokerage agreement without mandatory arbitration.

As of today, every court will uphold an arbitration clause, citing a general policy in favor of avoiding litigation by use of arbitration. Because of this standing rule favoring arbitration, arbitration clauses are an important exception to the principles discussed in chapter 3 about contracts of adhesion. This is one clause you really are stuck with.

Arbitration clauses are found not only in brokerage contracts. One recent Alabama case upheld the right of a pest extermination company to enforce an arbitration clause in its consumer service contracts. Arbitration clauses are becoming more common in consumer credit contracts as well. Companies like these clauses because arbitration is less expensive than litigation, and arbitration awards to consumers are usually less than jury awards.

If you are in a situation in which you do have some bargaining power—again, probably not in the securities or credit areas—you can try to make an arbitration clause as fair as possible. One way is to agree to arbitration only under AAA auspices, which are generally regarded as the fairest.

REQUIREMENTS FOR ARBITRATION CLAUSES

Different states have different requirements that an arbitration clause must meet to be enforceable. Some have no special requirements at all, reflecting a policy favoring arbitration. In California, however, consumers must *knowingly* waive their right to a jury trial. Furthermore, California now requires that an arbitration clause appear in a "clear and unmistakable form" in the contract, such as in highlighted or boldface type, or requires that there be a place for the consumer to sign, indicating that he has read it. Other states have similar laws. You should investigate your state's laws or speak to a lawyer.

Companies that are members of the New York Stock Exchange (NYSE) are also subject to specific requirements for arbitration clauses. NYSE rules require that arbitration clauses tell consumers that:

- arbitration is final and binding;
- the parties are waiving their right to seek remedies in court;
- prearbitration **discovery** (trading of documents and information) is different and more limited than that available in court proceedings;
- arbitrators are not required to spell out the legal or factual bases for their decisions, which are virtually unappealable; and
- a minority of the arbitration panel will be made up of current or former members of the securities industry.

FORUM-SELECTION CLAUSES

The "place" you go for legal relief—a court, for example—is a forum. In a forum-selection clause you are being told what place can adjudicate claims or disagreements about a contract.

Generally speaking, **forum-selection clauses** limit the parties (sometimes just one party!) to a certain state, or federal district, where lawsuits may be initiated. The right to choose the forum in which to sue can be very important. If there is no forum-selection clause, courts give the plaintiff the right, with some limitations, to choose which forum to sue in.

For example, let's say you are a resident of Biloxi, Mississippi, and you enter into a contract with the Waffle-Iron-of-the-Month Club in Brooklyn, New York. You get into a dispute with the company when, in response to your order for a Barney the Dinosaur waffle iron, they send one shaped like Dino the Dinosaur. Junior is horrified, and you complain to the company. They refuse to refund your money or even exchange the iron, claiming that all purple dinosaurs are alike. You decide to sue. Legally you could, at the very least, choose to sue the club in either Brooklyn, where the company is, or Biloxi, where you are. The courts traditionally defer to the forum choice of the person who starts the lawsuit, if the chosen forum is technically correct.

So where would you choose? Chances are, even if you felt completely comfortable with the New York court system, you wouldn't want to take the time and expense to find a New York lawyer or trot over to New York yourself to make your case—especially for a $13 waffle iron. Even on principle. But in Mississippi you might be willing to go to the trouble.

But take a good look at your agreement with these wafflers. Is there a forum-selection clause? If there is, it might require you to bring a lawsuit only in Kings County (Brooklyn) in the State of New York. For you, in this example, that's as good as taking away your right to sue. It's now utterly impractical.

Forum-selection clauses aren't always so strict, but they can be. The courts almost always enforce them, although a smidgen more scrutiny is applied to them than with arbitration clauses. It's not enough to matter, for our purposes.

There is an important difference, though, between forum-selection clauses and arbitration clauses. There is more variation of forum-selection clauses among types of contracts. If you're in a position in which bargaining is not practical, you may very well be able to get what you want from another service or goods provider without a forum-selection clause or without one as limiting. And, of course, remember that if the forum-selection clause requires you to use the courts of your own state, you're probably not giving up much by agreeing to it.

CHOICE-OF-LAW CLAUSES

Another common kind of waiver in form contracts designates which state's legal doctrines and substantive laws will govern interpretation of the document or any dispute over it. This is called a **choice-of-law** clause. Because it is so frequently found in form contracts used by big companies, it is also hard to negotiate away. You should therefore understand what these clauses do.

Every state in the Union, as well as the District of Columbia and each territory and other jurisdiction in the United States, has its own laws. Making those laws is what each state's legislature, courts, and administrative bodies do. Part of the system of federalism is that the democratically elected lawmakers of each state make laws, which, within the bounds of the U.S. Constitution, reflect the policy preferences of the people of that state. In many states the substantive law reflects a traditional approach in that state, which, short of a voter uprising, remains central to its legal tradition. States also must consider what their legal regime offers to businesses that have the right to set up shop wherever the legal climate is most favorable to them. Therefore, different states have different approaches to contract interpretation, consumers' rights, and the like. Some are very pro-consumer, others very pro-business.

For a company doing business all over the country, having to contend with the laws of many states is fraught with difficulty. Designating a choice of law provides a measure of predictability for these companies when they know that they only have to consider the legal doctrines of one jurisdiction instead of some greater number whose law might be applied without an agreement. For companies that have many thousands of similar contractual relationships, that can mean a considerable cost savings as well.

The traditional rule regarding contracts is that, regardless of where a lawsuit over that contract is begun, the law that will be applied in the suit is either the place where the contract is made or the place where the parties intended it to be performed. The latter is often more persuasive if the contract was signed in a geographically convenient neutral ground or a place that has little to do with the contractual relationship.

The choice of which law applies in interpreting and enforcing a contract is called the choice of **substantive** law. Substantive law is contrasted with **procedural** law. The applicable procedural law is always the law of the forum. Thus, a Pennsylvania court could apply California law to a contract, but the procedural law—the technical rules and procedures by which a court proceeding is governed—will remain Pennsylvanian. (Understanding this, incidentally, can give you some insight into one reason a party might prefer a given forum, as discussed above: choice of forum equals choice of procedural rules.)

As a consumer, you obviously would prefer to make your legal claim in a pro-consumer state. The **choice-of-law** clause often gives businesses their preferences. Typically, the clause will simply say, *All disputes arising out of this contract shall be determined in accordance with the law of the State of New York.* The choice in the example was no accident, by the way. Most lawyers agree that New York's law is very favorable to business, especially in areas such as insurance and employment. That does not mean, however, that its *juries* are favorable to business. So a business can have its cake and eat it too, by not designating the New York courts as a forum—or by designating another forum—but requiring the application of New York law to interpretation of the contract.

On the other hand, going back to brokerage contracts, the application of New York law could be detrimental to a consumer. Most states have **Blue Sky Laws**, which, to the extent not preempted by federal law, add some requirements and often more effective remedies to the federal system of securities regulation. New York, which is home to most of the brokerages, doesn't; it has only an antifraud law. A New York choice-of-law clause could pull your state's more protective blue sky laws out from under you.

Some courts have balked at applying choice-of-law clauses in consumer contracts. They reason that a company should not be able to escape the consumer-protection laws of its customer's home state with such a clause. If that were allowed, eventually those laws would be rendered less meaningful. Thus, they hold that as a matter of policy, such clauses will not be enforced when they deprive consumers of coverage under their state's consumer-protection laws. Some state laws dictate this result. Other courts, however, take a more traditional approach. If there is no evidence of fraud or abuse of bargaining power, they will enforce the clause. Again, if your bargaining position is such that you can't get away from this clause or you don't know if you would want to, only a lawyer is qualified to advise you about your options.

WAIVERS IN GENERAL

A waiver, as we said above, is the voluntary relinquishment of a known right. By "voluntary," the law does not mean you necessarily *wanted* to give the right up, but rather that you were *willing* to give it up to make the deal happen. In that sense, a waiver of a right is merely a type of consideration, little different from money. You don't, in an absolute sense, really *want* to give up your Edsel, but for $1,000, you're *willing* to do it.

We have been talking about waiver clauses in contracts, which are a kind of **express waiver**. An express waiver is a written or oral statement that the party is willing to forgo one of his or her rights. Some consumer contracts provide, however, that no waiver of any of the contract terms will be effective unless indicated in writing. This is not an evil provision, but it means that any oral promises concerning one party's right to enforce a specific contract provision are unenforceable.

Even then, there are courts which will, given all the circumstances, decide that the "no oral waiver" clause *itself* was waived! The most common example of this is when a homeowner tells a contractor to do additional work not covered in the contract. The contractor goes ahead with the work, but the homeowner refuses to pay, pointing to the "changes in writing only" clause. Most courts will say that, by authorizing the work and watching as it is done, the homeowner has waived the right to rely on that clause.

In the last example, watching the work as it is done, without protest, is called an **implied waiver**. That means that one party's behavior is "as good as" an explicit statement that he or she does not intend to enforce a certain condition or requirement of the contract. For example, let's say you rent an apartment under a lease that requires payment of rent by the first of each month. One month you forget to pay on time but send the check a week later in the hope that the landlord will accept it, which happens. By accepting the rent, the landlord has implicitly waived the right to evict you for failing to live up to the contract. The landlord cannot, after accepting the check, evict you for violating the lease. (Most leases and state laws are not this simple, but we will discuss this more in chapter 7.) That is an implied waiver. Alternatively, if you wrote and asked the landlord to take the check, and the landlord wrote back saying that he or she was willing to give you a break this time only, it would be an express waiver limited to the one late payment.

Many contract forms have another kind of nonwaiver clause. It says that, even if, as in the above example, the landlord accepts late payment once, the landlord has not waived the timely payment requirement for all time. That means the landlord could insist on strict adherence to the contract terms next month, even after letting you slide this month. This is a fundamentally fair clause and may actually result in a looser, more forgiving relationship between the parties. They don't need to fear that giving the other guy a break from time to time will alter their long-term expectations under the contract. But it does mean that you shouldn't get into the habit of paying late, because any time—the second or the fourteenth—you miss the contract deadline, the landlord could claim you are in breach of the lease. That pattern could, however, lead a court to say you were entitled to notice of a return to strict enforcement before breach is claimed. As soon as the landlord claims a breach, you should consult a lawyer.

What other waivers are frequently contained in form contracts? Here are a few:

• **Consequential damages.** Consequential damages, as discussed more in chapter 15, are compensation for the harm that a person suffers as a consequence of the actual wrong done. The best example is where you lose your term paper because your computer blows up. The warranty (a part of the sales contract, as discussed in chapter 8) will invariably state that consequential damages are not covered by the manufacturer. The manufacturer may repair your computer or even give you a new one, but under the contract the manufacturer will not write your term paper for you or compensate you for the time you'll have to spend recreating it. Most states will uphold limitations such as these, although compensation for other consequences, such as personal injury as a result of a malfunction, may be available under contract or tort law, notwithstanding the purported limitation as a matter of public policy. The idea behind these clauses is that the seller cannot know what use you intend to make of its product, nor the extent to which you take your own precautions. After all, considering all the things that can go wrong with a computer (as in our example), if you don't back up your data on a regular basis, you have only yourself to blame.

• **Punitive damages.** These are also discussed more fully in chapter 15. But a waiver of the right to claim punitive damages is a variation on the waiver of consequential damages. Some states will not enforce these waivers, regardless of the circumstances of the contract. The reasoning is that punitive damages cannot be waived as a matter of public policy.

- **Defenses.** It is common, especially in consumer credit contracts, for certain legal defenses—some of which we discussed in chapter 3, and some other more obscure ones—to be waived by the consumer. The enforceability of these clauses frequently depends on the state you're in and the overall situation of the contract. But you certainly would want to beware of a contract that takes important contract defenses out of your hands before you even start the relationship.

- **Jury trial.** This is one of the most common waivers found in contracts used by large businesses. They know that juries often start out more sympathetic to the "little guy." Jury trials are also more expensive, complicated, and time consuming than trials in which a judge makes both the legal and factual decisions. For that reason, if you decided to sue you might choose not to have a jury anyway. On the other hand, if a lot is at stake, you may not want to give up this right guaranteed in most cases by the Constitution. (Cases in which little money is at stake are often heard in small claims court, where jury trials are not available.)

- **Attorneys' fees and legal costs.** Many contracts, especially mortgages and other extensions of credit, require the borrower to pay any attorneys' fees and other legal costs (e.g., filing fees and other costs of litigation) incurred by the creditor in its efforts to collect money owed on the contract. This is usually an enforceable clause and in itself can amount to a substantial penalty on a party that breaches a contract.

As we said before, there are as many possible things to waive as there are rights of parties in a contract. Certainly there is no reason for you to agree to, say, an attorneys' fees clause in a contract to sell your Edsel, paint your house, or provide oboe lessons. But in many of the cases we've discussed, you may have no negotiating power. Then you must decide how valuable the right you'll be waiving is, compared with what you stand to gain by negotiating it away or walking away from the whole deal. In other words, waivers are just like any other contract provision.

SECURITY INTERESTS

Jerome thought he was only having his kitchen rebuilt. The price seemed right, and the contractor was prepared to finance the work, too, so Jerome could avoid dealing with bankers. When the steel sink turned a greenish gray, however, he was disappointed. When the contractor refused to return his calls, he was angry. When Jerome stopped making payments, he was smug. When he got a notice of foreclosure, he was shocked.

In this example (which admittedly is a little extreme), Jerome didn't appreciate the fact that his financing agreement for the kitchen remodeling included a mortgage. Perhaps he should have, because both federal and some state laws provide disclosure about this, but many consumers ignore this information. Under that document he made his house **collateral** for payment of the contract. A consumer's breach of a contract that includes a mortgage or a **security interest** allows the creditor to turn to the collateral to make sure the money is paid. "Turn to" means "take it and sell it." Even without foreclosing, as long as someone holds a security interest, or **lien**, in your home, you will be unable to pass on clear title—that is, you will have a hard time selling it. If Jerome wanted to sell his house with a lien on it, to go back to our example, he might have to pay off the debt just to clear the title and make the sale possible.

Is it worth risking your house for new kitchen cabinets? Maybe. Analyzing that risk is up to you. It may be a better deal for you to get a home-equity line of credit from a bank to pay for the repairs rather than financing through the contractor, although you should beware of overspending if you have an equity line of credit that gives you checks and easy access to your home's equity. Look out for security-interest clauses in consumer credit contracts so you'll at least have the chance to do your analysis before you're bound by contract. In this example, federal and some state laws may give you a right to rethink and cancel the deal, but not every transaction carries that right.

COSTS AND FEES

The most fundamental contract terms, of course, tell you what the thing you're bargaining for is going to cost you. But beware of terms that subtly change the economic formula behind your back and give away what you worked so hard for in negotiating the fundamental deal. Even if the deal is one in which you have had little need to negotiate—say an agreement to open a credit line or some other kind of "take it or leave it" transaction—you must find, read, and understand these clauses to determine whether you can afford the transaction at all.

Typical fees of this type include:

- high deductibles in appliance service contracts, which often negate their practical value;

- service charges on checking and savings accounts, including fees for returned checks of $20 or more—meaning that even a temporary inability to cover your checks could cost you big dollars in returned-check fees; and

- credit insurance, very costly decreasing term life insurance to cover the amount of credit you're getting.

The possibilities are endless. Other kinds of costs that consumers should be aware of will be discussed later in this book. But again, the idea is that it does pay to read the whole contract and see what a transaction will really cost before you sign.

■

CHAPTER FIVE

Step Right Up

Advertising and Your Rights

A N ADVERTISEMENT IS NOT OFTEN the basis of a contract. We learned that a contract can only be formed when
there is an offer, acceptance, and consideration. Store advertisements are not usually offers. The law, perhaps somewhat arti-
ficially, classifies them as "invitations to bargain." But there are
exceptions.

Suppose a store advertises that it will give a free gift or a special
discount to "the first one hundred customers" or a person who has
made some other special effort. If so, the store has made an offer.
You can accept it by successfully making the special effort, which
constitutes consideration. This could be the making of a contract. In
fact, a major department store got in hot water a few years ago by
carelessly advertising, "Be among the first one thousand shoppers at
our store tomorrow to win a $1,000 shopping spree." The wording
suggested to some people that all one thousand would win—a
million-dollar proposition for the store.

FALSE ADVERTISING

False or deceptive advertising has legal implications beyond contract
law. False or deceptive advertising is a kind of deceptive act or practice forbidden under federal law and in most states, notably under
the consumer fraud laws (discussed in chapter 15).

In false or deceptive advertising the merchant's intent isn't important. The overall impression conveyed is what counts. False or

deceptive advertising may mislead a consumer about a product's place of origin, nature or quality, or maker. The product can be property, services, or even credit (federal and some state laws regulate credit ads so you can shop for credit). An example of creating a misleading impression about a product's place of origin is putting French labels on sweaters made in Arkansas.

TRADEMARKS, TRADE NAMES, AND UNFAIR COMPETITION

Unfair competition law is meant to prevent merchants from engaging in practices that deceive the public about the origin or quality of goods. One way this is done is by the enforcement of **trademark** rights. A trademark is an authenticating symbol or mark that assures the consumer that a commodity or good comes from a certain source—i.e., a brand. The best-known trademarks are worth millions of dollars. For example, if just anyone could put "Coca-Cola" on a soft drink (and in years past many tried), people would never know what they were buying. But because of that company's vigorous enforcement of its trademark rights, when you buy a Coke, you know you're getting a Coke. That benefits Coca-Cola, and it benefits consumers. Similarly, a **service mark** is a symbol meant to convey the source of services, as opposed to goods, and it is protected by the trademark laws as well. A **trade name** is the name under which a merchant does business.

Trademarks that are **registered** with the federal government are often designated with the symbol ®. The ™ mark usually indicates that the merchant claims common-law trademark rights but has not met the legal requirements needed to secure federal registration. Registration of a trademark enhances its owner's ability to prevent infringement.

Illegal use of a trademark is called **infringement**. Willful infringers are subject to serious court action and possible criminal penalties for violation of protected trademarks. Because trademark infringement is a fraud on the public, and because companies have a strong incentive to protect the value of their trademarks, it is one of the most-litigated areas of unfair trade practices.

Similarly, promising first-quality socks and delivering irregulars or seconds is creating a misleading impression about an item's nature or quality. Claiming a cheap counterfeit watch is a Rolex creates a misleading impression as to its maker. That particular kind of **palming off** is also a violation of federal trademark law, which is a special type of unfair competition law (see "Trademarks, Trade Names, and Unfair Competition"). As for services, false advertising might lead you into thinking that someone has qualifications (such as being a master carpenter) that he or she actually does not have.

To avoid state and federal strictures against false or deceptive advertising, advertisements must be accurate about material aspects of the product or service offered. **Material** means that a representation, statement, or depiction in the ad would likely affect a consumer's purchase or use of the advertised product or service. In other words, it is important to your decision to purchase. If an advertisement led you to expect green spark plugs and you got gray ones, the ad probably did not materially mislead you. The standard would be what would be material to a reasonable consumer. Most of us would say the color of spark plugs doesn't really matter, no matter how serious an "interior" designer a car buff is.

That doesn't mean you get to stop thinking for yourself. There may be nothing wrong with an advertisement that features a dress that looks better on a fashion model than on a normal person. That's why we have fashion models. (There might be a problem if something special was done to make the *dress* look better than it really does.) And it's also okay for an advertiser to claim that it makes the best tasting fried chicken on the market. This kind of claim is "puffery"—that is, exaggerated sales talk. Consumers need to regard such claims with skepticism.

But it might be deceptive advertising to portray a toy in a way that suggests performance far beyond reality. And if the spark plug ad said the plugs would last fifty thousand miles and they failed early on, the advertisement was probably misleading. If you are not satisfied, complain to the company, report the matter to the state or local consumer protection office, or contact the National Advertising

Division of the Council of Better Business Bureaus or a self-regulating industry body.

BAIT AND SWITCH

The *bait* is an advertisement luring you with the promise of an unbeatable deal, say on an appliance or car. The *switch* happens at the dealer, when the salesperson tells you that the advertised model isn't available or is "not for you." Invariably, a more expensive model *is* for you. The salesperson has "switched" you from the one you wanted to buy.

Bait and switch is illegal in most states and under federal law if the advertised model was never available in reasonable quantities, although stores are not necessarily bound by *honest* mistakes in newspaper ads, such as misprints. It's also bait and switch if disparagement of the advertised product is used to discourage you in favor of another model. You probably have the right under state law to see the model that appeared in the newspaper ad. If the store is "fresh out" and refuses to offer you a raincheck, it also may be guilty of false advertising. You're allowed to be persuaded, but keep up your guard, and don't let someone talk you into buying a model you can't afford. If insisting on your rights gets you nowhere, keep the ad, get the salesperson's name (and that of anyone else you spoke to), and let the merchant know that you'll be contacting the state (and, if there is one, local) consumer affairs authority or attorney general. And then *do it*! If a misprint claim sounds fishy, the local consumer protection authorities may know if this store has a history of such sloppiness.

PRICE TAGS AND WINDOW SIGNS

You get to the store and find an incredible bargain—a dress you know is worth at least $100 is marked $10. You take it to the register, where the salesperson does a double take—there's been a mistake, he or she says apologetically.

Although certain stores would sell you the dress for $10, the general rule under state law is that you're not entitled to get the dress for

$10 when there's every indication that an honest mistake was made. After all, what have you lost, besides the chance at a windfall? Disappointment by itself is not consideration.

On the other hand, if the same dress were displayed in the store window with a prominent sign reading "FINAL CLEARANCE— $10!!," state law might well give you the right to insist on the advertised price (watching out again for the bait and switch). Although the FTC might consider both displays and price tags ads, the state may consider a store window display more like a public advertisement than a price tag, because its intent is to induce you to do something you wouldn't have done—go into the store.

Keep in mind that advertising watchdogs are out there—your local Better Business Bureau, the state attorney general's office, and the Federal Trade Commission. The FTC routinely monitors advertising for false, deceptive, and unfair claims. Once the FTC required a mouthwash manufacturer to stop claiming its product prevented colds when there was no evidence that it did. Besides having to stop making the claims, the advertiser had to run counteradvertising to educate the public that its previous ads were wrong.

In a similar vein many cities and states have laws regulating "Going Out of Business" sales. Merchants who want to run one of these ads may need a license, because in past years there was a rash of decade-long "Going Out of Business" sales that deceived consumers, who thought they were getting unique opportunities. Now you can't run such a sale in these jurisdictions unless you're really going out of business.

But don't wait for the government to act before you turn a skeptical eye on advertising. Advertising is one of the great areas of modern media creativity and is as old as free enterprise. Your job is to use your head while appreciating the adman's craft. Remember to take advertisers' claims with a grain of salt, comparison shop, and watch out for the bait and switch.

If, despite all your care, you are victimized by false or deceptive advertising, you may be entitled to do more than complain to the authorities. Under the consumer fraud laws, you may be entitled to extra damages when you are victimized by deceptive trade practices. We will discuss this in greater depth in chapter 15.

■

CHAPTER SIX

The Postman's Knock

Buying by Mail, Phone, Fax, and Computer

SHOPPING VIA MAIL ORDER AND CATALOGS has grown tremendously in the last few years. Shopping by television is also very important to some consumers. Most of the rules for ordering by mail apply when ordering by phone for delivery by mail or another common carrier, such as United Parcel Service or Federal Express. Thus, consumers who order merchandise through TV shopping channels such as QVC or HSC are usually as well protected as those who buy by mail—often better, because they usually use credit cards to order. (Your rights as a credit card customer are discussed in chapter 10.) Many consumers are also ordering products through their computers (see chapter 14). All of this has been a blessing for consumers with little time to browse in stores, but there are occasionally some drawbacks, including delays in receiving orders, uneven customer service, and inconvenience if repair or replacement is necessary.

In addition there is a risk of fraud, because it's hard to assess the company without seeing a showroom or salespeople. Computer merchants are even more ephemeral than TV merchants—and possibly more fly-by-night. At least with a phone number or post office box, there is a paper trail to follow if you have a problem. But a computer merchandiser's web site may, for all practical purposes, be no more concrete than cyberspace itself. The business may not exist at all. Also, remember that every time software developers claim they've come up with the hacker-proof way to securely transmit credit card information across the Internet, the hackers have the last laugh. Using your credit card by modem may be one wave you should not be so quick to surf. Therefore, in addition to the rules we've already learned about contracts, there are special rules that protect consumers involved in mail or telephone transactions, including fax and computer sales by modem. (Mail-order buying clubs, such as music, video, or collectible clubs, are discussed separately in chapter 13.)

SPECIAL MAIL AND TELEPHONE ORDER RULES

The FTC's Mail or Telephone Order Rule covers goods you order by mail, telephone, computer, and fax. Under this rule, goods you buy through these means must be shipped within the time the seller has advertised (e.g., six weeks). This covers goods that you understand not to be available until a certain time, such as magazines or flower seeds. If no time period is specified, the goods must be shipped within thirty days of your order. If not, you should have received a notice (by letter, postcard, phone, or fax) informing you of the delay and when to expect delivery. The seller also has to offer to cancel your order and send you a refund within one week if you don't want to wait any longer. Many states have laws that protect you even further than the federal law.

What about substitute goods? Unless the seller has your consent to agree to a substitute, you don't have to accept one. You can send it back and ask for a refund. If you keep it, though, you have to pay the usual price, unless the company offers it for less. Pick up a pen or the telephone and try to negotiate. Because mail-order firms depend more on goodwill than other companies do, a reputable company may be willing to strike a deal with you.

UNORDERED GOODS

A frequent problem with mail orders is that you don't get what you ordered. With unordered goods, the problem is the reverse—you get goods you didn't order. Federal law requires the sender of an unordered item sent through the mail to mark the package "Free Sample." (The law permits charities to send you Easter Seals,

Hanukkah candles, and the like and ask for a contribution. You can keep such shipments as gifts.)

Consumers who receive unordered merchandise in the mail should consider it a gift. You have no obligation to pay for the merchandise, and you may keep it. Although you're not required to by law, you could write the seller a letter stating that you never ordered the item and therefore have a legal right to keep it for free. (The letter will help you establish that you never ordered the merchandise and may discourage the seller from sending you bills or dunning notices.) But first make sure you or a family member didn't actually order the item in question. And be sure that you didn't inadvertently join a "club" with regular purchasing requirements when participating in a sweepstakes or ordering "trial" or "free" merchandise.

Sending you a bill for unordered merchandise may be fraud, which is a federal crime. If you can't resolve the problem by talking with the company, report such practices or any harassment or threats to force you to pay the bill to the FTC, the Postal Service, and your state consumer protection bureau. You also may get help from the Better Business Bureau in your area or the Direct Marketing Association, 1120 Avenue of the Americas, New York, NY 10036.

CHOOSING WISELY

The different ways of pitching by mail and phone seem to multiply every day. How do you go about finding the best mail-order values?

INTEREST FREE, BUT NOT FREE

Some credit card companies send a catalog to their customers every couple of months, featuring "the best" and "the finest" appliances, exercise equipment, etc., for their "discerning" customers. The glossy catalogs feature color photographs of each product and offer "no-interest" financing with your credit card. The payout periods are often very long terms, although you can hardly tell by the way they're phrased ("34 months").

WHILE YOU'RE IN A SPENDING MOOD

Have you ever wondered why there's an offer for a pocket-knife set on the flap of the return envelope of your credit card bill? Or why your department store statements smell like perfume? Or why a mail-in form for Star Trek commemorative plates stands between you and your phone bill?

Companies that offer credit often supplement their income with offers like these, which may or may not be related to the service the company offers. They're hoping that while your checkbook is open, you might be inclined to order some more stuff. It's also so convenient—just use the same envelope and a stamp you have to pay for anyway.

But keep your eye on these offers. Because their sponsors are hoping you'll make a casual purchase while in your spending mode, they may try to blindside you. For example, one offer advertised two dirt-cheap folding pocket knives with stainless-steel blades for $2, but in the fine print charged an absurd postage and handling fee of $6.95. Compare this with the postage and handling fees in a reputable mail-order catalog. Regardless of the overall value of the product and the postage, it's fair to assume that anyone who structures a pitch like this is not interested in giving something away.

Also don't assume that the company whose statement includes the offer stands behind it. Trying to resolve a problem with one of these products by calling your credit card issuer's 800 number will often get you no further than a computer that tells you the status of your account, a dead end, or some "order fulfillment" number—a toll call often far from where you live. And sometimes it's even worse: the offers are from companies unrelated to the one that "introduced" you to them, which offer the use of their credit as a "service to you."

Finally, do you need it? It's one thing to be inspired when you open a catalog, looking for something interesting. But there's a time to pay bills and a time to shop by mail. They may not be the same time.

But the prices—on appliances and products routinely discounted at superstores and even department stores—may be marked up; charging interest would just be gilding the lily. Be sure the markup is not more than the interest you would pay even on routine retail financing of a discounted appliance. Also, in two or three years, when the joy of that new theater-size television has worn off, how much will you appreciate paying $46 a month, with another year of payments to go? You won't care how much of the payment is interest. It's still a bite that comes every month, for a long time.

THE LOW END

At the other end of the spectrum is the "super value" mail-order company that specializes in appliances, computers, cameras, and/or fax machines. Their catalogs are printed on newsprint or they offer their wares right in the Sunday paper. Their prices are cut-rate too, although as often as not the one product you're looking for has no price in the catalog—it says, "Call for latest price." They don't offer credit themselves, although they gladly accept major credit cards on their order forms or over the phone.

These are often great places to buy what you want. But you'd better be sure you want it and always will. Companies like this rarely accept returns of their products, or they limit the return period to ten or fourteen days—return postage on you. If you want to take that risk, at least make sure that you do get that short period, because often these deep discounters are selling factory-reconditioned appliances or returns. You want to make sure the product basically works. But often, after that you're on your own.

One more thing: Beware the mail-order company that won't accept in-state phone orders. That's a red flag. It means that although they're willing to sell to out-of-towners as opposed to having the sale go somewhere else, they'd rather get local folks into the store. If you're thinking bait and switch, you're getting the idea.

PLAYING IT SAFE

So what should you do? A rule of thumb in mail-order sales is to find established merchants that have been in business for at least a few years. As with any other business, recommendations from friends are the best assurance of integrity you can have.

Ideally, the merchant you find specializes in what it's selling you (as opposed, again, to an "established" credit card merchant which sees an opening in mail-order sales). Although it is by no means a requirement, it's great if, in addition to its mail-order operation, the seller has a real store in a real place (or, if it's an out-of-the-way place, you can visit it yourself or have a friend check it out). That way there's some stability and substantiality. The business shouldn't disappear overnight.

The converse of that is to never do mail-order business of any substantial size with an unknown place that has only a post office box. It might be gone and untraceable the day after you order.

Placing an order for an inexpensive item is another way to check a company's performance before investing in more costly merchandise. Payment by credit card is also highly recommended—it usually makes it easier to resolve disputes (see chapter 15).

CONTACTS FOR RESOLVING PROBLEMS

If you have problems with mail- or phone-order purchases, first try to resolve your dispute with the company. If that doesn't work, the following resources may be helpful:

- The Better Business Bureau (BBB) in your area or near the company.
- State and local consumer protection offices near you and those near the company.
- Action-line and consumer reporters. Check with your local newspaper, TV, and radio stations for a contact.
- The Direct Marketing Association (DMA). Write DMA Mail-Order Action Line, Suite 1100, 1111 19th Street, NW, Washington, DC 20036.
- Postal inspectors. Call your local postal office and ask for the inspector-in-charge.

You may want to have your name removed from direct mail or telephone lists. Be aware, however, that if you purchase goods by mail after your name is removed, it may be added again. You may want to make a new request to have your name removed every few years. You also may want to ask mail or telephone order companies to retain your name on in-house lists only.

To remove your name from many national direct mail lists, write DMA Mail Preference Service, P.O. Box 9008, Farmingdale, NY 11735-9008.

To avoid unwanted telephone sales calls from national marketers, send your name, address, and telephone number to: DMA Telephone Preference Service, P.O. Box 9014, Farmingdale, NY 11735-9014.

TAXES AND FEES

Mail-order forms frequently leave a space to add sales tax for in-state residents; i.e., people who live in the same state as the company from which they are ordering. (Some companies have stores in many states and usually list them on the form. Take a good look to see if yours is listed. The order might be delayed if it's sent back to you with a request to add the tax, or you might be billed separately for the tax.) One of the big advantages of buying from a catalog is that, in most states, you don't have to pay sales tax if the company doesn't have a retail establishment in your state. Sales tax usually applies only to sales made in person if you take the merchandise with you or have it sent to an address within the state, as well as to within-state mail orders. Thus, you might owe no sales tax if you buy merchandise in person in a neighboring state and have it delivered to your home. (Be sure the shipping charges don't eat up the tax savings!) This is completely legitimate, but understand the limitations of the rule:

- It is illegal to send merchandise to a false address, such as that of a relative or friend who lives in a state where the seller doesn't do business, to avoid the tax. It is also illegal to walk out with the merchandise while having an empty box sent to your home.

- Most states have "use taxes" meant to capture the "lost tax" on these transactions. The use tax is frequently identical to the sales tax and would have the same effect on consumers if enforced. Although not often enforced against individual consumers, beware: some revenue-hungry states have been known to send inspectors to malls over the state line and take down license plates from their own state for later checking against tax-reporting rules.

- Some neighboring states, such as New York and New Jersey, have mutual sales-tax collection pacts.

Always remember that merchants don't "charge" tax—they only collect it.

Another little box on that mail-order blank is for postage and handling ("P & H"). Catalog shoppers don't necessarily expect discounts, but there is no reason to pay inflated postage and handling. Almost every mail-order company adds more than the amount of postage, usually pegging postage and handling to the amount of your order, often a completely arbitrary measure. A recent published report noted that a well-known lingerie catalog charges an extra $11.95 for the couple of dollars it costs to ship that *very* lightweight stuff to that someone special. Similarly, a popular catalog of inexpensive novelty items often makes its profits on large postage and handling fees and "personalizing" charges (that couple of extra dollars for a dime's worth of thread and labor in sewing someone's initials on an item).

In response to increased consumer awareness of this issue, some well-known catalogs now offer very low, flat, or even no fees, at least on a test basis. Obviously this is a test you should try to take.

■

CHAPTER SEVEN

The Lease You Can Do

Residential Leases

A LEASE HAS ALL THE ELEMENTS OF A CONTRACT, as explained earlier. The difference is that rather than buying something, a lease is a contract to *rent* it for a specified period of time, at a specified price. There are two main kinds of leases. The first involves real estate, such as a lease for an apartment, which is discussed in this chapter. The second includes all other kinds of property, such as leases for vehicles, which are discussed in chapter 9. Someone who leases property to someone else (an owner) is a **landlord** or a **lessor**. The person who takes out the lease is called a **tenant** or **lessee**.

The advantage of leasing is that it doesn't usually require you to invest as much of your money as buying, because you are not paying for ownership of the property. A lease cushions you from the risk of owning property that may **depreciate**, or decrease in value, but there is the chance that it might **appreciate**, increase in value, a gain that won't belong to you. You must return the property to the owner at the end of the lease period, and your payments never add up to **equity** (an ownership interest) in the property unless you have an option to purchase with a rent credit toward the purchase price.

Most states have laws that protect tenants—people who lease their homes. But these laws vary substantially from place to place. Big cities, which have the most tenants and many social problems related to housing, are usually the most protective of tenants' rights. Still, there are certain fundamental points that can be of aid no matter where you live.

CHOOSING A LANDLORD

As with any contractual relationship, the first decision in a rental relationship is when the landlord and tenant "choose" each other. The landlord-tenant relationship can last for years or decades, and indeed many have outlasted the marriages in the rented property. But short of an unhappy marriage, there's little that can make life more miserable than an unhappy landlord-tenant relationship.

So, when you go to check out a prospective rental property, don't just evaluate the space and amenities (number of rooms, baths, etc.). Evaluate the landlord. It is ideal if you can talk to the tenant who's vacating the property. If the apartment or house is vacant when you look at it, ask the landlord to give you the previous tenant's name. Make a note of the landlord's cooperation in this regard. In an apartment building, speak to other tenants you see in the lobby, on the elevator, or outside. You might even want to knock on doors. What do you want to find out?

• **Putting in the fix.** A tenant is entitled to have everything in the apartment in good working order. This is the single most important question needing an answer. One way to get an answer is to look at the condition of the property. Does it need major repairs? If so, see if you can discern how long it's been that way. An above-average landlord will, when told of flaws that you find, be willing to sign a written list of problems and promise to fix them. An average landlord will make an oral promise. The one who won't even promise is certain not to do it. Stay away.

Remember that repairs are not the same as improvements. You can negotiate for a post-1966 refrigerator, but you're not entitled to one.

• **Check the record.** You can look for a record of the landlord and this property with the local building management association, apartment association, Board of Realtors, the local office of the Institute of Real Estate Management, and the agency that handles tenant complaints in your area. The best preparation is to look at the public records available in the courthouse (has the municipality sued the landlord for code violations?) and the local code inspection agency (look for a pattern of *serious* violations).

• **Divinity in the details.** Obviously, repairs made outside of your own property, such as in the lobby of an apartment building, bear on the above as well. But there are also little hints that tell you how much the landlord cares. One quick way to judge the quality of a building is to look at the doorbells at the front entrance. Are the tenants' names uniform, generated by a label gun or, even better, miniature engraved tabs? If so, they were put there by an above-average landlord who cares about the appearance of the building. On the other hand, if the names were written on slivers of index cards, cardboard, and looseleaf paper—or they're missing altogether—this landlord doesn't care.

Similarly, how are the names written on the mailboxes? What is the condition of the mailboxes and the surrounding area? The elevator? How clean is the glass in the lobby? What do the grounds look like? The parking area? These little items don't necessarily bear on your own life in your own cubbyhole, but they can bear on your overall feeling about where you live, which is not to be underestimated in your overall feeling about life. Just as important, they tell you about your prospective "living partner." When it comes to building maintenance, it's not even a close choice—take Felix over Oscar.

OWNER OF A BROKER'S HEART

If you use a broker or Realtor (see chapter 11) to find an apartment, he or she won't be your best source of information about this match. The broker's commission—which, in rentals, is *almost always paid by the tenant,* and is usually equivalent to a month's rent—is riding on making you a match somewhere. If you need the broker to find exclusive listings or unlisted properties, this service may be worth every penny. And if the broker or Realtor is well established, you should take any recommendation seriously. But you've got to do the footwork of checking out the landlord yourself.

THE LEASE APPLICATION

A landlord is also entitled to learn a little about you. The main tool for doing this is the **lease application**.

The application is usually on a standard form available at stationery stores, although larger organizations may use their own form. One thing the form does is authorize the landlord to confirm the information you give and run a credit check. Landlords are most concerned about your ability to pay the rent, so they will ask for three to five years' worth of rental and employment history and will likely call your former landlords and employers. What landlords want to see here, above all, is stability. Keep in mind that a landlord who runs a check like this on you also ran it on your prospective neighbors. You want stability there, as well.

Landlords may also use credit bureaus and special agencies that specialize in tenant records, specifically evictions and rent-defaults.

THE SUITABLE TENANT

Remember throughout this process that a landlord has every right to be concerned about your suitability as a tenant. "Suitability" includes straightforward matters like tenancy history, income, credit history, and whether you have a criminal record. It may include purple hair and nose rings, too. This kind of discrimination is permissible.

On the other hand, there is *impermissible* discrimination, such as that based on race, religion, ethnic origin, sex, handicap, or family status. Impermissible discrimination is prohibited in most situations by the federal Fair Housing Act. (There are some exceptions for small, owner-occupied buildings, where a tenant is almost a member of the family.) The Fair Housing Act also forbids landlords from refusing to rent to families with children (except in certain retirement communities) or from evicting or harassing a tenant for any of these reasons (or for threatening action over discrimination). In addition, the Civil Rights Act of 1866 prohibits discrimination based on race, ethnic origin, or color of a tenant or prospective tenant, without exception.

Some states and cities have extended these protections to other classes, making it illegal to discriminate on the basis of sexual orientation, old age, or source of income (e.g., welfare, social security, alimony, or child support).

If you think you have been a victim of illegal discrimination in applying for a rental, you can file an administrative complaint with a local, state, or federal agency—the U.S. Department of Housing and Urban Development (HUD)—or you can sue the landlord in court. Because of the high burden of proof faced by a claimant in this kind of case, you would be well advised to seek the aid of a lawyer if you sue. Ultimately, if you prove your claim the agency or the court may require the landlord to rent you the premises and perhaps pay damages, including attorneys' fees.

THE LEASE

All leases are contracts by which the landlord grants the tenant *exclusive* use of the premises in exchange for rent for a certain period of time. Leases fall into two broad categories:

• **Tenancy for years.** This is a lease for a *fixed* period of time, called a **term**. No notice is required to terminate a tenancy for years, because the term defines when it ends. These leases are usually written and must be written if they are to extend beyond one year. They give both parties maximum security and predictability, with rent and even rent increases spelled out. Of course, they reduce tenants' flexibility—they can't just move out in the middle of the term.

• **Periodic tenancy.** This is also called a **month-to-month** tenancy. These leases are often for an indefinite period of time and require some notice to terminate. The notice period is usually the equivalent of one rent period, usually a month. Periodic tenancies may be oral. A periodic tenancy gives both landlord and tenant maximum flexibility and minimum security.

These two types of leases often meet at the end of a tenancy for years, when no renewal is signed and the **leasehold** (the status of the tenancy) switches to month-to-month. This is commonly called a **hold-**

over tenancy. In many leases, if the tenant holds over after the lease expires, the rent is doubled. If the lease does not address holdovers, in some jurisdictions, at the option of the landlord, a tenant's holding over may simply operate as a renewal of the lease, usually for a one-year term. Because giving the proper form of notice is highly technical in some places, landlords often scramble to avoid holdovers.

THE LEASE FORM

Most tenants and landlords prefer to deal with written leases. Tenants know their rent cannot be raised except as provided by the lease, and of course it's nice to know you'll have a place to live for the term. Landlords know they will receive rent throughout the term and need not risk an extended vacancy or the time and expense of listing and showing the property. Landlords also like the fact that the lease will set out or refer to the rules and regulations for the premises and will bind tenants to obey them. In addition, written leases usually provide for a late fee if rent is not paid on time (legally required to be reasonable in amount). See "Read Before You Sign!" on page 76 for other key lease clauses.

In a written lease the landlord may give up the right to increase rent. In most urban areas this could be a substantial concession. There are drawbacks to a written lease from the tenant's perspective, too. Leases are almost always provided by the landlord and are drafted with the landlord in mind, so the landlord can get you to sign away rights you would otherwise have. But, local law often "cancels out" waivers of certain tenants' rights (as discussed below). Also, in most areas where rental properties are scarce, your bargaining power is uneven, so courts are inclined to deem these as contracts of adhesion and to construe ambiguous terms against the drafter—the landlord.

But you've already learned that if you are presented with a preprinted form, it does not mean you cannot negotiate the terms. (Indeed, many landlords will give you a preprinted lease with scratchouts of their own.) If you have any leverage to negotiate, negotiate. Remember to get both sides to initial all the changes—that's proof that the changes weren't written in later.

READ BEFORE YOU SIGN!

Leases vary widely. Below are explanations of clauses found in a typical pro-landlord lease and in a lease that is more balanced between the rights of landlord and tenant. Leases similar to these are available in many stationery stores. The pro-landlord lease has few rights for the tenant and many tenant obligations; the balanced lease has obligations for both landlord and tenant and rights for both. Whether you are a landlord or a tenant, make sure you read and understand any lease before you sign it.

CLAUSE	PRO-LANDLORD LEASE	BALANCED LEASE
Interest on security deposit	No interest unless required by law.	Interest at a fair passbook rate.
Return of security deposit	Will return after deducting for tenant's failure to comply with terms of lease.	Landlord required to provide a written statement of repairs done to premises, with receipts.
Condition of premises/repairs	By signing lease, tenant acknowledges that premises are in good repair, except as noted in lease. No specific space provided on lease to write in repairs that are needed.	Landlord expressly warrants that premises are fit and comply with all applicable codes. Space provided for repairs needed and date repairs will be completed.
Limitation of liability	Restricts or eliminates landlord's liability for failure to keep premises in repair (e.g., damage caused by plumbing failures or leaks in roof). Landlord not responsible for damage caused by his or her actions or by neglect of his or her duties to keep premises in repair.	No clause waiving landlord's liability.

CLAUSE	PRO-LANDLORD LEASE	BALANCED LEASE
Default	If tenant fails to pay any part of rent, or breaks any other part of lease, landlord is authorized to terminate lease without notice; to enter premises without process of law to remove tenant; to possess and sell tenant's property to recover rent owed; and to have a first lien on all personal property of tenant as security.	No comparable clause.
Fire and casualty	Landlord has thirty days to repair damage that makes dwelling unfit for use, or landlord can simply terminate lease.	Tenant has right to terminate lease in case fire or other casualty makes unit uninhabitable.
Confession of judgment	In the event that landlord sues tenant, tenant appoints landlord's attorney to represent tenant in court; tenant waives right to be served and to notice of the suit; tenant confesses judgment (admits to the complaint filed against him by the landlord); agrees to pay landlord's court costs and attorneys' fees; waives all errors that might be made at trial; waives all rights to appeal; consents to immediate eviction.	No comparable clause.
Option to renew lease	None.	Tenant has option to lease for another period of time, at a stated rent. Landlord cannot arbitrarily refuse to renew lease.

(continued on page 78)

(continued from page 77)

CLAUSE	PRO-LANDLORD LEASE	BALANCED LEASE
Duty to maintain/ warranty	None (no part of lease says that landlord will make repairs if something breaks during the tenancy).	By warranting that premises are fit and meet code requirements, landlord promises to keep them that way.
Entry by landlord	Landlord has free access without notice.	Only with 24-hour advance notice and only for specified purposes.
Additional landlord obligations	None.	Spelled out in detail (e.g., adequate extermination services for unit, adequate locks, screens, secure mailboxes).
Tenant remedies if landlord does not maintain premises	None.	Tenant has right to hire repairpersons and buy materials, and deduct costs from rent, after giving landlord adequate notice of the need for repairs.
Tenant's right to terminate	None.	Tenant has right to end lease in event of job loss or transfer.

REGULATION OF LEASES

As mentioned above, many states and municipalities place limitations on what landlords can put in their written leases. For example, state courts have struck down lease clauses that provide that the tenant accept an apartment "as is" and that the tenant must pay full rent regardless of the condition of the property. Most states also frown on **confessions of judgment**, which were legal blank checks for the landlord.

They allowed the landlord to walk into court *and as the tenant's agent* "confess judgment"—admit to whatever the landlord said and agree to a legal judgment for whatever amount the landlord said the tenant owed or an amount in the confession of judgment.

The most pervasive form of rental regulation is **rent control**, which limits the amount of rent or rent increase landlords can charge. It exists in certain municipalities in New York, New Jersey, Massachusetts, California, and the District of Columbia. On the other hand, many states have specifically forbidden municipalities from enacting rent control. Rent control is a controversial policy.

NEW THINKING

For hundreds of years common-law courts regarded leaseholds as a type of interest in real estate called an **estate for years**. Under this approach the renter or lessee's rights against the landlord were comparable to a home buyer's rights against a seller—very few. (The best-known but least understood tenant's right was the **covenant of quiet enjoyment**, which had nothing to do with noise or fun but guaranteed that no one would interfere with the renter's right to remain in the property during the term.)

In modern times, however, the courts (and to a large extent legislatures) have come to view real estate leases as more like a *contract for shelter and services* than the transfer of a land interest. The fundamental difference is that every such contract includes an implied (unstated) **warranty of habitability**, a promise that the premises are fit to live in. The warranty of habitability imposes a continuing obligation on the landlord to keep the property in decent condition: at a minimum standard of safety and sanitation, defined by local codes. The landlord's failure to comply "substantially" with this warranty can entitle the tenant to withhold or reduce the rent owed or even to declare the lease terminated and move out. (In some jurisdictions laws permit the tenant to pay rent held by the court in the event of a dispute with the landlord.) In return, the tenant is obligated not to "trash the place" and to generally follow the landlord's reasonable rules and regulations.

Supporters claim that it keeps housing affordable and prevents the working and middle class from being priced out of living in urban areas where they work. Opponents say it is an unwarranted interference with the market that kills the incentive to build and maintain rental housing. Because rent control varies so widely from one locale to another, it is beyond the scope of this book to explain it in detail.

SECURITY DEPOSITS

One of the unpleasant aspects of renting property is the payment of a **security deposit**. The security deposit protects the landlord if the tenant damages the property or fails to pay rent. Usually the tenant pays the security deposit at the time the lease is signed. The landlord may ask for any amount—this is also subject to negotiation—but, again, many local laws restrict the amount to the equivalent of one or two months' rent. This money, then, is refundable as long as the tenant complies with the lease. But it may not normally be applied to rent, even the last month's rent before a tenant moves, because that undermines the landlord's "security blanket."

MONEY FOR NOTHING

The shift away from the "real estate" approach to renting (see "New Thinking") has also resulted in an important change in a landlord's obligations to replace a tenant who leaves in the middle of the term. Under the old approach, the landlord was entitled to keep the apartment empty during the tenant's leasehold, and the tenant had to keep paying rent. Now traditional contract principles apply, including the principal of **mitigation of damages**. As applied here, this principle requires that, even if the tenant wrongfully violates the lease, the landlord has to make a good faith effort to **re-let** the property—find a new tenant at the market rate. The old tenant only has to pay rent for the time the premises were vacant and, after the property is re-let, the shortfall if the new rent is less than the old.

Because security-deposit abuse by landlords is a problem, many states and localities require that the deposit be kept in a separate account for security deposits, with interest payable to the tenant. (You can negotiate for interest on your security deposit if the law does not require it when you are renting. It's a reasonable request, because the idea is to give the landlord security, not an interest-free loan.) Some states also require that the bank and the account where the security deposit is held be designated on the lease or by letter within thirty days of the lease. States and localities often require that the security deposit be returned within a certain number of days after the tenant moves out and that the landlord specify what repairs were necessary and what they cost before money can be withheld from the deposit. If the landlord violates these requirements during tenancy, he loses the security deposit, and the tenant is permitted to apply the amount of the deposit to the next month's rent. Because of the abuse problem, a tenant who succeeds in convincing a judge that the security deposit was withheld may often receive extra damages.

LANDLORD-TENANT CONFLICTS

SELF-HELP

Those who watch reruns of *The Honeymooners* from the 1950s will remember Ralph Kramden being "put out on the street" by his landlord—literally out on Chauncey Street with all his and Alice's worldly belongings. There was a time when self-help was an approved remedy in landlord-tenant relations. If you didn't pay the rent, the landlord simply changed the locks and kicked you out. That's illegal now, as is turning off the utilities, much less—as happened on another old TV show—removing the tenant's door from the apartment for nonpayment of rent. Now *only a court can order an eviction*—and only the sheriff can carry one out. We will briefly discuss the eviction process in the next section.

On the other hand, a number of self-help remedies may be available to *tenants* when landlords don't keep their end of the bargain, mainly by failing to do proper maintenance. These rights vary according to state and local law. Even before you read this list, keep in mind that a judge is likely to have the last word as to whether you have acted correctly in taking matters into your own hands.

- **Repair and deduct.** This law sometimes permits the tenant to make *essential* repairs that the landlord refuses to make in a reasonable time and then deduct the cost from the rent.

- **Reduced rent.** When the premises do not comply with the standards of the local building code, the law may permit tenants to serve notice on the landlord that they intend to pay reduced rent unless specified repairs are made by a reasonable time. If the repairs aren't made, tenants can pay the landlord a rent amount that is less than the contract rent.

- **Unilateral termination.** "Unilateral" means one-sided—here, the side being you, the tenant. There are three possible bases that could justify unilateral termination:

  - **Illegal lease.** If the landlord has been cited for gross code violations, it may be illegal for you to even live there. If occupancy is illegal, so is the lease.

  - **Constructive eviction.** The landlord never sent you an eviction notice or brought an eviction action in court but has made life on the premises so miserable that you can't really live there. "Constructive" means it's "as if" the landlord went ahead and evicted you.

  - **Material noncompliance.** This is reduced rent taken a step further. You give the landlord notice that if things aren't fixed within a reasonable time, you're leaving.

If you do any of the above, if permitted by the law in your state—or if you complain to the code-enforcing agency or join a tenants' organization—the landlord may not have the right to evict you. In fact, if the landlord does so for any reason other than a breach of the lease (which, if you are acting justifiably and legally, you have not committed), the landlord may be liable for **retaliatory eviction** in many states. In these jurisdictions, retaliatory eviction is assumed whenever a landlord evicts you (or even threatens to), refuses to renew your lease, increases the rent, or decreases building services within a legally fixed period (usually several months) after you exercise any of your legal rights as a tenant.

If the landlord thinks you've acted improperly, he or she generally has no self-help remedies. To get you out of the property, written notice must be served that the lease will be terminated unless you pay any back rent claimed to be due (or cease violating a building rule). To evict you, the landlord must take you to landlord-tenant court or housing court.

HOUSING COURT

Whether it's called "landlord-tenant court," "housing court," or something else, a special court is set up in most states for the **summary disposition** (quick resolution) of disputes between landlords and tenants. This usually precludes the right to a jury trial.

A landlord files the lawsuit in court and then **serves**—delivers in a legally specified way (sometimes mail in this case)—a copy of the **summons** (notice that you must come to court) and **complaint** (description of the claims against you). In this summary procedure you may have a court date within two weeks or so. If you show up, this is the kind of courtroom where it is easy to make your case—judges are usually helpful and do not expect all tenants to be able to afford lawyers. The proceedings also tend to be rather informal, as court proceedings go.

If you choose to defend yourself, you can assert most of the contract defenses we discussed early on, as well as the special protections for tenants discussed in this chapter. Keep in mind that most states have very specific requirements for lease-termination letters. Find out what yours are; if the letter you received doesn't conform—or if you didn't get one—the landlord's case is automatically tossed out. The landlord has to start again. Some states require registration of all rental property. Find out if your landlord has complied; if not, the landlord may be out of luck.

If, alternatively, you don't show up, the court gives the landlord a **default judgment** and sets a deadline, sometimes a few weeks, sometimes a few days, for you to move out. If you don't move out, though, the landlord can arrange to have the sheriff or other local official physically remove you. The law will bend over backward to give tenants the benefit of the doubt, but sooner or later a contract *is* a contract.

THE LONG AND WINDING ROAD

Considering all the technical requirements of suing in landlord-tenant court—properly serving the papers on the tenant, the processing and backlog in many courts and sheriff's offices, and housing-court judges' disinclination to order people out of their homes—eviction is usually a slow process, often many months. And in many courts the judge will "call off the dogs" if the tenant pays the rent owed, even at the last minute—at least this time. There's a point, though, where a landlord will convince the court not to let a habitual nonpayer make the landlord go through hoops each month just to get the rent that is due. (Some leases even make "habitual nonpayment or late payment" a separate kind of breach.) And then you really will be out on the street.

CHAPTER EIGHT

Guard Duty

Warranties

WHAT A WARRANTY IS

Y OU MAY HAVE SEEN the terms "warranty" and "guarantee." Both words have the same root, which means "to guard." For consumers, the two terms mean essentially the same thing: Each represents a bundle of obligations taken on by the provider as part of the purchase contract or imposed on the provider by law.

EXPRESS AND IMPLIED WARRANTIES

The law classifies warranties as "express" or "implied." **Express warranties** are promises to back up the product expressed by the seller either orally or in writing. Suppose your friend bought your Edsel, and you said, "I guarantee you'll get another ten thousand miles out of this transmission." That's an express warranty. An express warranty is a specific statement of fact or a promise. It isn't an opinion about quality or value, such as, "This Edsel is the best used car for sale in town." "Best" could mean anything to the speaker—best color, best looking, best status symbol. You as a consumer are expected to understand that.

In contrast, a **warrantor**—the person making the warranty—does not state **implied warranties** at all. They're automatic, or implied by law, in certain kinds of transactions. There are two main types of implied warranties: the implied **warranty of merchantability** and the implied **warranty of fitness for a particular purpose**. (There also is an implied **warranty of title** in a sale and **an implied warranty against interference** in a lease.)

- **The implied warranty of merchantability.** When someone is in the business of selling or leasing a specific kind of product, the law requires that the item be adequate for the purpose for which it is purchased or leased. This is a general rule of fairness—that what looks like a carton of milk in the supermarket dairy case really is milk that is drinkable and not sour or unusable. The implied warranty of merchantability applies only if the seller is in the business of selling the item that is the subject matter of the sale. So it wouldn't apply to someone buying your Edsel, unless you were in the business of selling cars. What you should remember, however, is the converse: Someone who is in the business of selling cars is always assumed to warrant that they "go"—though not necessarily much more.

- **The implied warranty of fitness for a particular purpose.** Another type of implied warranty is the implied warranty of fitness for a particular purpose, which means that any seller or lessor (even a non-professional) is presumed to guarantee that an item will be fit for any particular purpose for which it is being sold, as long as the buyer makes that purpose known and the seller knows that the buyer is relying on him to provide a suitable item. When you sell your used Edsel to your friend, you make this warranty if you understand your friend's purpose is to race the car, and you understand that she is relying on you to provide a car for that purpose, as opposed to basic transportation. Or suppose your friend told you she needed a car that could tow a trailer full of granite up steep mountains in the snow, and that she was relying on your Edsel to do the job. When, with this knowledge, you sell the Edsel to your friend, you make an implied warranty that it can do that. When the car fails in that purpose, your warranty will have been breached. On the other hand, if your friend tells you she's buying your car only because she needs spare Edsel parts, you can sell your Edsel—even if it's sitting out back on cinder blocks—without breaching any warranty.

KINDS OF EXPRESS WARRANTIES

Some express warranties deal with the quality of the goods: Will they do a specific job or meet certain specifications? Are they reasonably fit for their intended purpose? How long after the purchase will the manufacturer make repairs or replace parts and under what terms? Other warranties might deal with the ownership of goods: Does the seller have good title or ownership rights that may be lawfully transferred to the buyer? (These express warranties of title are part of a home purchase contract, for example, which is covered in chapter 11.)

Durations of warranties may vary considerably, depending on the type of transaction and warranty involved, and the applicable law. In most states, you have up to four years to enforce an implied warranty after the start of the transaction. In cases involving written warranties, the period may be much shorter. And unless prohibited by state law, the duration of the implied warranty can be limited to the duration of the written warranty. A written warranty will disclose how long it lasts. It may be as short as ninety days for a portable radio. A warranty on a new car, on the other hand, may last several years or thousands of miles.

THE MAGNUSON-MOSS WARRANTY ACT

A federal law, the **Magnuson-Moss Warranty Act**, covers written warranties for consumer goods costing more than a few dollars. It does not require that merchants make written warranties. If they do make such a warranty, however, it must meet certain standards. The warranty must be available for you to read before you buy. It must be written in plain language and must include the following information:

- the name and address of the company making the warranty;
- the product or parts covered;
- whether the warranty promises replacement, repair, or refund, and if there are any expenses (such as shipping or labor) you would have to pay;

- the length of the warranty;
- if the warranty does not cover certain legal damages—usually conse-quential or "out-of-pocket" damages, beyond the cost of the product—then a statement of that fact;
- the action you should take if something goes wrong;
- if the company providing the warranty requires you to waive certain rights in a dispute or submit to arbitration, then a statement of that fact (see chapter 4);
- a brief description of your legal rights.

Some states have warranty laws that provide consumers with more protection than the Magnuson-Moss act. A typical example is state **lemon laws**, which mandate new car dealers to refund con-sumers' money when a new car is so defective that it meets the statu-tory definition of a "lemon." Some states even have lemon laws for used cars. (See chapter 9 on auto purchases.)

WARRANTY SHOPPING

Consider different manufacturers' warranty terms when you shop. But keep in mind that the terms of a warranty are seldom negotiable, especially the length of the warranty, whether it covers only certain parts or certain problems, and what you must do to use your rights. You are virtually never buying the product from the manufacturer, after all, and retailers are usually not the ones offering the first-line warranty service themselves (although some stores that offer service plans do take over even the early warranty service).

On the other hand, you should know the retailer's return policy for defective merchandise. Mail-order and other deep-discount sell-ers frequently offer five or ten days for returns of defective mer-chandise but then require you to turn to the manufacturer with any problems that arise after that initial period. Other merchandisers such as appliance superstores often offer a thirty-day "no questions asked" return policy, which is very desirable. You don't even have to find a flaw; just change your mind, and they'll give you a full refund. And still other stores will ultimately stand behind all products they sell, even beyond the technical cut-off date for returns. The length of that commitment tells you about the strength of that commitment—to you.

FULL AND LIMITED WARRANTIES

The difference between a **full warranty** and a **limited warranty** can be the difference between night and day. The Magnuson-Moss act requires all written warranties for consumer products costing more than a few dollars to be designated as either a "full" or "limited" warranty.

FULL WARRANTIES

A full warranty is a promise that the product will be repaired or replaced free during the warranty period. State and federal laws require that if the warrantor repairs the item, it must be fixed within a reasonable time without charge and it must be reasonably convenient to

---

THE "FACTORY"

In the language of appliance retailers, warranties, packaging, and service often come from "the factory." That doesn't really mean, however, the place where the appliance is manufactured. The *real* factory might be in China, Mexico, or Singapore, while the factory they mean—the location of the executive offices, warehouse, or service center—is in a New Jersey office park or a Houston skyscraper. For that matter, the company whose brand name is on a product may not even *own* a factory. You'd be surprised which well-known brands of appliances are merely nameplates, distribution networks, and marketing strategies. Thus, a "factory" warranty is really the warranty offered by the company that distributes the appliance under its name, whether or not there's a factory by that name at all.

---

get the item to and from the repair site. If the company can't fix the problem in a reasonable number of attempts, it must give the consumer a refund or replacement. In effect, this is a federal lemon law. Many stores will offer a short full warranty of their own (thirty to ninety days), above what the manufacturer offers, and some premium credit cards will double a warranty for up to a year for products purchased with the card. Repairs or replacement during the extended warranty period become the responsibility of the card issuer after the manufacturer's warranty expires.

LIMITED WARRANTIES

A limited warranty is much more common. Not surprisingly, it covers less—usually only parts and almost never the cost of labor beyond the first month or so. For more expensive appliances such as cars or computers, however, reputable manufacturers may offer limited warranties for a longer period of time that provide greater coverage. For example, you might be able to find a computer warranty covering everything during the first year and including on-site repair (where a technician comes to you) during that period. When such warranty coverage is available, there's no reason you should spend a lot of dollars on an important and trouble-prone product without it.

Don't wait until a product needs repair to find out what's covered in your written warranty. Compare the terms and conditions of the

---

WARRANTY SENSE

The best-made products often have the best warranties, because they're less likely to need them. Thus, the manufacturer can guarantee a long period with little risk. A warranty is a statement about the maker's confidence in its products; because it involves the manufacturer's pocketbook, it's a statement you should take seriously. Try to figure the value of a warranty into the price of a product and make it part of your formula for purchase decision-making.

warranty before you buy, and look for the warranty that best meets your needs.

WARRANTY DISCLAIMERS

A merchant may not disclaim a warranty *after* you've made the purchase. But *before* you buy, in most states implied warranties of merchantability or fitness may be excluded or **disclaimed** if the contract or disclaimer is in writing and the relevant language is obvious. This may not be allowed under federal law, however, if there is a written warranty. For a disclaimer of the implied warranty of merchantability to be valid, the disclaimer must use the word "merchantability," or it must use language that in common understanding makes plain that there is no implied warranty. In contrast, the implied warranty of fitness for a particular purpose may be disclaimed merely by a less communicative written statement. If, however, a manufacturer has given a Magnuson-Moss full or limited warranty, the manufacturer may not disclaim any implied warranty. In any event, a person may not disclaim an express warranty that's written in the contract, but an oral one may not be enforceable in every case. If there is not a written warranty, a disclaimer is common. In many cases of consumer products, a warranty will be stated in the purchase contract you sign, which will also state a specific remedy if the product fails. This avoids giving no warranty while still protecting the seller or lessor to some extent. For example, the contract may provide that the seller will repair or replace the merchandise if necessary, but that the customer has no right to receive any money back. This protects the seller against the worst-case scenario (having to give you back money) while giving you some protection. This is called a **warranty limitation**.

Most warranty limitations exclude some or all forms of **consequential damages**. As explained earlier, these are losses caused by the product's defect, including your lost time and expense that result from the defect and repair costs. If, for example, your new computer crashes and destroys weeks of work, you may get a new computer. But under the terms of the wording in the warranty that came with the computer (as well as the disks), the warrantor will almost certainly not reimburse you for the lost time, work, or software—much less a lost job or client. At some point the law expects you to protect yourself, in this case by backing up your computer files. (Computer experts say that one in ten floppy disks is flawed!) An important exception to this is that you usually may recover damages in cases of personal injury that result from a product's defect.

ON-LINE WARRANTY SUPPORT

Most manufacturers of computers and other sophisticated equipment include **on-line** assistance during the warranty period; better manufacturers include it for life. (This is less impressive than it sounds, because many top-of-the-line computers and office equipment available five years ago are hopelessly obsolete today. If the products aren't in use, the on-line support won't be needed.) On-line assistance is also critical to get the most out of sophisticated computer software. No documentation provided with software has ever been able to anticipate every glitch that these powerful programs, running on powerful machines, can come up with.

On-line assistance consists of a staff of technicians (often called

---

SHORT-TERM SUPPORT

A computer software program gives users thirty days of free support. That might be adequate for most problems, because many arise during the initial installation and configuration of new software. But what if six months later you replace your computer, and, when reloading the software on the new unit, it starts spewing "garbage" onto the screen and won't work? After the first month, the manufacturer charges $15 a call for support. But the software itself only cost $30! It might be worth it to buy a newer program, perhaps from a different manufacturer, rather than pay 50 percent of the cost of software you already know has kinks in it.

"techs") who sit at banks of telephones and computer terminals and answer your questions about problems you're having with your computer. Look for these on-line features:

• **Long duration of free service.** As mentioned above, the difference between five years of free support and lifetime support may be meaningless. But while you're likely to have more problems in the first thirty days of using a computer application, thirty days isn't a long time to assume *all* your problems will be ironed out. And some problems can render the product worthless. Hardware and software manufacturers will often allow you to buy more time for support or will offer it on a charge-per-call basis. Once again, put these numbers and durations into the hopper when making your choice.

• **Toll-free calls.** It is amazing that anyone requires you to make a toll call for free support, much less that you might spend ten or twenty minutes or more on hold (see below) while the phone company is running the meter. Nonetheless, some major manufacturers continue to nickel-and-dime their customers this way. If all things are equal, or even close, go for the company that's brought its customer service into the modern age and offers an 800 number. You'll be glad you did.

• **Twenty-four-hour availability.** Or at least something like it. Some support staffs are available at least until midnight. After all, if you're working at that hour, you're likely facing some deadlines the next morning, and a technical problem could be fatal. Certainly, places that close up shop at 4:30 P.M. eastern standard time aren't of much use to customers in Oregon, who might not have eaten lunch yet.

• **Adequate coverage.** One of the biggest powers in computer software is notorious for the "virtual" impossibility of getting through to its technicians. Busy signals are followed by long Muzak-on-hold phone queues or even phone systems that just hang up on you after a while. Other, hungrier (not necessarily smaller) manufacturers provide better service. To find out if a company's support is accessible, try to get their phone number before you buy and make a sample call. Alternatively, ask present customers, read the computer-consumer press, or even ask a salesperson (as long as the store carries a range of competing brands).

- **Technical knowledge.** A few calls to most of these techs will impress you with their knowledge of their products and computing generally. But some staffs are better trained than others. Again, computer professionals and the computer press are the best guide for this kind of information.

- **E-mail option.** Many manufacturers offer an electronic mail address where their technicians can answer less urgent questions. This is an excellent option, because it saves you time on the phone and the frustration of trying to get through. Also, some of the better-known software programs are supported by on-line bulletin boards run by fellow users (and perhaps sponsored or moderated by the manufacturer) who know just what you're going through.

EXTENDED WARRANTIES AND SERVICE AGREEMENTS

Many companies offer **extended warranties** or **service contracts** for varying lengths of time and varying amounts of money (see below). Both of these will cost you extra. Take a hard look, and ask if the benefits are worth the cost. Consider how the extended warranty or service contract enhances your regular warranty. Find out where you'll have to send the product for repairs.

SILICON ALCHEMISTS

If an on-line technician's advice doesn't ring true, sounds radical, or still doesn't produce the hoped-for results, call again. You're 99 percent certain not to get the same tech and 50 percent certain not to get the same advice. There are many ways to skin an algorithm. Computing isn't as exact a science as you might think!

Keep in mind that some products tend to be durable, making service contracts less valuable, while others are trouble-prone. Some office managers swear by service contracts for facsimile machines or laser printers. Considering how temperamental computers can be, they may also be good candidates for extra coverage. Freezers, on the other hand, will usually last decades with minimal maintenance. Clock radios kept out of the bathtub are also long-lived. Appliances like these don't usually need service contracts.

Also look, especially in service contracts, at whether there's a deductible. For example, the contract might not cover repairs costing less than $50. The deductible amount, or a per-repair flat fee that you agree to pay, can add up, erasing all the expected savings. Sometimes it pays to wait until after the warranty has expired before deciding to buy a service contract, if you can. Then you have a sense of a product's reliability.

Be sure to take a good look at who's backing up the contract or warranty. Is it a well-known manufacturer? The store where you got it? Or a company you've never heard of with only a post-office box for an address?

Ultimately, don't be pressured by a salesperson into taking one of those contracts. They're frequently an important source of profit on the transaction. With the sale of a service contract, stores can get back some or all of what they've given up to a savvy negotiator. Think hard before you fall for this sales pitch.

PROTECTING WARRANTY RIGHTS

Just like any other right, there's no sense fighting for (or shopping for) warranty rights only to lose the ability to use them when you need them. Here are a few simple rules to follow:

• **Save the box.** Many warranties require shipping in the original packaging to service centers for warranty service. Sometimes this gets the manufacturer off the hook completely. But it also makes sense, because the original packaging is custom-designed to protect the product through the rigors of shipping. It's true that these boxes and all that Styrofoam take up a lot of space. If space is at a premium, you can collapse the boxes by cutting the tape or pulling out the large staples that hold the flaps together. New shipping (not masking!) tape will make the boxes as good as new. And any specially molded Styrofoam may store better out of the boxes; you may be able to get it to interlock or stack efficiently, taking up less space than it did in the original container. Also keep any documentation, software, or demonstration videos, etc., that came with the product in case you have to return the product for a refund.

• **Play by the rules.** Any violation of the manufacturer's operating and service instructions will probably void the warranty. If you think you can save the time and trouble of getting authorized warranty service with your own power screwdriver, that's your call. But doing so often voids your warranty coverage, because—with all due respect—most consumers are likely to make things worse once they start "poking around in there."

• **Keep good records.** Hang on to your receipts through the warranty period. They are your proof of when the warranty period starts and ends and are more important than the warranty return card. (That card is often just a marketing device that enables the manufacturer to learn more about you.)

If you do end up contacting the manufacturer, do so only as instructed in the warranty. It's a good idea to contact the manufacturer in writing, keeping copies of all correspondence, at the address specified in the warranty. That's especially true if you aren't getting quick responses. Your correspondence file will protect your warranty rights near the end of the coverage period. For more details, see chapter 15 on contract remedies.

If you do give in to the urge to use the phone, by all means keep a log of whom you've spoken to, with the date and time of the conversation and what they've told you. And, once again, if one telephone call doesn't do it, try another. You might get someone more helpful the next time around.

The quality of the retailer you're working with often comes full circle. Say a problem arises with warranty service, and after all the advice, repairs, or even replacements the manufacturer has sent you, you've had it with the product. You want a refund. But don't count on getting one from the manufacturer. They have little to gain—they've lost you as a customer either way.

At this point you might try the store where you got the item. It may be able to go around the warranty process, especially if it's fairly soon (say, a few months) after you bought the product. Stores are often able to ship back defective products that the manufacturer wouldn't have accepted from you directly. Manufacturers are, after all, more connected to retailers than consumers and must work with them. And, more than the manufacturers, the retailer *needs* you, and a better one will bend over backward to find a way to help. Doing so is an investment in a long-term customer relationship—the old-fashioned, and still successful, way to make money. That's why going to a more reputable dealer could be worth paying a reasonable premium over the place that charges—and gives—the least.

CHAPTER NINE

■

The Wheels of Life

Automobile Sales, Leases, and Repairs

BUYING A NEW CAR, TRUCK, OR VAN: The thought might excite you, or it might make you anxious. But no matter how you feel about it, the bottom line is that you're about to part with a substantial amount of hard-earned dollars for something that's going to be around for a while.

BUYING A NEW CAR

As with any other big-ticket item, it's important to do your homework in advance—before hitting the showroom. Decide what kind of vehicle you need, and how much you can afford to spend. Think about size: do you need a big family car, or will a sporty little coupe do the trick? How much head and leg room do you need? What safety features are important to you—antilock brakes, side air bags? (Check with your insurance agent to find out what discounts you'll get with these features. In some cases, such as car alarms, the insurance savings may make it much easier to afford the option.) Think about other options: do you care if you have power everything, or do you mind cranking open the windows yourself? Do you prefer cloth, vinyl, or leather seats? Are other features important to you? And what is a realistic budget for you?

After you've analyzed your needs and your finances, you're ready to begin looking. Before you start pounding the pavement, first check out some of the consumer-oriented publications that have information on cost, reliability, comfort, and other features of many cars. Such books and magazines include *Consumer's Guide, Consumer Reports,* and *The Car Book*. Many of these publications can be tremendously helpful to you in the negotiating process (see "Negotiating Tips When Buying," page 100). Your local library and bookstores should have many of these references. Then, as you zero in on a model or models, or even a make, talk to people you know and try to find out what kinds of experiences they've had with particular cars and dealerships.

ADVERTISING AND SALES PRACTICES

Advertising for motor vehicles is largely regulated by statute, and regulations vary from state to state. In some places ads must state the number of advertised vehicles in stock. Other items that may be required in an ad include price, dealer and factory-installed options, and warranty terms. In addition, if the vehicle is "on sale," the ad should state the date the sale ends. Be alert for scams. The bait-and-switch ad scam—where the dealer advertises a vehicle that he or she does not intend to sell—is particularly important to watch for. (We discussed this technique earlier, in chapter 5.) Also, if the dealer knows important facts about the vehicle but fails to reveal them, the law may consider that a deceptive act that could enable you to cancel the deal and even recover damages in court under consumer fraud laws. "Clearing up" the missing facts after the sale does not erase the dealer's deceitful act.

THE NEW CAR CONTRACT

A new car contract must be in writing, according to the present statute of frauds section of the **Uniform Commercial Code (UCC)**, in effect in every state but Louisiana. If the dealer has not signed the purchase agreement, you may not be able to enforce the contract.

The sales contract should

- describe the car and include the **vehicle identification number** (VIN), found on the driver's side of the dashboard, near the windshield;
- state whether the car is new, used, or a former demonstrator, rental car,

or taxicab, as well as the model year (e.g., 1996, 1997—it could be new but from a previous model year);

- include price terms consistent with your oral agreement and details on any trade-in you will supply, including mileage and the dollar amount credited;

- include a cancellation provision that enables you to get your deposit back if certain conditions occur, such as the car not being delivered by a certain date; this is required by law in many states;

- state the warranty terms very clearly;

- include financing terms that state price, deposit, trade-in allowance, annual percentage rate of finance charge (APR), monthly payments (including any taxes), and length of term.

NEGOTIATING TIPS WHEN BUYING

Do you like to negotiate and try to get the best possible price? Buying a car usually gives you plenty of opportunities to test your bargaining skills. A recent study by the American Bar Foundation found that the price of cars that are exactly the same can easily vary by $1,000 or more. A lot of that depends on the bargaining skills and tenacity of the buyer.

Unfortunately, lots of us *don't* like to haggle. And even if you do, salespeople at the car dealer do it all the time and are usually very good at it.

Experts recommend that you do some hard figuring *before* you even step into the showroom. How much can you afford for a down payment? For monthly payments? It may even help to shop for a loan before you shop for a car, so you know exactly what a loan for X dollars will cost. Then try to get the car you want for that price.

Go in armed with information. Books, magazines, and even on-line and fax services can tell you exactly what a *dealer* pays for a certain model and each possible option. Some will even calculate what a fair price is, given how much the dealer pays. This information gives you a solid base from which to negotiate (far better than looking at the sticker price and asking

By the way, don't let the dealer take back your solid negotiating gains in last-minute add-ons. For example, virtually no new car needs rustproofing; in fact, it voids most manufacturers' rust warranties. Is an alarm necessary or even useful where you live? Don't get one if it isn't. Credit insurance is an expensive way to guarantee that your family will be able to pay off the loan in the event of your death. Paying off your debts is one of the reasons to buy regular term or whole life insurance, and it's much cheaper per insured dollar than the credit insurance offered by finance companies. Remember that ultimately almost anything can be made to sound cheap if you divide its cost by twelve, twenty-four, thirty-six, forty-eight, or sixty (the number of months in your finance contract). But you could turn around after all those little add-ons and find yourself paying twenty

them to reduce it by 5 percent or some other arbitrary figure). Let the dealer know that *you* know how much the car and the options cost them. (You'll probably find that many options are marked up way more than the car itself.) Let them know, too, that you're comparison shopping and will be getting prices from at least three dealers. To make the comparisons simpler, keep your trade-in separate from buying the new car. Don't even mention your trade-in possibility until you've settled on a price for the new car and options.

Sound like a lot of hassle and work? You can avoid the whole problem by either going for a "one-price" model or going to a dealer who has promised not to dicker. Or you can use one of the auto quotation services that you'll find advertised in car books and magazines. These services say that they can get you very low prices because they work with an extensive network of dealers. For a fee they'll get price quotes for you from a variety of dealers, letting you compare and make your choice in privacy—and with the time to make a smart choice. Some of these services are available on-line, through the Internet or commercial services such as America Online, as well as by phone and fax.

or fifty dollars more a month than you thought for items that are overpriced to begin with and usually available cheaper elsewhere.

If the dealer presents you with a computer-printed form that has terms in it you don't agree with, don't be shy to make the dealer go back and run off another. Be sure that credit insurance is not included if you don't want it. Also watch out for "destination charges" and the notorious "dealer prep." These are just price add-ons, especially the latter. You don't have to pay them, and you should be able to negotiate them away.

Your old Edsel will almost certainly be accepted in trade for credit toward the purchase. Experts recommend separating new car negotiations from a possible trade-in (see "Negotiating Tips When Buying"), but if you do mix them, try to get the highest price possible on your trade-in while negotiating hard on the new car. Know the **blue book** value of your car. (The blue book—*National Automobile Dealers Association Official Used Car Guide*—is available at most public libraries, banks, and other lending institutions.) Given your knowledge of its condition and mileage, push hard for at least the blue book value. Make sure the value of your trade-in cannot be decreased when the car is delivered.

Better yet, negotiate a provision that enables you to pay cash or the trade-in amount for a down payment, then try to sell the car on your own. The dealer is interested in the "turnaround"—the profit that can be made in selling the car. Someone who really wants the Edsel for personal use is probably willing to pay more than the dealer, because the same car will—because of the turnaround calculation—cost more if it is bought from the dealer. Your only problem then is timing everything (and getting a ride to the dealership!).

The last step in the deal is to sign the purchase agreement. Be very careful at this stage. By signing it, you become obligated to the dealer to buy the car specified, with the features specified, according to the terms you've negotiated. *Before* you sign the purchase agreement, make sure you understand and accept all the contract terms. This is important, because not reading it won't get you off the hook—you'll probably have to abide by the conditions of the contract you have signed even if you have not read it. Read the contract carefully. Ask questions. Cross out blank spaces to avoid any additions after you sign. *Make sure that all of the dealer's oral promises made during negotiations appear in the contract.* Do *not* sign until the contract satisfies *you*.

Who should sign it for the other side? Either an authorized salesperson or a supervisor, the manager, or the owner. If for some reason the person is not authorized, the contract might not be enforceable, and the dealership might refuse to deliver the car you thought you had bought at the price you thought you had negotiated. A new car is a huge purchase. With that much money at stake, you should be sure that you've met the manager or owner, and that the person signing the contract is authorized to sign.

If you cancel the sales contract after signing, what happens to your deposit depends on the stage of the transaction and the contract terms you signed. The earlier in the deal, the more likely the dealer will refund your deposit and the less likely you will be sued. Some states entitle you to a refund if, for example, you decide to cancel before the dealer representative signs the contract. If you need financing, be sure that the purchase agreement states that you can get a refund if you cannot get financing, despite your best efforts.

DEALER FINANCING VERSUS OTHER OPTIONS

Most people don't have enough cash to buy a new or late-model used car and need financing. Banks, credit unions, finance companies, and car dealers are all potential funding sources. Interest rates will vary among these options, although some experts think you'll generally do better at a bank or credit union than at the dealer or finance company. Credit unions may have the lowest rates for used cars.

Shop around for the best deal by comparing the various terms and **annual percentage rates** (APRs). The APR is the unit price for credit that takes into account all the finance costs of the loan. The APR is expressed as a yearly rate. It may depend partially on your credit history. It pays to shop around.

The creditor (the person or institution who provides the money for the car) must inform you, before you are bound to particular financing, of:

- the APR (this must be conspicuous—for example, printed in red or much larger type than the rest of the document);
- the balance on which the creditor computes the finance charge;
- the dollar amount of the finance charge (this must also be conspicuous);
- the amount to be financed (the amount of credit);
- the total dollar amount to be paid (credit obtained plus finance charge); and
- the number, amount, and due dates of payments.

The APR enables you to comparison shop for credit. Don't make the mistake of automatically going for the arrangement that gives you the lowest monthly payment, because it could cost you more in the long run, as explained below. A good example of using APR to find the best deal is provided by shopping for financing for a car. Suppose that you're buying a $5,000 used car, putting $1,000 down, and planning to borrow $4,000. How might you use the credit terms disclosed to select the best credit contract? Before you sign a loan, the lender must show you the amount financed ($4,000), length of loan, monthly payment, total finance charge, and the APR. The table below compares four credit arrangements.

FOUR POSSIBLE CREDIT ARRANGEMENTS*

	APR (%)	LENGTH OF LOAN (YEARS)	MONTHLY PAYMENT	TOTAL FINANCE CHARGE	TOTAL AMOUNT PAID
Lender A	11	3	$131	$ 714	$4,714
Lender B	11	4	103	962	4,962
Lender C	12	4	105	1,056	5,056
Lender D	12	2	188	512	4,512

*These figures are correct, even though the arithmetic appears slightly different in some cases. Lenders frequently round off monthly payments to the nearest dollar and adjust the final payment to make up the difference.

Which loan offers the best terms? The answer depends partly on what you need. The two cheapest loans (those with the lowest APRs) are offered by lenders A and B. You will pay a higher total finance charge to Lender B because you're using borrowed funds for four years instead of three. However, if you can only budget $105 a month for car payments, and you can't find an APR less than 11 percent, you might have to take the longer term from Lender B. You will cut your monthly payments from $131 to $103, but you will have twelve more payments, and you'll wind up paying almost $250 more in finance charges.

You may not be able to shop for credit effectively if you merely compare APRs. The benefits of a low rate may have to be compared with those of a rebate—you can't have both. The less credit you need, the better deal the rebate may be.

For example, a major automobile manufacturer recently offered consumers a choice of a cash rebate of $1,500 or 5.8 percent financing for four years on certain models. Assume that the car that you want to buy under this offer costs $16,000, and that you have $2,000 for a down payment. You have the following choices:

1. **Finance through the dealer.** A $2,000 down payment, if required, would leave $14,000 to be financed over four years at 5.8 percent. Your monthly payments would be $327.51.

2. **Finance through a bank, credit union, or other lender.** With the $1,500 cash rebate and your $2,000, you have $3,500 to apply to the purchase price of $16,000. This leaves $12,500 to borrow ($16,000−$3,500 = $12,500). If you can borrow $12,500 for four years at 11.17 percent, you will find that your monthly payments are $324.10. This is the better deal.

Or let's say your car dealer is pushing "incentive financing" by offering a 4.9 percent rate, while your credit union may be charging 12 percent on new car loans. In such cases, you need to find out how much the dealer would charge for the car if you paid cash. By holding constant the down payment and the length of the loan from the dealer or credit union, you can see which arrangement would cost less in finance charges and be better for your particular situation. In essence, you make all the terms of the two credit arrangements the same, except for finance charges and monthly payment. Then favor the deal that gives you the lowest monthly payment for the same length loan.

THE PAPER CHASE

One way buying a car differs from buying a loaf of bread is that the buyer virtually never walks in with a checkbook and drives off with the car—especially where financing is involved. Part of the reason is that, even if the car doesn't have to be ordered for you, the dealer usually handles the paperwork with your state's motor vehicle administration, which makes it possible for you to hold title—legal ownership—of the car. (This is one area of the law in which possession is much less than nine-tenths of the law, because the technical title requirements are legally critical.)

Dealers are entitled to charge a fair fee for handling your paperwork, but keep an eye on these numbers—getting you a registration and plates shouldn't be a profit center for them. Use this opportunity, though, to have them order duplicates of the registration, as needed for your family, in states that issue them.

What if something happens to the car between the time you make your deposit and the time the dealer delivers it? The answer depends on who has the risk of loss. Usually, unless there is an agreement to the contrary, the party who possesses the vehicle bears the risk and is more likely to have insurance against the loss. Under the UCC, if the seller is a merchant (for example, a car dealer), the risk of loss passes to buyers only when they receive the car. If the seller is not a merchant, as in a private sale of a used car, the risk passes to the buyer on **tender of delivery**—when the seller actually tries to deliver the car or makes it available for pickup arranged by a contract.

REPOSSESSION

You may lose title if you fail to make your payments as they become due. The creditor is then permitted to repossess your car. When you buy a car on credit, you usually give the creditor rights to your property (the car) that are superior to the rights of your other creditors.

This is known as a **lien**. When you buy the vehicle on credit, you sign a **security agreement**, which gives the creditor a **security interest** in your car (the collateral). These liens are filed with the state, usually by noting the lender's interest on the title certificate. If you don't pay, the creditor may try to get the car back and apply its value toward your debt. That is **repossession**.

The only limitation on a repossession is that the vehicle must be taken without "breaching the peace," i.e., without violence or a significant potential for violence. The repossessor can, however, essentially break into the car or tow it away. In many states, the creditor does not have to sue the debtor or even notify the debtor of the default before reclaiming the vehicle.

If your car is repossessed, you usually have one chance to redeem yourself—or, more specifically, to **redeem** the property before it is sold to someone else. To do so, you normally must pay the entire balance due, plus any repossession costs and other reasonable charges. This is because of the contract's **acceleration clause**. This forces you, the debtor, to pay the entire outstanding debt, not just the amount of overdue payments. Some states, however, have laws that allow you to "reinstate" the contract by making up missed payments. But in most cases, once a default and repossession have occurred, it is unlikely that you will have enough money to pay the entire balance, even if you don't have to pay interest for the period after the car was repossessed. Redemption rarely takes place.

If you do not redeem the car, the creditor may keep the car to satisfy the debt fully (unless you have paid at least 60 percent of the purchase price). The law refers to this as **strict foreclosure**. There is no duty to return excess value over the amount owed in a strict foreclosure. You must, however, be provided notice of a proposal to strictly foreclose and may object to it. Creditors seldom use the option of strict foreclosure because dealers want to sell, not keep, cars.

More likely, the creditor will sell the car to satisfy the debt. If the profits from the sale are not enough to pay expenses and satisfy the debt, you would be liable for the difference. The only limitation placed on the creditor is that the sale be "commercially reasonable." In some cases, that may mean first getting court permission to hold a sale. The sale may be public or private. The creditor must, however, give you reasonable notice of the time and manner of the sale. If it is a public sale, you have the right to take part (bid on the car). If the sale produces too much money, the creditor must pass some of it along to you. For example, if the amount of debt and expenses totals $5,000, and the creditor gets $5,600 from the sale of the car, the balance of $600 is due to you, and the UCC obliges the creditor to refund the money to you.

BUYING OR SELLING A USED CAR

In recent years the used-car business has boomed, partly because consumers may resist the high prices of new cars and partly because the popularity of leasing has resulted in many clean, late-model cars on the used car market. The business is changing, too, with superstores promising low prices, no-haggle shopping, and good warranties on late-model cars. Some auto brokerage services, including some that are on-line and available through the Internet or a commercial service such as CompuServe, advertise that they'll get you low, no-haggle prices on used as well as new cars.

Legally, buying and selling a used car has some unique features, but it is similar to buying a new car. The advertising rules are largely the same, so you must still beware of bait-and-switch ads that look too good to be true. And you have to keep in mind—always—that unlike most auto dealerships, a private seller (the source of most used car sales) is not concerned about a commercial reputation. The private seller might leave town with your money and never be seen again—especially if you're the one looking.

Still, some experts believe you may be better off buying from a private seller, as alluded to in the discussion on trade-ins above. A private seller may give a more accurate description of the car's faults based on personal knowledge, and you may get a lower price from a private seller. (They're not in the car business, after all, and indeed are seldom looking for profit on the turnaround but rather need to raise cash for something new.) Private sellers, however, seldom give warranties, which dealers sometimes offer. Also, some states have regulations governing used car sales that may apply only to dealers.

You have to handle your own paperwork with a private seller. If you are paying more than $500, you should have a written contract. An oral contract to sell a car for over $500 may not be enforceable. Even under $500, it is always best to put the contract in writing if you are not going to conclude the deal immediately with a bill of sale. Many states require you to present a bill of sale to register your car. A bill of sale may also serve as a receipt. The bill of sale should contain the date of the sale; year, make, and model of the car; vehicle identification number (VIN); odometer reading; a statement of the car's condition; amount paid for the car and in what form (cash, check, and the like); and buyer's and seller's names, addresses, and telephone numbers. The seller should sign and date the bill of sale, and both you and the seller should get a copy.

SPECIAL RULES FOR USED CAR DEALERS

A hundred years ago horse traders had a reputation for shady dealings. Fair or not, used car dealers often have a similar reputation today. The inherent problem lies with human nature. Too many of us don't take to heart the natural risks of buying a used car—or a used horse. All too often, our unrealistic expectations lead to bad feelings and disappointment. All this could be prevented if we took some precautions up front.

Used car dealers have to make a profit, above the salesperson's commission, on a car whose real value is probably closer to what they paid for it than what they'll get for it. To improve their chances, they make sure that most cars, especially late models, are in almost pristine *cosmetic* condition. The car looks good, but you have to find out about structural defects, accident histories, and long-term maintenance problems. By all means, ask the seller about each of these matters. You also must take the car to a trustworthy mechanic for examination—one that you select, not one recommended by the dealer. *Anyone who does not permit this kind of inspection simply cannot be trusted—look elsewhere.*

The Federal Trade Commission has issued a **Used Car Rule** for dealers. Under the rule, "dealers" are those who sell or offer to sell six or more used cars in a twelve-month period. The rule prohibits them from representing that a car comes with a warranty when none exists. They must make available the terms of any written warranty they provide, and they must post a "Buyers Guide" prominently on the car.

The Buyers Guide must include the following information:

- whether or not the car comes with a warranty, and if so, an outline of the specific coverage; and
- whether the vehicle comes with implied warranties only or is sold "as is," that is, with no warranties at all.

The Buyers Guide also states

- that you should request an inspection by an independent mechanic before you buy;
- that you should get all promises in writing; and
- some of the major problems that may happen in any car.

If you buy a used car from a dealer, you must be given a copy of the actual Buyers Guide posted on your car. If you have negotiated any changes in the warranty, it should be noted on the Buyers Guide. The Buyers Guide becomes part of your contract, and its terms override any conflicting terms in that contract.

INSPECTION OBSESSION

The Buyers Guide sticker, which applies to used car dealers, urges you to take the car to your mechanic before the sale is final. If the seller, whether a dealer or a private party, will not allow your mechanic to inspect the car, don't buy it unless it's such a good deal that you won't mind paying for critical car repairs later. Some people choose to take this risk by buying used cars at auctions. But it is a high risk indeed.

There are other facts that a seller must tell the buyer. The seller, whether a dealer or a private individual, should be truthful about the car. If the buyer is disappointed because it is not as described or does not perform as it was supposed to, a breach of warranty action may arise against the seller, who has deceived the buyer. If possible, you should get the seller to provide you with the car's complete service records.

Federal law requires the seller of a used car to give the buyer a mileage disclosure statement, even if the seller is not a dealer. The statement also should certify the odometer's accuracy to the seller's knowledge. If the seller knows it is incorrect, the seller must admit it. Refusal to provide such a statement or illegally tampering with the odometer exposes the seller to stiff penalties.

LEMON LAWS AND OTHER SPECIAL PROTECTIONS

What can you do if the car you just bought is a real lemon? What if the car you purchased is in the repair shop almost as often as it is in your garage? To protect consumers from such situations, most states have passed some form of **lemon law**, which usually applies to *new* cars purchased for personal, family, or household use. Lemon laws entitle you to a replacement car or a refund if your new car is so defective that it is beyond satisfactory repair by the dealer. However, you must give the dealer a reasonable opportunity to repair the car.

Normally a lemon is a car that continues to have a defect that substantially restricts its use, safety, or value, even after reasonable efforts to repair it. This often means four repair attempts on the same problem or a directly related problem within six months or one year (the time period varies by state). Or it might mean the car is out of commission for more than thirty nonconsecutive days during either the year after the dealer sold it or the duration of any express warranty, whichever is shorter.

To get the benefit of your state's lemon law, you typically must do several things. First, you must notify the manufacturer (and, in some states, the dealer) about the defect. Second, you should keep a copy of *every* repair or service receipt you are given. This serves as your record that the required number of repair attempts has been made and is especially important if the defect had to be repaired at another garage or in another city because it was physically impossible to drive the car back to the seller's repair location.

Most states require that you go through an arbitration procedure before you can get a replacement or refund. Some states sponsor arbitration programs, while other states require you to use a program run by manufacturers. Arbitration is usually free, and results often are binding only on the manufacturer or dealer; if you don't like the result, you can still take the manufacturer to court. Some states require arbitration only if the manufacturer refuses to give you a satisfactory replacement or a refund. You may also have the option of bypassing arbitration and going directly to court.

You should be aware that many consumer advocates have serious misgivings about lemon laws. They say such laws are often of little use because the requirements may be extreme (i.e., car out of commission for thirty days in a year), and the statutes may build in considerable risk to the consumer, often under the guise of avoiding a litigation explosion. In some states, for example, if the manufacturer makes a settlement offer to the buyer that the buyer rejects, and then at trial the buyer does not get at least 10 percent more than the offer, the buyer must pay the manufacturer's legal fees and costs from the time of the offer. For many consumers this would lead to immediate bankruptcy. As a result, not many suits are brought under such laws.

If you do successfully pursue a lemon-law claim, you may get a refund of what you paid for the car, as well as reimbursement for taxes, registration fees, finance charges, and the like. If you choose, you may get a replacement car. Be sure that it is of comparable value to the lemon it is replacing and that it satisfies you completely.

Lemon laws cover used cars in a growing number of states. In some places the law applies both to dealer and private-seller purchases. The laws may have a connection with the safety-inspection-sticker requirement. These sticker laws usually protect you if two conditions occur. First, the car must fail inspection within a certain period from the date of sale. Second, the repair costs must exceed a stated percentage of the purchase price. Then you are permitted to cancel the deal within a certain period. You will probably have to notify the seller in writing of your intention to cancel, including your reasons. You must return the car to the place of sale even if it must be towed. If the seller offers to make repairs, you can decide whether to accept the seller's offer or get your money back.

Keep in mind that the car might pass the safety inspection and still be a lemon. And you may drive the car (if it is drivable), but be aware that if the car does indeed turn out to be a lemon, the law usually allows the seller to deduct a certain amount from your refund based on the miles you have driven. This applies to both new and used car sales.

In addition to lemon laws, other statutes protect car buyers:

- the federal **Anti-Tampering Odometer Law** prohibits acts that falsify odometer mileage readings;

- the federal **Used Car Law** requires that dealers post Buyers Guides on used cars;

- the federal **Automobile Information Disclosure Act** requires manufacturers and importers of new cars to affix a sticker called the "Monroney label" on the windshield or side window of the car. The Monroney label lists the base price of the car, the options installed by the manufacturer and their suggested retail price, how much the manufacturer has charged for transportation, and the car's fuel economy (miles per gallon). Only the buyer is allowed to remove the Monroney label.

By far, the statutes providing the strongest protection are the consumer fraud statutes prohibiting unfair and deceptive acts and practices, discussed in chapter 15.

RECALLS

The recall system identifies defective automobiles that are already on the road by notifying car owners about how to get them fixed.

Generally it includes defects that affect the car's safety, cause it to fall below federal safety standards, or both, and that are common to a group of the same kind of cars or equipment. The defect can be in performance, construction, components, or materials found in the car or in related equipment, such as child safety seats.

Many recalls result from the manufacturer's response to owner complaints. The National Highway Traffic Safety Administration (NHTSA), however, influences and orders many recalls. The NHTSA receives safety-related complaints through letters and its toll-free telephone hotline. (This hotline number is listed in "Where to Get More Information," on page 245). When the NHTSA registers enough complaints, NHTSA engineers perform an engineering analysis and then contact the automobile manufacturer. The manufacturer must either remedy the defect or launch its own defect investigation. Ultimately the NHTSA decides if a final defect determination and recall is proper.

The manufacturer must remedy the defect for free. This does not apply when the first buyer bought the car more than eight years earlier. In comparison, the standard for tires is three years. The manufacturer has the option of repairing the defect, replacing the car, or refunding the purchase price. If the manufacturer refunds the money, a certain amount may be deducted for depreciation (loss in value). The manufacturer reimburses the dealer who makes the repairs. If the manufacturer chooses to repair the defect, it must do so within a reasonable time. Otherwise, the manufacturer must replace the vehicle or refund the purchase price.

AUTOMOBILE LEASING

An alternative to buying a car is leasing one. Leases are becoming increasingly popular, with about a quarter of consumers choosing to lease a new car rather than buy one. This percentage rises to half in the case of luxury cars.

A lease is essentially a contract for the use of a vehicle for a specified time period. There are two types of lease contracts: the **closed-**

end lease (sometimes called a **net** or **walk-away lease**) and the less common **open-end lease** (sometimes called a **finance lease**). Leases usually are for at least a year; two- and three-year leases are common.

Leasing a vehicle is like renting an apartment—you know what your monthly costs are going to be, but at the end of the term you have no **equity** (ownership) in the property. Whether to lease or not depends on your situation and what's important to you. Purchasing a car might be more economical in the long run, but leasing may be attractive to people who want to avoid the hassles of ownership, drive a more expensive car than they could afford to buy, and drive a new car every two or three years.

Whether it is better to lease or buy a car depends on many factors. Monthly payments for a leased car may be lower than if you purchased it. Whether your lease payment is lower depends on four key factors:

- the capitalized cost of the vehicle (i.e., what the vehicle was worth new);
- the interest rate;
- the residual value of the vehicle (i.e., what it's worth at the end of the lease); and
- the length of the lease.

Your monthly payments cover an estimated amount for the depreciation of the car over the lease period (the difference between the vehicle's worth when new and at the end of the lease), so, unlike your monthly payments if you purchase a car, you are not paying off the vehicle's full value when new. When your lease is up, you can turn it in, extend the lease payments (or renegotiate another lease), buy for cash (typically at the residual value), or finance the purchase through an installment loan. The lease usually doesn't spell out these options, though it often does contain an option to purchase at the residual value. How you buy the car or extend the lease is often a separate negotiation.

With a lease you'll probably have to face another set of monthly payments once the lease has expired. On the other hand, if you buy on credit instead of leasing, you at least have the possibility of paying off the vehicle entirely over time and driving it for several years without having to make any monthly payments. You'll be driving an older car, but when you're done with it you can sell it and get some cash.

At one time leasing normally avoided a down payment and various taxes, but nowadays you often have to put up a down payment, sometimes called a "capital cost reduction." You may also face an acquisition fee if you ultimately choose to buy, or a disposition fee if you return it at the end. You may have to pay a documentation fee to the dealer to set up the lease. You'll have to put down a security deposit equivalent to one or two months' payments and in some states a monthly "use tax." But don't forget that there are fees associated with installment loans, as well as the possible headache of selling a car yourself (see page 108). And there may be some tax advantages if you lease mainly for business use.

It's hard to generalize with all these variables in the air, but sometimes you can get "more car"—a higher-priced model—under a lease than if you purchased it.

Usually the consumer is liable for damage to the vehicle, though a lease may include insurance. If not, you must provide your own. Damage done to the car while in your possession may cause the **lessor**—the bank or company that leases the car to you—to deduct an "appropriate" amount from your deposit.

Will you owe anything at the end of the lease? That depends on what kind of lease you have. Under a closed-end lease contract, the car's value when you return it may not matter unless you have put extreme wear on the car. But because lessors sometimes charge for minor damage, it might be a good idea to repair things like cracked windows (usually covered by insurance) and to address other cosmetic damage before you bring the car back. If all is well, you return the car at the end of the term and walk away. But your monthly payments are higher under this kind of lease than under an open-end lease, because the lessor (the leasing company) takes the risk on the car's future worth. An open-end lease involves lower payments. You gamble that the car will be worth a stated price, the **estimated residual value**, at the end of the lease. If its appraised value at the end of the term equals or exceeds the specified residual value, you owe nothing and may be refunded the difference if your contract provides for a refund. If it is worth less, you pay some or all of the difference, often called an "end of lease" payment.

LEASE FINANCING

As noted above, up front you'll probably have to pay a security deposit (returnable at the end of the lease) and a fee similar to a down

---

NEGOTIATING TIPS WHEN LEASING

With more and more people leasing vehicles, it's natural that a number of state and federal agencies should explore consumer protection in this area. One reform adopted by a number of states is to require the lease contract to include the vehicle's "capitalized cost," a figure that would be roughly the vehicle's sticker price if it were purchased. Because hardly anyone pays the sticker price on a new car, the thinking goes, why should they permit their monthly payments to be in part determined by this figure? (Your monthly payment depends in large part on the difference between the value of the car when new and its value at the end of the lease, as well as the interest you pay.) And even when it is not legally required, car dealers often voluntarily provide the capitalized cost in their standard lease contract, as well as simplify the contract generally and make it more reader-friendly. Consumers who know how to look for and use this information and comparison shop between dealers may be able to save $100 or more on monthly payments.

Yet one of the big attractions of leasing is that it is relatively hassle free. Many consumers may be more concerned about getting a monthly payment they can afford and may not want to do the work of trying to get it lowered. And a lease contract has many more variables than a straight purchase. All these variables actually open up more opportunities for bargaining, which could benefit you. As usual, it pays to do your homework, make the effort to negotiate, and not go ahead with a deal until you are fully satisfied.

---

payment when you buy a car, although it will have a different name. By paying a large amount up front, you could, in effect, reduce your monthly payments. But by doing this, you lose one of the advantages of leasing: lower up-front costs. Other expenses may include tax, title, and license fees, as well as a lease-acquisition fee. You might have to pay for repairs and maintenance after any warranty period expires, unless the lessor agrees to pay in your contract. At the end of the lease term you may have to pay an excess mileage cost if you have a closed-end lease. Excess mileage charges add up very quickly. For example, if your lease specified that you would drive no more than 15,000 miles a year and you exceeded that amount, you might have to pay twelve or thirteen cents a mile for the excess. It is essential that you get a lease that allows you to drive the number of miles that you typically drive before the excess mileage kicks in. (Under an open-end lease the final appraised value of the car will reflect any excess mileage.) Excessive wear and tear may also cost you.

You almost always may renew or extend a lease at the end of the term. Sometimes your lease may contain this option, or you can negotiate for it.

On the other hand, getting out early is something altogether different. You have signed a binding contract that obligates you to make payments for a stated term. Your contract may contain an early termination clause. This usually requires a minimum number of monthly payments before you may cancel, and the formula for determining the amount you owe in the event of early termination typically results in a very large payment. In addition, this early termination charge may apply even if the reason for early termination is the theft or destruction of the vehicle or even death or disability of the lessee or someone in the family who drove the car.

There are many ways of calculating the charge for early termination, and it is important that you understand the method that the dealer proposes so that you have the option of trying to negotiate better terms before you sign. You may also wish to have gap insurance included in the lease to take care of situations like owing more for a car that has been stolen than the market value that the insurance company will cover. Even if you have to turn a car in early under an existing contract, it may be possible to work something out with the company if they hope to get more business from you in the future.

Almost all leases include a **purchase option**, which allows you to buy the car when your lease term ends. Under such a provision, which you'd probably be well advised to bargain for, the lessor must state the purchase price or the basis for setting this price in the initial lease contract. Purchase options are common in both open- and closed-end leases.

PROTECTIONS FOR CONSUMERS WHO LEASE

The federal **Consumer Leasing Act (CLA)** offers protection not only to consumers who lease cars but to those who lease other items as well. It applied to leases of consumer goods of more than four months' duration. (It does not apply to leases of real estate, vehicles used for business, or total contractual obligations over $25,000.) The law requires the lessor to disclose information before you sign the lease. Among the most important items are:

- total amount of any initial payment you are required to pay;
- number and amount(s) of monthly payments;
- total amount for fees, such as license fees and taxes;
- any penalty for default or late payments;
- the annual mileage allowance and the extra charges involved if you exceed that allowance;
- whether you can end the lease early and the extra charge required;
- whether you can purchase the auto at the end of the lease and for what price;
- any liability that you may have for the difference between the estimated value of the auto and its market value at the time you end the lease;
- any extra payment that you must make at the end of the lease.

The Federal Trade Commission helps enforce the CLA and will take action if there is evidence of a pattern of federal law violations.

You can contact the FTC at the Correspondence Branch, Federal Trade Commission, Washington, DC 20580. The FTC has published a free booklet entitled *A Consumer Guide to Vehicle Leasing,* which explains your legal protections and provides checklists to help you decide whether to lease or buy and to help you compare lease offers. It also answers commonly asked questions. It is available from the FTC Public Reference Department at the address above. Your state may have laws protecting consumers who lease. Check with your consumer protection agency or the local office of your state's attorney general.

RENTING A CAR

Rentals may last as little as one day. They are never economical in the long run but have the advantage of, say, getting you from the end of a May lease to early autumn, when dealers are eager to make deals to move out cars of the waning model year. And, of course, people rent cars when traveling on business or pleasure.

A car-rental contract should list the base rate for the rental car and any extra fees. The length of the rental period should also appear. Special rates are frequent, and discounts are available through so many bodies—professional organizations, unions, frequent-flier clubs, etc.—that virtually no one should ever pay the full price for a car rental, at least without an upgrade to a larger or better-equipped vehicle. When you pick up your car, it may also be possible to negotiate a special deal or upgrade. It's always worth your while to try to get as large a car as you feel comfortable driving.

But the rental agencies giveth and quickly taketh away—or will, if you let them—through extras. The rental company might offer you the **Collision Damage Waiver (CDW)** option. The rental company covers damage to your rented car if you accept CDW. Coverage, however, does not include personal injuries or personal property damage. Similarly, they will offer you personal-effects coverage, i.e., insurance on your own property in case it is stolen from the car while you're renting it.

Before accepting these expensive options, make sure your own automobile, medical, and homeowners insurance policies do not already protect you in an accident involving a rented car or your own property loss. (Hint: If they don't, talk to your broker. This is standard coverage, though your deductible may be higher than that offered by the CDW. Also, coverage outside of the United States is not standard, but your credit card may offer insurance that does apply outside the country.) If traveling on business, your company's insurance policy might cover you. Sometimes, charging rentals on certain credit cards automatically covers you. Confirm this in writing, however, before you use the card and decline the rental company's coverage. Consumer experts consistently identify the CDW as one of the most unnecessary expenses incurred by consumers, perhaps vying only with credit insurance.

Other additional fees might include dropoff fees if you leave the car in a city other than where you picked it up. Other costs might be fuel charges, extra mileage fees, and fees for renting equipment like child-safety seats or ski racks, as well as fees for additional or younger drivers. Avoid the unnecessary ones, and by all means (as ever) shop around!

When you accept your rental car, and before you drive it off the lot, carefully check it for damage and note any damage on the rental agreement. In some parts of the country criminals prey on tourists driving rental vehicles. It's worth checking to make sure that your car cannot be identified as a rental.

Are you guaranteed a car if you have confirmed reservations? Not necessarily. Many companies now check driving records when customers arrive to pick up cars and reject customers whose driving records don't meet company standards. Even if you have a confirmed reservation, you may be disqualified from renting a car for any of the following reasons: moving violations within the last few years; seat belt law violations; accidents, regardless of fault; convictions for driving while intoxicated (DWI), driving under the influence (DUI), reckless driving, or leaving the scene of an accident; or driving with an invalid, suspended, or revoked license.

REPAIRS

Every car needs repairs or at least regular maintenance. If you don't regularly change the oil, plus the oil and air filters, you may as well skip this whole chapter; whatever money you save with purchasing savvy you're throwing away with maintenance negligence.

You can take it to a car dealer, which warranty terms may require. Your other choices include taking it to an independent garage or a franchise operation specializing in specific repairs, or repairing it yourself. Each option has its advantages and disadvantages.

Dealers may charge more. On the other hand, they are more familiar with your make of car than other repair shops and may have new and better equipment to service your car. Manufacturers want to ensure that dealerships run quality repair operations, so they invest in training mechanics. Dealers want you to be happy with the car you bought so you'll buy another in a few years—from them. You can take advantage of these strengths and save money by looking for seasonal specials on routine maintenance by dealers of your make.

A service station is a good option for nonwarranty work if the mechanics have adequate training and test equipment. Parts might cost more, but labor might be less expensive than dealer repairs. Certainly routine matters such as oil and filter changes can be done just as well at a service station as at a dealer. And though they don't have the leg up on your make of car that a dealer does, if you use a service station often, the mechanics get to know your car. Then they might spot potential problems early. There's also the angle that a local mechanic would like to develop such a good relationship with you that you'll make a point of buying your gasoline there and perhaps other products, like tires.

What about highly advertised repair chains? Specialty shops may repair one part of a car, such as brakes or mufflers. Or they may advertise complete car care services. Sheer size and volume means lower costs than dealers and independent mechanics. On the other hand, because they specialize in repairs that are usually one-time in nature, they have an incentive to make those repairs rather than to advise skipping them. Similarly, they are seldom in a position to develop a long-term relationship with you. If you know what repairs your car needs, however, franchise shops can be a good deal.

THE REPAIR CONTRACT

The repair contract, often called the **repair order**, is essential for getting a satisfactory repair job done on your car. The repair order describes the work to be done, and, once signed, creates a contract authorizing the mechanic to make the described repairs. The repair order should contain:

- the make, model, and year of your car;
- the mileage and repair date;
- an accurate description of the problem;
- a list of parts to be used and their charges;
- the estimated amount of labor needed (time to be spent fixing your car);
- the rate to be charged, either per hour or flat rate, to do the work; and
- your name, address, and telephone number.

The mileage and repair date are important. They verify warranty terms and simplify service records. Your telephone number is also critical should unexpected problems arise. If the mechanic cannot reach you, he or she must decide whether or not to proceed, and you may have to live with the results of that decision. But note that in many states, if you don't sign the repair order, you don't have to pay for any services done by the mechanic.

Getting a cost estimate for the repairs before work actually begins is a good idea. It's even required by law in some states. In those states, the final cost must not exceed a certain percentage or dollar value of the original estimate without the customer's consent. Repair shops generally have the right to charge for making an estimate, but you must receive advance notice.

The law may entitle you to some repair warranties. If the repair shop makes an express warranty, you are protected as long as you abide by the terms of the warranty. Likewise, if a manufacturer's warranty covers the car or part, you should not have to pay as long as you satisfy warranty conditions. Some state courts have held that the implied warranty of merchantability extends to car repairs. That means the repairs must be suitably performed. Beware of "unconditional" guarantees offered by many repair shops. There are always *some* limitations on written guarantees. Be sure to read the fine print; there may be special procedures that you are required to follow to obtain the benefits of the warranty.

FALSE AND DECEPTIVE REPAIR PRACTICES

Most of us don't understand how cars work. We certainly don't understand why they *don't* work, and as for making them work again—forget it! To protect consumers against fraudulent practices, mechanic incompetence, and overcharging, many states have enacted statues specifically governing car repairs or have included car repairs in their unfair and deceptive practices statutes.

Most of these statutes or the regulations issued under their authority require price estimates and repair orders. Many states also give you the right to keep or examine replaced parts and require repair shops to prepare a detailed invoice, which must state the labor and parts supplied, warranty work done, guarantees, and installation of any used or rebuilt parts. In some states you may have the right to same-day repairs unless you agree to a longer period or the delay is beyond the shop's control. Shoddy repair work must be corrected at no charge, especially in states where the implied warranty of merchantability has been extended to repair work. Finally, many states require repair shops to post price lists conspicuously.

If you think a repair shop has cheated you or made unauthorized repairs, keep in mind that for many mechanics—and the only ones you should deal with!—their business depends on a good reputation, which they will take care to maintain. So, you may wish to try to adjust the matter with them before you involve your lawyer and threaten legal action or complain to your state attorney general, the local branch of the Better Business Bureau, or even the Chamber of Commerce.

If you do not get satisfaction, you may wish to sue if, for example, the shop made unneeded repairs or reinstalled the original part rather than a replacement. If the shop tried its best to correct the fault by fixing something that *was* broken, although *not* the problem's ultimate cause, you should pay the shop. After all, the repair shop *did* fix one of your car's problems. It is not, however, a complete guarantor of your car's health.

THE MECHANIC'S LIEN

In most states the repair shop obtains a **mechanic's lien** on your car, which helps the shop secure payment for the work done. For example, if you have authorized extensive work but decide that the car isn't worth that much after the shop completes the work and refuse to pay for completed repairs, the shop may keep your car. The car's actual value and the actual cost of the repairs do not matter. If you abandon your car in this manner, the shop may ultimately sell your car so that it can recover as much of the cost of repairs as possible. But note that in states that require written estimates and repair authorization, the mechanic's lien does not attach if the repair shop has not complied with these requirements. In such states you are entitled to ask a court to order the car returned to you.

CHAPTER TEN

Something Borrowed

Consumer Credit

THE USE OF CREDIT is as American as apple pie. Americans routinely borrow money to buy, over time, homes, cars, appliances, clothing, vacations, and other goods and services. Frequently credit is available from the seller. A great deal of credit is sales credit, including automobile credit and retailers' cards. Credit on bank credit cards—except for cash advances—is usually sales credit too. It may be subject to different legal rules, but for the most part this chapter ignores such refinements and concentrates on generally applicable laws.

On average, about 11 percent of a family's after-tax income is absorbed by payments for consumer installment debts. There are three basic forms of consumer credit.

• In an **installment credit agreement**, a consumer signs a contract to repay a fixed amount of credit in equal payments over a specific period of time. Automobiles, furniture, and major appliances are often purchased on an installment basis. Personal loans are usually repaid in installments as well.

• In a **revolving credit agreement**, sometimes referred to as an **open-end credit agreement**, a consumer has the option of paying in full each month or making a specified minimum payment based on the amount of the balance outstanding. Department stores, gas and oil companies, and banks typically issue credit cards based on revolving credit. Visa and MasterCard, issued by banks and other companies such as AT&T, are examples of this type of credit.

- In an **open thirty-day agreement**, sometimes called a **noninstallment credit agreement**, a consumer promises to repay the full balance owed each month. This is old-fashioned charge account credit, which is rapidly disappearing. Travel and entertainment charge cards, such as American Express and Diners Club, as well as charge accounts with local businesses, may require that the full balance be paid on this basis.

The extension of credit is a service for which lenders, or **creditors**, charge money, which of course is called **interest** or a **finance charge**. Interest represents the price of money and is based on an amount representing a premium over what the lender could have made if the lender had invested the money, known as the **principal**, rather than lent it to you, plus the nuts-and-bolts cost of providing the credit. Interest can also be looked at as the amount you are willing to pay to have something now instead of later.

THE COST OF CREDIT

Many states regulate the amount of interest, or the **rate**. Some, particularly if the credit is extended by the seller, leave it entirely, or practically, to the market. That means it's up to you to shop for the best rate and credit terms, a task made easier by the **Truth-in-Lending Act (TILA)**. TILA requires that all creditors provide information that will help you decide whether to buy on credit or borrow and, if so, which credit offer is best for you.

Under TILA, before you sign a contract for credit, creditors must disclose to you in writing the following information:

- the amount being financed;
- the number of monthly payments required; and
- the critical annual percentage rate (APR).

The APR is an annual rate that relates the total finance charge to the amount of credit that you receive and the length of time you have to repay it. Think of the APR as a price per pound, like twenty cents per pound for potatoes. You can buy five pounds for one dollar or ten pounds for two dollars—either way the cost per pound, or rate, is the same, and the amount you spend depends on how many spuds you buy. When you buy credit, you buy a certain amount of credit for a number of months. The total dollar amount of your finance charge will depend on how many dollars' worth of credit you obtain initially and how many months you use those dollars.

TILA also regulates credit advertising, which makes it easy to credit shop. For example, if an automobile ad emphasizes a low monthly payment (giving a dollar figure), it also must tell you other pertinent information, like the APR.

The APR must always be considered in terms of the length of the loan. As noted in the chapter on automobiles, if you can only afford $100 a month for a car, you might have to take a longer term loan to get the payment down to that figure. Just be aware that at the end of the loan period, your **total finance charge**—the total amount of money you've paid just in interest—would be higher than if you'd

---

TAX DEDUCTIBILITY

Under current tax laws almost all homeowners have the option of deducting all their mortgage interest from their taxable income for tax purposes. Thus, from a tax standpoint, it often makes sense for those who own property and itemize deductions to refinance their installment and revolving credit—which is not deductible—by taking out a second mortgage (a lump sum) or a home equity loan (a line of credit). Tax advantages notwithstanding, this is not a step to be taken lightly. If you can't pay back the money, you'll risk losing your home. When you take out a second mortgage or a home equity loan, you are allowing another lien to be placed on your home. (You granted a lien when you took out your first mortgage.) While your home is the last thing an unsecured creditor can look to in satisfying, say, nonpayment on a credit card debt, or it may not be looked to at all, nonpayment on a home equity loan can easily lead to the loss of your home.

taken out a shorter loan. The choice of stretching out the loan is one you may rationally choose to make, but watch out for balloons, where the creditor sets low initial payments, but the last payment is a whopper!

There are other factors as well. Auto dealers, for example, frequently offer incentive financing with very low APRs or cash rebates. Often you can save money by skipping the low rate and taking the cash, then applying the cash to the amount you would have financed. (You might save even more by getting financing from someone other than the dealer.) By reducing the principal, even with a higher interest rate, you might end up with lower monthly payments for the same length loan and, at the end of the term, a lower finance charge. Similarly, taking the cash may make shortening the term of the loan attractive.

CHOOSING A CREDIT CARD

Many of us are bombarded with solicitations for credit cards such as MasterCard, Visa, Discover, and Optima, which are actually issued by banks, savings and loans, credit unions, and other companies but are part of a cooperative network. (American Express cards are not bank affiliated.) Basically these banks and other institutions are asking you to borrow money from them, assuming that you will use the cards' credit lines rather than pay off your balance in full. (The card issuers get a small return on every purchase, paid by the merchant, regardless of whether you pay your balance in full.)

Selecting a credit card is like selecting a suit or dress; you want a good fit. Because there are many card issuers, you have a wide choice of cards. In this section we examine terms typically offered to consumers by banks and other issuers of credit cards. It is illegal for card issuers to send you an credit card unless you've asked for it. Every solicitation must include a brief disclosure statement under the TILA. Any offer to extend credit that doesn't have full disclosure that's easy to find has something to hide. Put it in the recycling bin.

The TILA disclosure statement must tell you the card's APR and, just as important, how the credit grantor figures it. This depends on how you use the account and how payments are applied. A common system is to apply the APR to the **average daily balance** in your account over the billing period. Some retail credit cards compute the balance by subtracting payments made or credits given during the billing period from the total amount you owe; this is called the **adjusted balance** method. A very few credit grantors still use the **previous balance** method. They do not subtract from the balance any payments made during the billing period but apply them at the end. These little details can amount to a lot of money in the medium run, but it's hard to tell which is best without seeing how each system works with your account activity. (The previous balance method tends to be most costly to consumers.)

Many credit cards offer a **grace period** of twenty to twenty-five days for purchases. This is the time between the end of the billing cycle and the date by which you must pay the entire bill to avoid paying any finance charge. The grace period rarely applies to cash advances on your credit card, and if it does, it probably has a very costly up-front fee. The credit grantor may adjust the grace period under another method of assessing monthly charges on your bill, called the **retroactive**, or two-cycle balance method. Under this system, if the opening balance on your bill was zero and you then made credit purchases but did not pay your entire bill, your next monthly bill will include a finance charge for these purchases from the dates that they were posted to your account. Look closely at the disclosure statement or cardholder agreement to see if it uses the retroactive method. The retroactive balance system is not meant for your benefit, but if you usually don't pay your balance in full and continue to revolve, there is little difference between the retro system and the average daily balance.

The APR on a credit card can change if there is a **variable-rate provision**. More and more credit card issuers set APRs that vary with some interest rate index, such as the market rates on three-year U.S. Treasury bills or the prime rate charged by banks on short-term business loans. In their solicitation to you these issuers must state that the rate may vary and how it is determined. This may be done by showing the index and the **spread**. The spread is the number of percentage points added to the index to determine the rate you will pay. Thus, you will frequently see a disclosure such as this:

Variable Rate Information

Your annual percentage rate may vary quarterly. The rate will be the prime rate as published in *The Wall Street Journal* plus 9%. The rate will not go below 15.0% or exceed 19.9%.

Many new offers these days have "teaser rates," such as a low rate effective for six months, at which point the prime plus 9 percent takes over. Pay attention to how long the period in which you get the low rate lasts.

ADDITIONAL FEES

Your disclosure statement may refer to various fees. These include:

• **Transaction fees for cash advances.** These are typically in the neighborhood of 2 percent of the amount of the advance, with a minimum of several dollars. They should be capped at $10 or, at the most, $25, although not all are.

• **Late-payment fees.** You should not plan to pay late. Many card issuers are generous in this regard and do not impose the late fee every time, or only after a grace period, such as ten days. Fees of $5 to $15 are typical. Also note that late payments are a default that can lead to cancellation of the card.

• **Over-the-limit fees.** These bear watching, because a perfectly innocent mistake can result in your going above your preset credit limit and incurring a fee of $10 to $15 for each credit period in which you've exceeded your limit, even once. Again, doing so can be a default. Some accounts don't charge this type of fee.

• **Replacement card fees.** If it is more than nominal, this may not be a reasonable fee. Watch out for the provider who sticks you with a big fee in the agreement—there might be more surprises in there.

ANNUAL FEES

Whereas few, if any, credit cards issued by retailers have annual fees, many credit cards issued by financial institutions do. These fees, which must also be in the TILA disclosure, typically range from $15 to $25, or higher for gold or platinum cards. In the present competitive environment, you don't have to pay an annual fee, considering how many free cards are out there. But it might make sense to do so in some situations. For example, it might be important to you that a card provides separate benefits, such as airline miles. Another reason is that you do not pay off your balance in full each month and can get a lower APR with a card that charges a fee. What it boils down to is that you have to decide at the outset whether you will pay off the balance each month or typically carry a balance each month. Those who "revolve" should shop for a card with a low rate, even if it carries an annual fee. Those who really will pay off the balance each month or the great majority of months should shop for a low- or no-fee card.

SECURED CREDIT CARDS

Some people whose credit ratings aren't good enough to merit a credit card want the convenience of cash-free living enough to pay for a **secured credit card**. This is a credit card secured by a savings account on deposit with the issuer. The line of credit is usually limited to the amount on deposit or a little less. Watch for high APRs and fees on these cards, which are sometimes the refuge of the credit-desperate. Don't apply for any card that requires an application fee or that requires a call on a 900 number to apply. And avoid like the plague the ones that only work with catalogs provided by the issuer. That's not what you want the card for.

Having a secured card may be compared to using training wheels on a bike. After a year or so on your secured card, your demonstration of responsible use of credit may merit you a regular credit card. Look for cards that promise that you can convert to an unsecured card after a year.

Issuers make their money one way or another; if it's not on interest, it will be on fees. Thus, charge cards such as American Express, Diners Club, and other premium cards with very high lines of credit or no preset spending limits charge $35 to $75. Consumers will have to decide for themselves whether the "prestige" or carrying such a card is worth the fee.

APPLYING FOR CREDIT

When you apply for credit, there are legal rules to make sure that your application is handled fairly and confidentially. The federal **Equal Credit Opportunity Act (ECOA)** prohibits credit grantors from considering race, color, national origin, sex, marital status, age, receipt of public aid, or exercise of your legal rights as a credit-seeker in connection with your application or in setting the terms of credit actually granted you. As to age, once you have reached the age of majority (eighteen or twenty-one, depending on the state), credit grantors generally may not use your age against you—whether youth or old age—in determining your creditworthiness. They may, however, consider the future of your income stream if you are at or near retirement, although you may not be required to buy life insurance to qualify for credit. Your credit also cannot be canceled on your retirement.

Credit grantors may generally use any of the following factors to decide whether to extend credit to you and at what terms:

• **Ability to repay.** This depends on the stability of your current job or income source, how much you earn, and the length of time you have worked or will receive income. Credit grantors also may consider your basic expenses, such as payments on rent, mortgages, other debts, utilities, college expenses, and taxes. This analysis is typically done by mortgage lenders rather than companies that grant consumer installment credit.

• **Credit history.** This shows how much money you owe and whether you have large, unused lines of open-end credit. A very important consideration is whether you have paid your bills on time and whether you have filed for bankruptcy within the past ten years or had repossessions or judgments issued against you.

- **Stability.** Your stability is indicated by how long you have lived at your current or former address and how long you have been with your current or former employer. Owning a home is normally a big plus.

- **Assets.** Assets such as a car may be useful as collateral for a loan. Credit grantors may also look at what else you may use for collateral, such as savings accounts or securities, although this kind of analysis is found more often in business loans than in the typical application for consumer credit.

The Equal Credit Opportunity Act requires that the credit grantor notify you of whether it will accept or reject your application within thirty days of receiving it. If your application for credit is denied, the denial must be in writing and must give the reasons or allow you to request the reasons. And under the **Fair Credit Reporting Act (FCRA),** in the event of a credit denial (or withdrawal or reduction), the grantor must tell you if it based the denial on your credit report and, if so, the name of the reporting agency that prepared the report and how to reach them. If you think you have been denied credit for illegally discriminatory reasons and cannot resolve the problem with the institution, you may want to consult a lawyer. The Equal Credit Opportunity Act allows punitive damages of up to $10,000 in addition to any losses you can prove you suffered as a result of such activity.

CREDIT RECORDS

Just as it is frustrating to apply for your first job when they all say they want someone with experience, applying for your first loan or credit line without a credit history seems hopeless. You do need a credit record, even if you are married and your spouse handles "all that stuff." Your spouse could mishandle that stuff and tarnish your name, or your spouse could mishandle something else and become your ex-spouse. Especially if you have your own income, open an account or two in your own name and use it (wisely!) from time to time.

There are ways to build a good credit history. Start by opening and maintaining checking and credit accounts. The next step is applying for a credit card from a department store (it should be one of the national ones, because many smaller credit grantors and gasoline cards do not report to credit agencies) and using it. Another option is to have someone who does have a credit rating, such as a parent or spouse, cosign the loan with you. (It should be someone close, because a cosigner is fully liable on the loan.) Once you pay it back, you have, as in all these techniques, shown that you can do it. You can also try to see if you can borrow against money in your account at a bank or credit union, or get a secured credit card.

You should also know about credit bureaus, or credit reporting agencies, which keep computerized records of your financial payment histories, public record data (liens, lawsuits, and the like), and personal identifying data. (These agencies do not have medical information.) There are three main credit reporting services, though they may operate under other names in some communities: TRW Information Services, Equifax Credit Information Services, and Trans-Union Credit Information Company. They are regulated by federal law and in some states by state law.

The credit bureaus do not issue a "credit rating" as such, nor do they make credit decisions. They just provide information reported to them by credit grantors. The information is not provided to just anyone but is legally restricted to persons or organizations with a legitimate business need for it. (In applying for credit you usually give permission; you may also be asked to give permission when you apply for a lease or even a job.) Because the reports filed by credit bureaus have so much influence over your financial future, be sure the information you use to apply for credit is consistent. Decide on the form of your name to use and stick with it. Don't be shy about giving your social security number when you apply for credit—it's the best way to identify you and ensure that your data isn't mixed in with someone else's.

You can also see your credit report. If you are denied credit on the basis of your credit report, you are entitled to a free report from the bureau used by the credit grantor within thirty days of the denial. Thanks to laws in some states and the voluntary policies of some credit bureaus, it may be free in other situations as well. In any event, you shouldn't have to pay more than a nominal fee.

You are also entitled to know the identity of every creditor reporting to the agency on you and everyone who has gotten a copy of the report in the last six months. If you dispute the correctness of any information on the report, the Fair Credit Reporting Act requires the agency, if your dispute is "nonfrivolous," to verify or delete the information. If there is a sticking point with a certain creditor, you may be able to get the creditor to agree to set the record straight; if there is a good reason for the problem that occurred and you have since settled matters, they should be glad to help. The credit agency will automatically notify the other bureaus of any change and, if you wish, notify any creditor who has checked your files in the last six months. Thus, you can fix most problems without the help of expensive credit-repair "clinics" with their pie-in-the-sky promises and high-as-the-sky fees. (In contrast, credit counseling services, which help consumers figure a way out of deep credit holes, are often useful and affordable. You can get more information about nonprofit agencies from the National Foundation for Consumer Credit at 800-388-2227.)

How long does it take for a bad credit experience to fade away? Normally, most negative information may not legally be reported after seven years but may be made available for a longer time if you are applying for at least $50,000 worth of credit, life insurance with a face value in at least that amount, or a job paying more than $20,000 a year. And bankruptcies stay on the report for ten years.

DEBT COLLECTION

Besides harming your credit record, **delinquencies** (failure to pay debts on time) can cause you to end up in court. In some states, a successful lawsuit by a creditor could result in **garnishment** of your wages, especially if you have a decent income. That means your employer is ordered to pay part of your salary to the creditor until the debt is paid off.

A car, truck, large appliance, or other durable good purchased with credit may have a lien on it and be subject to repossession for nonpayment. Some states require advance notice before the creditor can **repossess** (take its stuff back). Remember that all credit agreements contain **acceleration clauses**, which say that if you are in default, the entire debt, not just the monthly payment or payments you missed, is due immediately. And if repossession and resale of the property does not satisfy the whole debt—which may be swollen by finance charges, late fees, and repossession costs—you are still on the hook for the deficiency (unless state law prohibits a deficiency, as some do in some cases).

The **Fair Debt Collection Practices Act (FDCPA)** regulates professional debt collectors who work as outside agents for creditors. It does not regulate creditors themselves, although many states have laws that do. Under the federal act a debt collector may only contact you by mail, in person, or by telephone or telegram during convenient hours. Unless you agree in writing (or a court grants permission), a collector may not contact you at inconvenient times or places, such as before 8 A.M. or after 9 P.M. Also, a debt collector is not permitted to contact you at work if the collector knows or has reason to know that your employer forbids employees from being contacted by collectors at work. You can tell the debt collector what times and places are inconvenient for you to receive calls.

A debt collector is not allowed to contact you if the collector knows a lawyer is handling the matter for you. And the collector must leave you alone if you instruct the collector, *by mail,* to do so. Once you do that, the collector may only confirm that there will be no further contact and that some specific legal action may be or will be taken (and only if they mean it). A collector must also leave you alone if you notify the collector in writing during the first thirty days after you are contacted that you dispute all or part of the debt, unless the collector provides proof of the debt.

Within five days of your first contact, a debt collector must send you a written notice stating:

- the name of the credit grantor to whom the money is owed;
- the amount owed;

- that the debt collector will assume the debt is genuine unless you challenge all or part of it within thirty days and what to do if you believe you do not owe the money; and

- that if you ask for it, the debt collector will tell you the name and address of the original creditor, if different from the current creditor.

A debt collector may contact anyone needed to locate you but may not speak to anyone more than once nor mention the fact of the debt. (That prevents the collector from mailing you an otherwise innocuous letter in an envelope indicating it comes from a bill collector.) A collector certainly may not, under the law, harass, oppress, or abuse anyone. Specifically, a debt collector may not

- threaten violence to you, your property, or your reputation;

- use obscene or profane language;

- annoy you with repeated phone calls;

- make you accept collect phone calls or telegrams;

- publish your name on a public roster of "deadbeats";

- misrepresent the amount of the debt;

- falsely imply that the collector is a lawyer; or

- threaten legal action that the collector does not intend to take or that is not available.

Debt collectors who violate these rules are subject to being sued for civil penalties by the Federal Trade Commission in Washington, which is particularly active in this area. You can also sue in federal or state court under the Fair Debt Collection Practices Act if you act within a year of the offense. You may recover your losses plus up to $1,000 per violation, but you are subject to paying the other side's attorneys' fees and court costs if your own suit is undertaken in bad faith.

If a retailer, bank, or other credit grantor misbehaves in collecting a debt, check with your state's consumer protection office or attorney general's office to see if help is available. (A letter to these agencies, with a copy to the offending credit grantor, may go a long way.)

■

CHAPTER ELEVEN

Where the Heart Is

Buying and Selling a Home

Ahome is the largest purchase most Americans will ever make. It's surprising, then, that people sometimes plunge into buying or selling a home with less care than they give to buying or selling a car.

If you are one of the millions of Americans about to buy or sell a home, it's important to understand the ramifications of the decisions you will make. For example, state and federal law, the economy, your personal preferences, your financial situation, the prevailing real estate market, current mortgage rates, and tax considerations are among the many factors that affect you as either a buyer or seller. You will also need to work with a variety of people—real estate agents, attorneys, lenders, home inspectors, appraisers, and insurance agents, to name a few. In short, buying and selling a home is not the simple matter it might appear to be.

Whether you are buying your first home or selling your tenth, you will want to make sure that you understand how the law affects your decisions. This chapter begins with questions related to buying and selling a home. It's a good idea to become familiar with the legal aspects of both the buying and selling process. This is particularly true if it has been a while since you bought or sold a home. Practices and laws change, so you'll want to be aware of how these changes affect your responsibilities as a buyer or seller.

Remember, someone must be willing to buy a home before you can sell it, and vice versa. The sale will involve negotiation and have legal consequences. Like any other contract negotiation, it's a good idea to understand the goals of both parties in the transaction.

ELEMENTS OF REAL ESTATE

When you own an interest in real estate, you own the land and every-thing under it, including minerals and water; anything of value on the land, such as crops or timber; the airspace over the land; and im-provements on the land such as buildings, for example, a garage, barn, or fence. Each of these elements may be separate or shared and may also be subject to legal claims or **liens**—claims against property representing an unpaid debt of the owner or an unpaid judgment en-tered against the owner by a court.

Several different persons can have a legally recognized interest in the same real estate. For example, a farmer leases land owned by a school district. Although the district owns the land, the farmer owns the crops he or she plants on the land. The district may also have sold mineral rights in the land to another person.

REAL ESTATE TRANSACTIONS

Transactions involving real estate are different from buying anything else, and that difference is reflected in complexity. Possession of per-sonal (movable) property is a strong indicator of ownership. With real estate, on the other hand, the property cannot be moved, and possession does not necessarily mean ownership. To illustrate, un-less property is fenced in, it may be difficult to distinguish a neigh-bor's property from your own. And while you may own real estate, you may not have possession of it, if, for example, you are renting the property to someone else.

Other factors that distinguish real estate from personal property are: many different people can have an interest in the same real prop-erty; foreclosing on real property is much more difficult than repos-sessing a car; and real estate is taxed differently than personal property.

Most people buy a home because they want to own it and reduce their living expenses as they get older. Other benefits include favor-able tax considerations and more control over one's personal living environment than might be possible in the context of renting.

MEETING THE PLAYERS

Although it's possible for a home to be bought and sold strictly be-tween **principals**—the buyer and seller—this rarely happens today. Often a home buyer will want to use the services of a real estate agent, an attorney, and a home inspector to check out the property. To obtain financing, home buyers will consult the staff of one or more lending institutions. They also may consult with a financial planner or accountant about financing and an insurance agent to ob-tain homeowners insurance.

Sellers often use a real estate agent and an attorney. The seller also may turn to a financial planner or accountant for assistance in sort-ing out the tax consequences of selling.

Typically, two real estate agents are involved in the sale of the home: the **listing agent**, with whom the seller lists the property, and the **showing agent**, who shows the property to prospective buyers. Buyers should keep in mind that *both the listing agent and the agent showing properties are agents for the seller*. This means that both of these individuals work for and on behalf of the *seller*, not the buyer. For a prospective buyer this is an absolutely crucial point. It means, for example, that neither the listing agent nor the showing agent is permitted to disclose to a buyer confidential information supplied by

---

HOME OR INVESTMENT?

A common view of prospective home buyers is to think of a home solely or, at least, primarily as an investment. However, this view may be mistaken. There is no reason to assume that home prices will always rise. As many owners have discovered in the last five years or so, home prices can fall, sometimes dramatically. And, depending on the home prices in your area of the country, renting may be far more economical than buying, particu-larly if the renter invests the difference between a mortgage payment and rental payment. Nonetheless, while the decision to buy a home is not just an investment decision, it may be wise to give it the same care.

the seller that is adverse to the seller's interest in selling the property. (The seller and agents are, however, obligated to disclose material defects in the property if specifically requested to do so by a potential buyer, and, under some states' laws, even if not specifically asked. See page 157.)

As a buyer you can avoid this information gap by hiring a **buyer's agent**. You will, of course, have to pay something for this person's services, but the fee will probably be negotiable, or it may even be taken out of the commission that would have been paid in any event. Because this individual represents you as the buyer, he or she will be required to disclose to you all relevant information—bad as well as good—about the property you are considering. In addition, a buyer's agent is there to negotiate the best possible purchase terms for you.

Under recent changes made by the National Association of Realtors, a buyer's agent can be compensated from the total commission generated by a sale. This change is expected to increase the number of buyer's agents and thus expand the level of information available to buyers. It could also lead to a slight increase in house prices. Because this is an area of law that is rapidly changing, it is important for the buyer to have a knowledgeable attorney review a buyer's agent agreement before anything is signed.

The seller's listing agent helps determine the price of the home, suggests how to market the home, schedules advertising and open houses, shows the home to prospective buyers, and otherwise facilitates the sale. The showing agent works with buyers to show homes, contacts the listing agents, monitors the transaction, and, perhaps, helps obtain financing. In most cases the seller pays the sales commission, which is shared by the two agents.

Before starting the search, the buyer's lawyer should prepare a contract form on which to make an offer. The one supplied by the showing agent is likely to be seller-oriented. If the buyer does not have such a contract, he or she will want an attorney to review an offer to buy before it is signed, or at least be sure the offer has an attorney-approval provision so that an attorney can review it before it is final. If you are a seller, you probably will want to consult an attorney early in the process and before signing a listing agreement with a real estate agent.

Buying and selling real estate almost always entails a contract. So keep in mind that a typed or handwritten "letter of agreement" or "letter of understanding" signed by the parties will be binding if it meets the legal requirements of a contract. Don't sign something assuming it's not a contract and therefore not important. If something goes wrong, you don't want to discover too late that you've signed away important rights, failed to include important protections, or failed to receive what you expected. And beware of making oral promises. For example, if a seller orally promises to update the electrical system, the buyer might be able to insist that the system be updated even if the matter doesn't arise in later negotiations. Legal advice will be much more helpful—and less expensive—before rather than after signing a purchase contract.

SELECTING A REAL ESTATE AGENT TO SELL YOUR HOME

Experienced, reputable agents can be an invaluable asset to a seller. Real estate agents can offer advice on the suggested listing price, give you an educated guess as to how long it may take to sell, and offer valuable suggestions about how to best show your home. The major advantage, however, is that by listing with an agent, information about your home is immediately available to hundreds of other agents and buyers in your area through a Multiple Listing Service (MLS), which may also be available over the Internet.

The agent with whom you sign a listing agreement is known as the listing agent; most are members of the local MLS. Usually, within twenty-four hours of signing an agreement with an MLS agent, all MLS offices in your area will get a notice that your home is for sale. Because most home buyers work with agents, this makes information about your home available immediately to a wide range of potential buyers. (You should think twice before hiring a real estate agent who is not a member of the MLS.)

Choosing an agent requires that you do your homework both on the qualifications of the real estate firm and the individual agent who will handle your sale. You may want to interview several agents from various local firms with the following in mind:

• Is the firm a member of the National Association of Realtors? The association is a national voluntary professional organization whose members exchange information and hold seminars in order to enhance their skills and improve the services provided to buyers and sellers of real estate.

• Ask about sales for the last six months or one year. How do these figures compare with the sales figures of other real estate agencies?

• How long do homes stay on the market?

• How much and where does the agency advertise?

• How close is the actual sale price to the listing price for homes sold over the past six months or year?

• What does the agent think you should do to make your home more saleable?

You also may want to know how familiar various firms and agents are with your area. How well do they know its schools, facilities, and public transportation? The answers to these and similar questions can help you select someone who is knowledgeable and interested in working for you.

It's a good idea to avoid agents who want to list your home at a much higher price than other agents suggest. This may be just a device to get the listing. Within a few weeks you may find yourself being pressured to reduce the price drastically. Thus, make sure you are comfortable with the agent you choose. You should have confidence in your agent's ability. Your agent should be responsive to you by telling you who has expressed interest in the home and following up on the visits of potential buyers. For example, if many buyers have seen your home but no offers have been made, your agent should be trying to discover why. Is the price too high? Is the decor detracting? Should minor repairs be made?

THE LISTING AGREEMENT

Once signed, the listing agreement is a binding contract between the seller and the listing real estate firm. Its provisions include length of the listing period, commission rate and payment date, responsibilities of the firm and its agents, and who is responsible for the cost of advertising and other costs associated with the home sale.

Read the listing agreement carefully. Discuss any provisions you would like to change. To further protect your interests, resist signing an agreement until your attorney has reviewed and approved it, especially if you have requested changes that have been resisted.

One final suggestion could save you a lot of money. Before signing a listing agreement, let your friends and neighbors know you're selling. If any expresses an interest in buying, exclude them from the listing agreement. Then, if one ultimately buys the property, you won't be required to pay any commission.

Most real estate firms prefer **exclusive right to sell** listings, also known just as "exclusives." An exclusive guarantees that a commission will be paid no matter who sells the property as long as it's sold during the time period covered by the listing. Exclusive listings require that the listing agency work the property and actively promote its sale. Other types of listings include **open** listings and **exclusive agency** listings. Most real estate agencies avoid open listings for residential sales because these listings allow sellers to list with other agencies or sell the homes themselves. Under an open listing the commission is paid only to the agency who finds the buyer. In some states an exclusive agency listing may be offered, under which the seller can avoid paying commission if he or she sells the house personally and not through an agent.

MLS-member real estate firms combine their exclusive right to sell listings. This makes the home available to a wide variety of prospective buyers. The multiple listing agreement defines how the firms share the sales commission when the property is sold.

Typically, real estate firms charge 5 to 7 percent of the sale price. On some higher-priced homes a firm may charge the full commission on the first $100,000 or $200,000 and a lower percentage of any amount above that price. If the agency that lists the home is also the agency that sells it, the commission is shared by the agency and the individual agent who actually handled the sale. If the listing firm and the selling firm are different, the commission is shared by the two firms.

Other less common forms of fee payments include the flat-fee method, in which a set fee is charged regardless of the home's price, and the net method. The net method, which is not favored and is illegal in some states, allows the broker to retain any amount of the selling price higher than an agreed sale price.

Remember: All commission agreements are negotiable, particularly in a seller's market. So are the other terms in the listing agreement. At the very least, the real estate agency should be willing to negotiate provisions on:

- **The length of the contract.** Many of the standard forms provide that the contract renews automatically. Many firms want a six-month listing. If you're in a hurry to sell your home, try to get a sixty- or ninety-day listing.

- **When the commission is earned.** You should insist that the listing agreement provides that this occurs only when the seller and buyer actually complete the sale, not when they sign the purchase agreement.

- **Who will be responsible for the advertising expenses**—the seller or the agency?

You should always remember that the listing agreement between a seller and a real estate firm carries a **fiduciary responsibility**. This means that the firm and all of its agents act for the seller. They owe the seller care, obedience, accounting, loyalty, and notice. Your agent should promptly return your telephone calls, keep you informed about the progress of your home sale, schedule open houses, and generally appear interested in the sale. On the other hand, do not be unduly upset if you are presented with offers that seem unreasonably low. Your firm and its agents have an obligation to present you with all offers, even those that may seem insulting. Of course, you are not required to accept any offer presented, although you may be required to pay a commission to an agent if you refuse to accept an offer at the precise price and terms set forth in the listing agreement. But if you feel that undue pressure is being applied, it may be time for a change—another reason to limit the length of a listing agreement.

BUYING A HOME

If you're a prospective buyer, postpone offers and negotiations until you get a feel for various neighborhoods and the style of home you are seeking. Visiting open houses is an excellent way to do this. You also may want to be prequalified by a lender for a mortgage before you have a specific home in mind. This will require filling out financial statements, making the necessary financial disclosures, and having your credit record checked. This will give you a rough idea of how much money the lender will lend you, making it easier for you to pinpoint your price range.

MAKING AN OFFER: THE PURCHASE CONTRACT

Negotiations are handled in various ways in different parts of the country. Typically, most transactions begin with negotiation over price, although other items, such as date of possession, may also be negotiated. The real estate agent will provide a form, usually called a **preliminary agreement** (there is nothing legally preliminary about it, however), a **contract to purchase** or, simply, a **real estate contract**. In any case, this is a formal, written offer that conveys your terms to the seller. If you wish to have the home inspected, the contract should include an **inspection rider**; if you intend to apply for a mortgage, it should include a **mortgage-contingency clause**; if your attorney has not reviewed the contract, it should include an **attorney-approval rider**. (Each of these is discussed in more detail below.) In other words, it should cover the basics. Remember, once this document is signed by both parties, it is legally binding.

BUYING A HOME FROM A BUILDER

A buyer purchasing a new home from a builder may or may not work through an agent. If you are not working with an agent, you should consult your lawyer to ensure that the purchase contract with the builder contains no surprises. In addition, you may want to consider having the finished structure inspected, notwithstanding its newness. Remember, it's the quality of the construction, not its newness, that is important. An independent inspection can give you this assurance.

If you are contracting with a builder on a home that is not yet built or finished, you will want to make sure you will get what you think you are buying. For example, model homes typically include options, rather than standard features. Along with superior windows and siding, these could include better-quality kitchen cabinets, higher-grade carpeting, and more expensive lighting fixtures. In a large planned-unit development it is not uncommon for developers to switch to cheaper finishing materials as different phases of the construction continue. Make sure that the builder provides you with a complete list of standard and optional features. If you are choosing options, make sure the purchase contract includes the specific cost of all options.

You will want to know other facts as well, such as the type and extent of any landscaping to be provided by the builder, plans for development of surrounding property, and the exact provisions of any warranty from the builder. If possible, you will want a warranty that is insured by an insurance company rather than a warranty guaranteed only by the builder. Finally, the builder should provide you with evidence that the subcontractors and material suppliers have waived any liens they might have against the property in the event the builder does not pay them for their work.

Specified dates for completion and occupancy should be included if the home is not yet built. You can provide for a penalty or the right to cancel the contract if the builder exceeds these dates. You can also insist on an escrow or holdback for incomplete items that are discovered just before closing.

The offer should specify a date after which it is no longer valid. This period may be as little as twenty-four hours from the time the seller or the seller's agent receives it. The offer to purchase also is usually valid only if both the buyer and seller sign it within a certain time period. As a general rule, an **earnest money** deposit accompanies the offer to purchase.

When the buyer signs the offer to purchase, he or she usually deposits a sum of money—perhaps $500 or $1,000—with the seller, the seller's real estate agent, or the seller's attorney. This is earnest money. The offer should specify that the earnest money deposit will be placed in an interest-bearing account with the interest credited to the buyer. Earnest money is not the same thing as the buyer's down payment, although if the sale goes through, it will be applied to the down payment. Earnest money symbolizes the buyer's commitment to take the necessary steps to complete the purchase, for example, obtaining a loan. Thus, if a prospective buyer does little or nothing to complete the sale, he or she risks losing the earnest money deposit.

THE PURCHASE CONTRACT

The purchase contract may be called a sales contract, real estate contract, purchase agreement, sales agreement, purchase and sale agreement, or preliminary agreement. Whatever it is called, it is a legal document that, when signed by both parties, is a legal contract that will govern the entire transaction. Some states automatically allow you to void such a contract within seventy-two hours or a similar period—a statutory "attorney review period" (see below). Ideally, though, *before* signing such a contract, you and your attorney should review it carefully. Remember, once signed, you are obligated to fulfill your part of the contract. A purchase contract, in most cases, is a standard form contract with any necessary riders attached. As usual, you can change any terms on a preprinted form. The contract can include many provisions but should include the following:

- the date of the contract;
- the purchase price of the home;

- the amount of the down payment;

- all items to be included in the sale, such as wall-to-wall carpeting, window treatments, appliances, or lighting fixtures;

- any items to be excluded from the sale, such as an heirloom chandelier;

- the date when the deed will be transferred (also called the closing date);

- an inspection rider, which allows the buyer to have the home inspected, usually within ten days of the date of the contract. Various types of inspections, such as structural, termite, roof, etc., may be specified. If the inspection is unsatisfactory, the buyer ordinarily is released from the contract. However, the buyer may not be released if the contract allows the seller to make repairs, and the repairs, when made, meet applicable standards of workmanship;

- an attorney-approval rider for both the buyer and the seller if either or both parties sign the contract before it is reviewed by their respective attorneys;

- a legal description of the property;

- a provision that the seller will provide good title to the home or what is sometimes called **marketable title**. Generally, the seller fulfills this obligation by providing an abstract of title, certificate of title, or a title insurance policy. This indicates that the seller has the authority to sell the home. In some states, for example, Connecticut, the seller is required to deliver good title, which the buyer is expected to verify at his or her own expense by securing an abstract of title, certificate of title, or a title insurance policy. If the buyer encounters problems in establishing title, he or she can reject the title at closing;

- any restriction or limitations that could affect title;

- a provision for paying utility bills, property taxes, and similar expenses through the closing date;

- a provision for return of the buyer's earnest money deposit if the sale is not completed as, for example, when the buyer has been unable to obtain financing after reasonable or good faith efforts to do so;

- a provision for taking possession. Along with a firm date for transferring possession from the seller to the buyer, the buyer should include a provision that requires the seller to pay a specific amount of rent per day if the seller does not leave the home by the agreed date. If the buyer and seller already know that possession will be delayed, the buyer may ask for a certain amount of money to be held in escrow at the closing to cover the rent for the expected time period;

- a provision for a walk-through inspection within a specified period before the date of closing to allow the buyer to make sure conditions are as they should be according to the contract;

- terms of any escrow agreement;

- a provision for who is responsible for maintaining insurance until the closing. The Uniform Vendor-Purchaser Risk of Loss Act applies in some states, which means that the seller assumes the risk of loss until either transfer of title or possession. In some states the common law requires the seller to assume this risk;

- signatures of the parties.

Many buyers like to inspect the property within twenty-four hours of the closing to be sure it is in the same condition as it was when they signed the offer to purchase and to make sure that all property to be included in the sale remains in place. This is called a **walk-through**. If something has been removed that was included in the sale under the terms of the purchase contract (such as a chandelier or appliance), the buyer should quickly notify his or her attorney or the seller's agent to see if the item will be returned before closing. Or, if agreeable to both parties, the buyer and seller may decide to reach a financial compromise instead.

SPECIFIC CONTRACT RIDERS

One common rider, the **attorney-approval** rider, makes the purchase contract subject to approval by the buyer's and seller's respective attorneys within a short period of time, usually five to ten days after acceptance of the offer. In such cases the standard contract form should include the phrase *"Subject to the Approval of the Attorneys for the Parties Within __ Days,"* with the number of days written in.

Without such a condition in the contract, both the seller and the buyer are bound by the terms of the contract, which may be unclear or may differ from the parties' intent.

Like the inspection rider and the mortgage-contingency rider, this language allows a buyer to get out of a purchase contract. In fact, this is the reason some sellers will not accept such clauses, although it is mandated in some states. An attorney-approval rider could specify that a lawyer must state such disapproval in writing, with the seller having the option to correct the problem causing disapproval. This type of rider ensures that the contract need not bind the parties if their lawyers find an unsatisfactory provision in the small print. Meanwhile, the buyer and seller can sign the contract knowing that

AN AGENT OR NOT?

There are advantages to selling your home without an agent. If you sell your home on your own, you will not have to pay a sales commission. While this may seem like a large savings, you must prepare yourself to assume all the responsibilities and costs associated with selling your home. These include advertising your home, spending time with potential buyers, and negotiating the sale. Sellers familiar with local sales procedures and the real estate market may choose to sell their homes themselves. Various books can help guide you through the process. Experts generally recommend that the seller hire both a lawyer and appraiser at the beginning of the process. An appraiser can help you establish a price for your home, and the attorney can help you with the legal issues, legal filings, and other necessary documentation.

There are three distinct disadvantages to doing it yourself, however. First, you will lack the many resources that real estate agents have to attract buyers. For example, your home will not be listed in your local Multiple Listing Service, so it is likely that fewer buyers will see your home. Second, you will have to find time to show your home and talk to potential buyers, and you will need to pay for all advertising. Third, you will be directly involved in negotiating the sales price and other contract provisions.

the other party may not easily back out of the contract because of a minor defect or objection.

The **mortgage-contingency rider**, a common provision, allows the buyer a certain period of time to obtain a commitment for financing at a specified interest rate for a certain amount of money. This is usually thirty to sixty days, depending on the average time needed to obtain a loan commitment. The clause might read, for example, that the contract is contingent on the buyer's obtaining approval for a thirty-year mortgage for $100,000 at no more than 8 percent interest within forty-five days. For additional protection, the buyer might specify the type of loan he or she prefers, for example, fixed, variable, FHA, or VA.

A mortgage-contingency rider provides critical protection to the buyer. For example, it allows the buyer to void the purchase contract without penalty in those cases in which the buyer is unable to obtain

---

At first glance this last task may seem easy enough. Yet many sales fall through without the mediating influence of a third person with the experience to bring the buyer and seller together on a variety of issues. A professional real estate agent is on the alert for "deal-breakers," the kind of petty disagreements over small items that break up negotiations.

If you've decided to sell on your own and also don't hire an attorney to negotiate for you, remember that settling on the terms and conditions of sale, including the price, is a give-and-take process. The fact that you love your renovated kitchen won't influence a potential buyer who intends to remodel anyway. If, after some reflection, you conclude that you lack the necessary experience, it may be wise to turn to a real estate agent or your attorney.

The major advantage of buying a **For-Sale-by-Owner**, or **FSBO**, home should be a lower purchase price, because the seller will not be paying a commission on the sale. The truth is, however, that many FSBOs are priced as high as they would be if they were listed with a real estate firm. If you are interested in a FSBO, make sure you check the prices of comparable homes on the market as well as recent sales in the area.

---

financing on the terms specified in the contract after making a reasonable or good faith effort to do so within the time provided. Because this type of clause favors the buyer, some real estate agents suggest that the buyer obtain a prequalification from a lender, which gives the seller a degree of confidence that the buyer will not use the clause to void the contract unless some extraordinary circumstance arises.

The seller may refuse to agree to a mortgage-contingency rider. This can and does happen in a very hot seller's market, in which case, there's not much the buyer can do. But the absence of a mortgage-contingency rider might mean that the buyer will be forced to finance his or her home purchase at an unfavorable interest rate. Because of this risk, buyers should be cautious about signing a purchase contract that does not contain this clause. Sellers should ensure that the

---

THE FAIR HOUSING ACT

A homeowner may legally refuse to sell a home to a potential buyer for many reasons (e.g., shaky credit), but not for **prohibited** reasons (race, gender, etc.). The **Fair Housing Act**, Title VIII of the **Civil Rights Act of 1968**, covers housing discrimination. This law prohibits housing discrimination by real estate firms and homeowners. This means that homeowners may not refuse to lease or sell property based on race, religion, gender, color, or national origin. In some localities, special housing discrimination ordinances or laws also cover sexual orientation. This does not mean, however, that sellers must sell *you* their home. It means that you could take legal action if the seller refuses to sell and you believe it was due to discrimination.

A homeowner can face serious financial penalties if found in violation of this law. The potential buyer could sue for actual monetary losses as well as attorneys' fees, court costs, and even punitive damages.

A homeowner *may* lawfully "discriminate" on economic grounds. Without too much fear of legal action, a seller could refuse the bid of a buyer with a poor credit rating or inability to obtain a loan. The homeowner's

---

proposed interest rate is reasonable and based on current rates, and allow a limited but reasonable time for the mortgage commitment. Similarly, most sellers accept an inspection rider but should make sure that this rider expires relatively quickly—say, ten days from signing. Unlike a mortgage commitment, there's usually no reason that an inspection can't be done within a week or so.

UNCOMPLETED SALES

What happens to the earnest money deposit if the sale is not complete? Generally, the purchase contract allows the buyer to get back the earnest money and any interest earned on it, unless he or she has in some way violated the contract. If the seller refuses to return

---

argument could be that he or she cannot be forced to remove the home from the market while waiting for a loan commitment that has little chance of materializing. Perhaps the safest thing for the seller to do if the economic viability of an offer is in question is to tell the buyer that the offer might be accepted once the loan commitment is obtained—if no other offers were received in the interim.

Real estate firms and agents also are covered by the Fair Housing Act, which prohibits them from **steering**, a practice of showing potential buyers homes located only in certain neighborhoods. For example, a firm or agent might be accused of steering if the homes shown to prospective black buyers were located only in neighborhoods with a high concentration of black residents.

If you suspect that someone has discriminated against you, request a complaint form by calling the federal Department of Housing and Urban Development (HUD) at 800-424-8590. HUD's job is to investigate such complaints. You also may contact a local civil rights organization to find out if your area has specific organizations to contact. Usually, you will have to consult a lawyer about possible legal action against the homeowner.

the deposit, the buyer may have to sue the seller for return of the deposit.

If the seller violates the terms of the contract or refuses to close the sale, the buyer can sue to force the seller to complete the transaction. It is also possible for the buyer to sue for damages. For example, a buyer who had incurred costs for obtaining a mortgage or costs for renting temporary housing caused because the seller broke the contract would have a case for damages.

THE HOME INSPECTION

A professional home inspection varies among localities, but generally the aim is to discover any problems with the home that might not be readily apparent. Most inspectors check to make sure that there are no material defects or problems with such items as the electrical, plumbing, heating, and air-conditioning systems. The inspector may also check for termites, estimate the age of the roof and when it might need replacement, and look at the condition of the basic structure, including the foundation, evidence of basement seepage, and other problems. Some inspectors check for radon, lead paint, or other environmental hazards.

A professional inspector should not be an alarmist. The idea is to point out problems without exaggerating defects. It's a good idea for the buyer to accompany the inspector during the inspection. In this way the buyer can ask questions and get an idea of the cost of any repairs that are necessary or advisable. The inspector may also suggest ways to better insulate the home or offer maintenance suggestions that can prolong the life of systems such as heating and air conditioning.

Most buyers do not want to pay for an inspection until they have settled on other terms with the seller. To do this, the buyer often uses an inspection rider to provide that the offer to buy is contingent on a favorable inspection of the home. It is unethical for home inspectors who are contractors or architects (as many are) to angle for corrective work on defects they find.

DISCLOSURES

Disclosures about real estate are covered—or not—by state law. In other words, disclosure is treated differently among the states. Some states require sellers to fill out a long form that explicitly asks about the seller's knowledge of various material defects that might be present in the home. Most states, however, do not require disclosure, although in many of these states the listing agent will require it anyway. It is certainly wise for the buyer to beware. In some jurisdictions, unless the buyer asks specific questions about defects, the seller is not required to disclose them, even if he or she has specific knowledge that one or more substantial defects exists. As a result, any problems discovered by the new owner after the sale is closed are his or her problems. There is a trend for courts to require disclosure if the buyer does not ask. But do not rely on this possibility. As a buyer, when in doubt, ask.

As a seller you may want to disclose known material defects that seriously affect the home's value even if your state does not mandate such disclosure. This will help you avoid any future legal problems involved with the sale of your home. Many lawsuits involving real estate transactions are due to the seller's misrepresentation or failure to disclose. Responding honestly to the buyer's questions and either repairing material defects or disclosing them is an effective way to avoid future litigation.

SETTING A PRICE

As a buyer or seller, how do you establish the value of a home? First of all, there is no "right" price. The value of a home is almost entirely dependent on what someone is willing to pay for it and how long the seller is willing to wait to find that person. Most sellers are not in the position to wait for the ideal buyer who will pay their ideal price. They want to find the optimum price at which their home will sell in a limited amount of time. To do this, they typically rely on comparisons with recently sold homes in the neighborhood. A real estate agent can help you by giving you a list of homes sold through the local Multiple Listing Service during the past year or so. For example, if the home in question is a three-bedroom, two-bath ranch on a typical lot, your agent can point out sales prices of similar homes to determine a listing price. Try to limit your study to homes that are similar to the one you are seeking to sell or considering bidding for. If Victorian homes are prized in your area, even a Victorian needing work will be priced higher than other styles of homes of similar size.

Amenities are a big factor in the price. An attached garage, wood-burning fireplace, updated kitchen and baths, large lot, and spacious rooms are among the factors that generally increase a home's price. Location is also a factor. Most buyers want good schools, good transportation, quiet neighborhoods, and little or no commercial activity. The presence or absence of these factors all affect the selling price of your home.

Perhaps equally important are personal reasons for selling and how long you can wait to buy or sell. Typically, the most interest is generated in the first few weeks a home is listed. If the seller wants to sell a home fast, it should be priced so that it stands out among comparable homes on the market. If the seller is willing to wait (and willing to keep the house in tip-top shape during the time it remains on the market), the seller will likely price it above the competition. Sellers who try to hold out for the highest price, however, may find themselves reducing the price down the line. A house that has been on the market beyond the average marketing time generates little interest from buyers, even when the price is reduced dramatically. Most buyers will assume that the home has problems, which they, understandably, want to avoid.

As a buyer, you have to consider the following factors to determine whether or not you can afford to purchase a home:

- How much money have you saved for a down payment?
- What is the status of your current income and expenses, such as car payments?
- Do you have a good credit history?
- What are the current interest rates on mortgages?
- What are your priorities and lifestyle?
- How much home can you afford?

AFFORDING A HOME

This is one of the first things to consider when buying a home. First of all, knowing what you can afford will narrow your range so you will not waste time looking at homes that cost too much. First-time buyers often are disappointed when they find the home of their dreams only to discover they cannot afford it. Unless you are paying cash for a home, how much home you can afford depends on your income, your assets, your expenses and debts (including automobile or education loans and outstanding credit card balances), prevailing interest rates on mortgages, the cash needed for a down payment (10 to 20 percent of the purchase price), and closing costs (4 to 6 percent of the purchase price).

There is a formula for determining what you can afford. The prevailing rule says that a home should cost no more than 2.5 times your annual income. Thus, if your income is $50,000, your price limit would be $50,000 multiplied by 2.5, or $125,000. Typically, a lender expects you to pay no more than 28 percent of your gross income for housing, which includes the loan payment, property tax, homeowners insurance, and estimated utility costs. A lender will look at your debts. As a general rule, your total indebtedness, including monthly housing expenses, should not exceed 36 percent of your gross income.

Along with these guidelines, consider your lifestyle and priorities. If costly vacations, dining out, and entertainment are important to you, you may want to buy a less expensive home than the lender says you can afford. Many people, however, find that they are willing to give up some luxuries or even stretch their budget for the home they want. In an era of corporate downsizing and job insecurity, however, this may be unwise. Luxuries can be cut back in an emergency; a mortgage payment cannot.

The total loan amount a lender will agree to provide is directly tied to your income and expenses. As a homeowner, you will be making a monthly loan payment, along with the cost of insurance, property taxes, utilities, and maintenance. A lender looks for a solid history of income, employment, and credit. The lender also will review your expenses, including automobile payments, credit card debt, education loans, child support, alimony, etc. If you are borrowing money for your down payment, the lender will treat the interest payments on that loan as expenses or perhaps even decline the loan unless most of the down payment is your money.

DOWN PAYMENTS AND OTHER CLOSING COSTS

Some people may qualify for special government-insured loans offered through the Federal Housing Administration (FHA) or Veterans Administration (VA). The down payment needed for these loans is minimal. But, unless you can qualify, you will need a down payment equal to 20 percent of the purchase price to avoid paying the extra cost of **Private Mortgage Insurance (PMI)**. With less than a 20 percent down payment, banking regulations require the buyer to carry PMI. This insures the lender against nonpayment of the difference between the customary down payment and the down payment actually paid. The charge for PMI may be as much as $50 or $60 per month, although the amount declines as the loan ages and you begin to pay off more of the principal. It is not tax deductible.

If you cannot put down 20 percent, the only way to end the PMI payments is to demonstrate in the future that your equity in the home has increased to 20 percent. This can sometimes be done if you refinance and your home has increased in value to the point where the balance of your loan is less than 80 percent of the home's value. Or, if you have owned your home long enough to build up equity through principal payments, you may be able to eliminate PMI. Be aware, however, that the insurer will need written support from a certified appraiser as to the value of your home. The value assessed by a municipality for real estate tax purposes is seldom considered in evaluating home equity.

Along with the down payment, you will need between 4 and 6 percent of your loan amount to pay for closing costs, unless you are obtaining an FHA or VA loan. These costs include fees for your attorney, the lender's appraisal, lender's title insurance, title search, escrow deposits for property taxes and/or homeowners insurance, as well as other expenses, such as recording fees. If you are obtaining a loan from a federally insured financial institution, the law requires the lender to provide an estimate of these costs at the time you apply.

The seller has to cover some closing costs. He or she is responsible for paying the commission on the sale and must pay any taxes owed on the property, any money due his or her lender, and any liens that may be outstanding on the property. Usually the seller is required to pay the cost of a title insurance policy for the buyer that insures the buyer against any defects in the title to the property.

MORTGAGES

The interest you pay on your loan is part of the cost of owning a home. For example, a 1 percent increase in the interest rate on a $100,000 loan adds approximately $75 to your monthly loan payment over the life of a thirty-year loan. Obviously, the lower the interest rate, the more you can afford to borrow. Be aware that home interest rates can change quickly. They usually are the last rates to decline when other interest rates are falling and are among the first to rise when other rates are climbing.

If you are unsure about your price range, and especially if you are a first-time buyer, **prequalifying** for a loan can help smooth the purchase process. You will know exactly what you can afford and avoid the disappointment of being unable to buy the home you thought you could afford. To prequalify for a loan, you will need to go through most of the steps entailed in applying for the actual loan. If you decide to prequalify, be sure to do so through a loan originator, that is, an actual lender. A mortgage broker, who brings together borrowers and lenders, cannot prequalify you for a loan.

FINANCING A HOME PURCHASE

Few people have enough cash to buy a home outright. Most need to finance their purchase by borrowing money. Usually, this is done by contracting with a financial institution or mortgage company. The buyer agrees to pay interest on the money borrowed and the lender retains a lien on the property, called a **mortgage** or **deed of trust**. Today, a wide variety of financing mechanisms exist to finance a purchase. Some buyers may qualify for federally insured loans, which permit smaller-than-normal down payments and lower interest rates than prevailing market rates.

It pays to watch trends in interest rates and shop around for the best deal you can find. Lenders are very competitive. Interest rates and fees charged to originate a loan vary among financial institutions. Typically, lenders charge the prospective buyer a fee, called **points** (as in percentage points), to obtain a loan—this may be a flat fee or a percentage of the loan (one point is 1 percent of the loan amount). One lender might offer an 8 percent, thirty-year fixed-rate loan with a flat fee of $200. A second lender might offer a 7 percent, thirty-year fixed-rate loan with two points. A third lender might offer the loan without points or other fees but at a higher interest rate. This could be advantageous for a buyer who wants to put as much as possible into his or her down payment. Another buyer might prefer to pay higher points in exchange for a lower interest rate because the Internal Revenue Service allows points to be deducted against taxable income in the year the home is purchased. The Truth-in-Lending Act helps you make a choice by requiring information that will help you understand the options and make comparisons.

There is an alternative form of financing in some states called a **land contract**. A land contract is a common form of seller financing. The buyer pays the seller a down payment and agrees to make payments of interest and principal on the outstanding balance. In other words, the seller acts as a lending institution. This is often referred to as "the seller taking back a mortgage" or "taking back paper." Typically, the buyer takes possession of the property, but the seller retains the right to sue to recover the property if the buyer fails to fulfill his or her contractual obligations. This is sometimes used when the buyer does not have a large amount of cash to buy a new home and is generally considered undesirable from the buyer's point of view, because the buyer can be quickly ousted for default (more so than under a bank mortgage) and may lose the built-up equity. Other drawbacks include inability to finance home improvements, inability to borrow on built-up equity, and possible problems in obtaining clear title from the seller when the time comes to transfer ownership.

Sometimes a **bridge loan** is needed to allow a buyer to buy another home while waiting to sell his or her present home. You can obtain a bridge loan if you have a contract to sell your present home and you need the loan only for a specific, relatively short period of time. It is much more difficult to obtain a bridge loan if you do not have a buyer for your home and thus need to pay loans on two properties. Bridge loans usually carry a higher interest than a traditional home loan, because they are for a short duration. But because they're only for a short time, the interest bite is not as painful as it would be under a long-term mortgage.

FIXED-RATE LOANS

Some prospective buyers prefer a **fixed-rate loan** because the interest rate cannot be increased during the term of the loan, typically fifteen, twenty, or thirty years. Under a fixed-rate loan buyers can feel more comfortable knowing the exact amount of their monthly loan payments throughout the life of the loan. (Much of the same comfort, however, with some of the benefit of a variable rate, may be obtainable with a variable rate capped over the loan life and even capped each year.) Although the interest rate does not change with a fixed-rate loan, the way in which the payment is divided changes over the loan period. At the beginning most of the payment is applied to the interest owed to the lender. As the loan progresses, more money is applied to the principal—the face amount of the loan. This process, called **amortization**, also means that the amount of interest deductible for federal income tax purposes will decline over the life of the loan.

The major difference between a fifteen- or twenty-year fixed-rate loan and a thirty-year fixed-rate loan is that the borrower will make higher monthly payments (which include more of the principal) on the shorter term loans than would be the case with a thirty-year loan for the same amount of money. Over the life of the loan, however, the buyer pays far less interest because he or she is using the money for a shorter period of time and is paying off more principal each month.

ADJUSTABLE-RATE LOANS

Adjustable-rate loans vary, but they all share one common factor: Some aspect of the loan terms can be changed by the lender during the life of the loan. The specific type of adjustable mortgage is tied to whether the change is in the rate of interest, amount of payment, or length of time for repayment. If you are considering applying for any type of adjustable-rate loan, make sure you understand exactly how the mortgage works, including the spread between the interest rate and the index to which the rate is tied, how often the loan can be adjusted, and the maximum allowable increase (or decrease) each year as well as over the life of the loan.

Adjustable-rate loans include:

• **Adjustable-rate mortgages (ARMs).** These loans typically offer a lower interest rate than fixed-rate loans at the start and often come with a "teaser" rate—a lower-than-market interest rate in the first year. After the initial period the interest rate will usually be adjusted annually and is tied to an index that may move up or down but is not under the control of the lender. The index might be the one-year U.S. Treasury bill (the "T-bill") rate or some other rate that reflects the changes in interest rates. Note that the rate is *tied* to the index— it is not the same as the index. The mortgage might specify, for example, that the future rate would be two points above the average T-bill rate. Typically, ARMs are adjusted once a year on the anniversary date of the loan. In addition, ARMs usually have a provision for a cap, that is, the highest rate that can be charged. Some may include a minimum rate as well. When considering an ARM, consumers should never take one without a cap and should insist on an example of what the highest possible payment would be under a particular ARM.

- **Convertible ARMs.** These loans usually offer a conversion factor that allows the borrower to convert to a fixed-rate loan at a specified period of time. For example, a convertible ARM could allow the borrower the option to convert to a fixed-rate loan once a year over the first five years of the loan. The interest rate to be paid would also be tied to an index.

- **Renegotiable-rate mortgage (rollover).** These loans typically set the interest rate and monthly payments for several years, sometimes as if the loan were being amortized over a much longer period, and then allow both the rate and principal payments to be changed, depending on general market conditions. If the new terms are unacceptable to you, you can pay the loan in full or refinance at prevailing interest rates.

- **Graduated payment mortgage (GPM).** With this type of loan, typically sought by young buyers who expect their incomes to rise, the payments are low in the first couple of years and gradually rise over the years thereafter.

- **Shared-appreciation mortgage.** These loans offer lower-than-market rates of interest and low payments in exchange for a lender's share in appreciation of the property. Usually the lender will require that its share of equity be turned over when the home is sold or at a specified date set out in the loan agreement.

BALLOON LOANS

With a **balloon loan**, the buyer is expected to pay off the loan completely within a short period of time, usually in three, five, or seven years, but the loan is amortized over a longer period, so the payoff amount is large. In other words, this is a short-term loan with a large (balloon) final payment. The interest rate can be fixed or variable, but in all cases the unpaid balance on the principal is due at the time specified. The borrower must either refinance or sell the home to pay off the loan.

To attract buyers, builders often offer balloon loans during periods of high-interest rates when home sales are sluggish. In most cases the interest rate will be lower than prevailing home loan rates. But if interest rates are high when full payment is due, refinancing may not be possible. The balloon will "burst," resulting in foreclosure and loss of the home.

FHA AND VA LOANS

The Federal Housing Administration offers insured low-interest loans made by the federal government and approved lending institutions. The cost for this loan insurance varies and is charged at the closing. While FHA loans are not available through all lenders, in some areas they are very popular and can make the difference in obtaining a loan for some potential buyers who do not qualify for conventional financing. The Veterans Administration offers government-insured loans to qualified veterans.

Income qualifications, required down payments, and the maximum allowable loans under these plans change periodically. Currently the maximum FHA loan is about $150,000 in certain high-priced areas of the country.

For first-time home buyers, the federal government as well as state governments offer loan assistance to prospective buyers who meet eligibility requirements. For current information about these loan programs, consult local FHA and VA offices as well as your real estate agent.

JUMBO LOANS

Jumbo loans exceed the amount of loans allowed by the Federal National Mortgage Association (Fannie Mae) and the Federal Home Loan Mortgage Corporation (Freddie Mac), the federal agencies that oversee the secondary market in mortgage loans. The maximum mortgage amount for Fannie Mae and Freddie Mac can go up or down. Recently it stood at $203,150.

Fannie Mae and Freddie Mac are not loan guarantors; they are purchasers from primary lenders. These agencies purchase loans from lenders and then resell the loans to other organizations, such as insurance companies and banks. On the other hand, FHA and VA are loan guarantors. Many FHA and VA loans are purchased by Fannie Mae and Freddie Mac.

Interest rates on jumbo loans typically are slightly higher than other loans, but this isn't always the case. Lenders who intend to keep the mortgage in their portfolio tend to offer competitive interest rates.

NEGATIVE AMORTIZATION

In a typical home loan, the borrower pays off the interest and principal in installments. This is known as amortization, because the debt is gradually reduced. **Negative amortization** can occur when the installment payments do not cover all the interest due each month. This unpaid interest is added on to the principal that is owed, resulting in a debt that increases, rather than decreases.

The worst problem with negative amortization occurs in a market in which home values decrease. Then the size of your debt could increase to the point where it would exceed the equity in your home. Sadly, you could sell your home and not be able to repay what you owe. Most professionals advise buyers to avoid a negatively amortized loan. The risks outweigh the benefits of the lower payments. It may be better to postpone buying a home until you can make higher payments or investigate a lower-cost loan from the FHA or VA.

APPLYING FOR A HOME LOAN

Obtaining a loan requires a lot of paperwork and sometimes a lot of fortitude. The savings and loan scandals and the large number of foreclosures in recent years have forced lenders to take a much more critical look at their lending practices. While you won't be asked for your blood type, it's a good bet that you will be asked about everything in your financial history.

Loan applications vary, but most require the following information:

- employment history, salary history, and proof of employment;
- outstanding debts;
- assets;
- source of your down payment.

This last point requires some explanation. The lender will want to make sure that you are not borrowing money to make your down payment. (If you are borrowing money and will be making interest payments, this will be taken into consideration.) If you are receiving a gift from relatives for a down payment, the lender will expect proof that the gift will be forthcoming.

When you apply for the loan, ask the lender how long the approval process is expected to take. It can take anywhere from twenty-four hours to three months, depending on a variety of factors. If you have included a mortgage-contingency clause in your purchase contract, be sure to inform your lender when you apply for the loan of the date the clause expires. Usually your lender will work with you to meet the deadline or alert you that approval will take more time. At that point you may be able to get an extension from the seller on the contingency.

Although illegal in many states, if permitted, many home loans include a **prepayment penalty**. This is a charge imposed if the borrower pays off the loan ahead of schedule. This penalty is usually 1 or 2 percent of the loan. It is not unusual for home loans to include a prepayment penalty for the first few years; however, you should avoid mortgages that require a prepayment penalty beyond the third year.

Once your loan is approved, the lender will provide you with a **loan commitment**, in which the lender agrees to lend a specific amount of money on specific terms. A copy of this commitment can be provided to the seller for assurance that your financing is in place. A substantial amount of documentation is provided by the lender, or **mortgagee**, before closing. Much of it is mandated by federal law and is meant to disclose the true cost of the loan to the borrower, or **mortgagor**.

Ultimately the borrower will sign many documents; however, two are essential to completing the loan transaction. One is a **promissory note**—a contract under which the borrower agrees to repay the lender the money borrowed plus interest. The borrower may be responsible for repaying the note even if he or she later sells the home to a buyer who assumes the mortgage. The second document is a **mortgage,** or **deed of trust,** the document that gives the lender a security interest in the real estate. Having a security interest in your home means the lender may enforce repayment of the loan by selling the property. If you do not pay, you could lose your home.

INSURING YOUR HOME LOAN

Several types of insurance contracts pay your home loan if you die or become disabled. This type of insurance establishes an annual premium cost for the life of your loan. Because your loan declines as you pay down the principal (main amount of the loan), the amount of insurance coverage decreases each year, although the cost stays the same. That makes it a poorer deal as time goes on. You are getting less and less for your money each year—like a lease in which the rent stays the same but the apartment gets smaller.

In almost all cases, a term life insurance policy that can be used to pay off the loan in the event of your death is preferable to a mortgage insurance policy. Term life insurance is less expensive and offers better protection and more flexibility. (For example, if your spouse has a regular source of income but little savings, he or she may not want to pay off the house but might prefer to keep the life insurance proceeds in the bank.) All insurance products are relatively complicated. You may want to consult a financial professional or an attorney to check these policies before you buy one.

Because temporary or permanent disability can threaten your ability to pay your home loan, you may also want to consider buying a disability policy or participating in any disability insurance offered by your employer. Disability insurance can add to your peace of mind and that of your lender. Again, however, *credit* disability insurance may not be your best choice.

THE CLOSING

The real estate closing is the final stage in the process of buying a home. The closing is a meeting at which the buyer and seller, usually accompanied by their respective lawyers and real estate agents, complete the sale. At this meeting the buyer usually makes all the required payments. The seller produces all documents necessary for the transfer of good—that is, marketable—title and delivers a deed that transfers the title to the buyer.

Before the closing the parties and their lawyers will review all documents to see that everyone is fulfilling all conditions and promises of the contract. A closing statement or settlement sheet is prepared, fully listing the financial aspects of the closing. The **Real Estate Settlement Procedures Act (RESPA)** will apply in any transaction in which a buyer is obtaining a mortgage from a federally insured financial institution. This requires the use of a settlement sheet developed by the Department of Housing and Urban Development. In other closings in which the buyer is not obtaining a mortgage, another form of settlement sheet is usually prepared.

Both buyers and sellers should expect to sign a lot of papers at the closing. Buyers should expect to sign the following:

- a promissory note promising to pay in full the loan and interest;

- the mortgage document;

- a truth-in-lending form, which requires the lender to tell you in advance the annual percentage rate of the loan over the loan's term and other information about payments;

- a payment letter telling the buyer the amount of the first payment and when it is due;

- an affidavit that the buyer's various names all refer to the same person (mainly relevant to buyers who have changed their names after marriage);

- a survey form stating that the buyer has seen and understands the survey of the property and that it fairly depicts the property;

- a private mortgage insurance application, usually required on loans with a down payment of less than 20 percent;

- a termite inspection or other inspection form, indicating that the buyer has seen a report of any inspections that were made.

The seller can expect to sign the following documents:

- the deed transferring title in the real estate from the seller to the buyer;
- a bill of sale transferring ownership of any personal property that may be included in the sale of the real estate;
- an affidavit of title in which the seller states that he or she has the legal right to sell the real estate and that there are no liens or encumbrances (judgments, mortgages, or taxes owed) on the property;
- an affidavit as to mechanic's liens and possession indicating that the seller has not had any work done on the property that would give rise to a mechanic's lien and that no parties other than the seller are entitled to possess the property;
- an occupancy certificate indicating that a new home complies with the local housing code.

Both buyer and seller will also sign the following:

- An affidavit specifying the purchase price and indicating the source of the purchase price. (This affidavit assures the lender that the buyer has not received any undisclosed loans from the seller or others that could negatively affect the buyer's ability to repay the lender's loan.)
- A RESPA form developed by the federal Department of Housing and Urban Development and sometimes a separate closing statement specifying all costs associated with the transaction.

At the time of closing the seller and buyer will total up various credits to determine how much money the buyer must pay. The seller will receive credits for such items as fuel on hand (such as oil in the home heating tank), unused insurance premiums, prepaid interest, and paid taxes and public utility charges such as water and sewer fees. These credits also will include any other items prepaid by the seller that will benefit the buyer.

The buyer normally will receive credits for such items as the earnest money deposited and taxes or special assessments that the seller has not paid. The settlement sheet will also specify who is responsible for the payment of various expenses. These will include the sales commissions and the costs of the survey, title search, inspections, recording fees, transaction taxes, and the like. The allocation of such expenses will depend on the terms of your contract as well as the law and customs in your area. Your real estate agent or attorney should advise you ahead of time of how much money you will need at the closing. Typically you will be required to have a certified or cashier's check in the amount required to meet these expenses.

Other common fees include a loan origination fee to cover the lender's administrative costs in processing the loan, a credit report fee, a lender's appraisal fee, a mortgage insurance application fee, a mortgage insurance premium, and a hazard insurance premium. Buyers also may have to put money into escrow to ensure future payment of such recurring items as real estate taxes. This amount is regulated by federal law. Also there often are separate document fees that cover the preparation of final legal papers such as the promissory note and mortgage or deed of trust. Sometimes, if the buyer has used a mortgage or loan broker to secure a loan, that person's fee will be paid at closing.

SAVING MONEY ON PMI

Private mortgage insurance (PMI) is usually a must on low down-payment loans to cover the lender's risk in the event of a foreclosure.

This insurance is paid for by you, the borrower, but you may not have to pay for it indefinitely. Some lenders are willing to allow PMI to be canceled once there is no longer a need for it—for example, after you've accumulated equity in the house equal to 20 percent of the value. Check to make sure this is the case *before* you commit to a lender. The ability to cancel this insurance can save you a lot of money.

CONDOMINIUMS AND COOPERATIVES

There are ways to be a homeowner without buying a piece of property outright. **Condominiums** and **cooperatives**, or **co-ops**, offer certain advantages over traditional home ownership.

A condominium is a common-interest community in which individual units are separately owned, but the owners share an interest in common areas, for example, hallways, roofs, and exteriors. With a cooperative, or co-op, buyers purchase shares of stock in a corporation that owns a building. A condominium owner has title to his or her unit; a co-op owner receives a proportionate amount of shares in the corporation that owns the building, based on the unit's proportion of the building. He or she signs a lease with the corporation.

For the purposes of income tax laws and other laws regarding real estate, a condominium is treated as a single-family home. But an association has the right to impose maintenance fees, demand escrow payments for large repair bills, and manage the overall operation of the entire building. Owners of co-ops also must abide by the corporation rules; additionally, if they fail to pay their fees, they may be evicted.

There are important differences between common-interest home ownership and single-family home ownership. In single-family home ownership, the control, decisions, and expenses are the responsibility of the owner, subject to zoning restrictions established by local law and any restrictions contained in the declaration of the builder who originally developed the property. As a general rule, multi-unit ownership is subject to more extensive regulation than single-family ownership. For example, there are statutes, rules, and regulations governing what you may and may not do with your condominium, co-op, or other multiunit dwelling.

If you are considering a common-interest purchase, be sure to obtain all the information on the terms of sale and such regulations. Ask to see the bylaws, operating budget, management agreement, and regulating agreement, and then give them to your lawyer to review. Many states require disclosures to the purchasers of units in a common-interest community. Some states have a central agency that licenses and regulates the development and sale of common-interest community units.

The cost of the unit is not the limit of your financial obligation with multiunit real estate. There will be monthly assessments to cover maintenance and related expenses for operating the common areas. These assessments will be in proportion to the percentage you own of the total complex. If all the apartments in a ten-unit building are the same size, each owner would have a 10 percent ownership stake. This means that each owner will pay 10 percent of its assessments.

These costs will almost certainly increase over time; decreases are considered newsworthy. You should determine the amount of the monthly assessment and the potential increase before signing an offer to purchase. In addition, unit owners are subject to special assessments above and beyond the basic assessment, to pay for unforeseen improvements or repairs. Always ask about pending projects and their approximate costs. You should also be sure that there is enough liability insurance coverage for the entire development.

CHAPTER TWELVE

■

Security Nets

Insurance

IF LIFE WEREN'T FULL OF RISKS, it wouldn't be life. That doesn't mean, however, that you can't reduce your exposure to risk. Insurance is one way to reduce that exposure. Fundamentally, a consumer insurance contract provides that, in return for regular payment by the insured of **premiums**, the insurer is prepared to **indemnify** the insured for a covered loss—that is, pay money equal to the damage sustained, minus a predetermined amount called a **deductible**. (Most commercial insurance policies operate on a similar basis but often with more complex formulas.) Deductibles make insurance more affordable because they reduce the insurer's costs. Through them, the insurer avoids both the indemnification and administration of small claims.

Deductibles also help reinforce the idea that insurance is meant to protect against significant loss, not routine loss. As discussed below, keeping this in mind will help you adequately plan your insurance needs while keeping the cost of insurance economical. It also helps you maintain the state of caution necessary to avoid losses in the first place, saving insurance for unavoidable or catastrophic loss.

INSURANCE SALES

One goal of this chapter is to give you the sense of perspective that is necessary when dealing with insurance brokers who are, to give them the benefit of the doubt, very excited about the insurance "products" their companies have to offer. Two terms are used to describe insurance salespeople: **brokers** and **agents**. Generally an insurance broker represents many different companies, although most have relationships with only a handful. An agent typically represents only one.

Insurance salespeople, even at their most aggressive, are not bad. They are working for a living, just like everyone else. And many mutually satisfactory insured-broker relationships have been built on aggressive cold calls by agents. On the other hand, you might prefer to buy from a friend, relative, or acquaintance who sells insurance. Trust is the cornerstone of any business relationship, especially one with technicalities the consumer is unequipped to master. So it's a good idea to buy from someone you know or—if you prefer not to do business with friends—someone who is recommended to you.

No matter who ends up getting your insurance business, remember that they make their money by commission: the more you pay in premiums, the more they make. Competition, of course, counteracts the incentive to oversell, so there is no reason not to talk to several brokers or agents, especially since most have a relationship with only one or two insurers. You might be quite surprised how big a difference there can be between two comparable companies' virtually identical policies. Keep in mind, though, that a company's claim-handling history and long-term financial stability can have an impact on the overall value of a policy. The least expensive policy gets very expensive if the insurer denies valid claims or goes out of business, leaving you without coverage.

Some states allow insurance companies to offer insurance directly to consumers, without brokers. In many cases you can achieve substantial savings by this route, but not always. Unless a company completely dispenses with its commissioned salespeople, it will usually be reluctant to undersell them. This is not an unreasonable policy, because insurers rely on their cadres of agents and brokers to sell their line of policies. In that case, their price level may just reflect a slight discount. Then, instead of the commission going to a neighbor who sells insurance, it goes to the insurer itself. Also, any independent judgment a broker, or even an agent, can offer you is lost when you deal directly with the company.

Having said that, you must strive not to be manipulated by an insurance salesperson into buying more insurance coverage than you need. There *is* such a thing as "overinsurance." Of course there is usually no reason to pay for redundant coverage. Also, seemingly small premium additions for unneeded coverage can add up to hundreds and thousands of dollars over the years. Breaking your budget for insurance almost never makes sense. You must sit down and figure out the point where premiums stack up high enough to undermine the value of the policy, given the risks involved.

This calculation is especially valuable when considering how high a deductible to take. For example, you can easily spend thousands over a few years for the privilege of a $100 deductible on automobile collision insurance instead of a more economical $250 or $500. You would have to make quite a few claims to get back those premiums, more than most people ever make and more than most insurers will pay before asking you to take your business elsewhere.

THE INSURANCE CONTRACT

Once you have done the basic comparison shopping and are working out the details of your coverage with an insurance salesperson, you will reach a point where you need to fill out an application for insurance. Besides basic identification information, the insurer will want to know all about the property you want to insure or the risk you want to insure against. It will want to know a lot about you as well, because with this application it will attempt to determine how much risk to take on by issuing the policy. The insurer may get a credit report on you. On an automobile policy, the company will want to know all about your driving record.

The answers you write in those little blanks determine whether the company will **bind**, or write, a policy for you at all, and if so, at what cost. They become part of the contract under the policy terms. People with an innocent little fender-bender that really wasn't their fault would not have to be very bad to be *tempted* to fudge these answers. But answering untruthfully is wrong, and it is fraudulent. A false answer on an insurance application, if material, will usually *invalidate the policy* if it is discovered. In this case, a material misrepresentation is one that caused the insurer to issue a policy it would not have issued or whose terms would have been substantially different if you had been truthful.

Misrepresentations on insurance applications *are* discovered, and frequently, because insurers faced with paying a large claim have a big economic incentive to make thorough investigations. The obligation to uncover promptly a misrepresentation is on the one who knows it best—the one who made it—not the insurer. (That means that a material change in circumstances relevant to the policy, such as a new job that results in an increase in the distance you drive to work, must be reported to the insurer even after the application process.) For want of a few hundred dollars a year in wrongfully "saved" premiums, people have lost the right to make claims in the tens and hundreds of thousands of dollars when insurers discovered the insured did not really live where they claimed to live or similarly lied on their applications. Many states require insurers in such a situation to return the premiums paid—cold comfort indeed when a large, otherwise legitimate claim goes out the window.

Insurance contracts are the very definition of contracts of adhesion, defined in chapter 3 as "take it or leave it" form contracts with no room for negotiation. Although you can change terms such as the type and amount of coverage and deductibles, the insurer will not negotiate the price with you; based on the kind of coverage you want, the insurer follows a rigid formula. Other terms of the policy, such as definitions and requirements under the policy, are nonnegotiable in consumer insurance. They have been carefully drafted by insurance company lawyers based on court decisions and regulatory requirements. Sometimes these terms are so technical that even

---

TRUTH AND CONSEQUENCES

Fraudulent misrepresentations on an insurance application may save you in premiums but, besides being wrong, they put you at risk of having your entire claim denied. Fudging the answers on the application isn't just bad, it's bad sense, and could lead to financial disaster.

most lawyers who are not insurance law specialists would be hard-pressed to read a policy and come away with an accurate understanding of coverage and claim requirements. Because many states now mandate (or companies are using) plain-English policy forms, your contract may be easier to read. It pays to read your policy carefully, try to understand its terms, and ask questions. Whether your contract is jargon-filled or plain English, in the event of a conflict with the insurer, any ambiguity in the policy terms will be held to favor you, but this is not a reason to avoid trying your best to understand them beforehand.

TYPES OF INSURANCE

It is beyond the scope of this book to give in-depth advice on selecting insurance. But there are some insurance basics that you should know. They'll make your shopping more knowledgeable and give you a starting point for intelligent questioning of your broker or agent.

GROUP VERSUS INDIVIDUAL INSURANCE

Many people are eligible to purchase life, disability, and supplemental health, accident, and disability insurance through groups. These include employees of a company and members of unions, professional associations, and automobile clubs. Group rates are usually lower than individually rated policies. Like off-the-rack clothes, they come in a certain variety of sizes and styles but no more. A minimum of advice is available, at least compared with what your own broker should be doing for you, although a phone number is usually available to connect you with the group's broker or an officer of the group in charge of choosing insurance.

In contrast, individual policies are easier to customize. You can probably get more flexibility as to the **term,** or length of the insurance contract, and other aspects of the policy. You can also choose which company you want to insure you. But like a custom-made suit, it will cost you. If, based on your other calculations, you can get a good fit off the rack, there's no reason not to take advantage of it.

PREMIUMS

Paying insurance premiums is not a lot of fun, no matter what, but make sure you have control over the situation. Many kinds of insurance are billed quarterly or twice a year, making budgeting tricky. Some insurers will permit you to make monthly payments, although they often require automatic withdrawal from a bank account. Some also charge a small service fee for extended payment.

Most states don't allow insurers to drop your coverage simply because you've missed a premium payment. They are usually required to send you a notice of cancellation, giving you an absolute deadline by which time you must make the payment. Often your agent or a representative of the company can help you with a tricky situation, such as where the check really is in the mail. All things being equal, neither wants to lose you as a customer.

It's usually wise to avoid premium financing, where an insurer will let you extend payments by means of a high-interest loan. If the insurer won't let you extend payments without interest (but with a

---

GROUP THINK

Many members of groups are offered types of group insurance that are rarely sold to individuals by agents and brokers. These include policies that may cost you very little and pay a certain amount per day if you end up in the hospital or provide cash payments to you in the event of accidents or if you contract a particular disease, such as cancer. Remember, the primary purpose of insurance is to protect against serious risk. As inexpensive as these policies are, what are your chances of spending time in a hospital or becoming ill in a specific way? Always remember that ready-made policies like these are testimony to the insurer's own estimation of your likelihood of recovering more money than you put in: very little.

modest service fee), or if the premiums are too high for you to buy insurance on your current budget, you probably should take a fresh look at your insurance situation and see if you can reduce your premiums by changing carriers, raising deductibles, or reducing coverage.

HEALTH INSURANCE

One of the biggest areas of insurance is health insurance. Most Americans are covered by health insurance at their place of employment, although what was once a fringe benefit is now a major concern. The plight of those who are not covered and the increasing cost to everyone in the system is an ongoing political fracas. Some basic points about today's health insurance system, however, are worth learning.

There are two types of traditional, **indemnity**-type health insurance, in which you go to the doctor of your choice, pay the bill, and submit it for reimbursement or indemnification:

• **Basic coverage** is what it sounds like. It pays for basic medical expenses, such as doctors, hospitals, and related expenses, including the cost of a hospital stay. Typically these plans pay 80 percent of these expenses once a deductible is met. You may have to pay the doctor or other provider first, then submit a **claim form** with a statement of

---

COBRA

Employers don't have to provide medical insurance, but if they do, many are required by federal law—the Consolidated Omnibus Budget Reconciliation Act, or COBRA—to offer employees who are terminated or quit the right to purchase eighteen months of coverage at their group-rate cost plus up to 2 percent. This right to purchase coverage also applies to divorced spouses and noncustodial children. This coverage may not be cheap, but it may be less expensive than an individual or conversion plan.

---

services in order to be reimbursed, or the doctor may be paid directly by the insurer. The deductible can be from $200 to $500, depending on the plan; there are often separate deductibles for individual members of a family if you have family coverage. The 20 percent not covered by the plan is called the **coinsurance** or **copayment** amount.

Payment under basic coverage is made only up to an amount determined by the insurance company as reasonable for a certain procedure. Thus, if your doctor charges $250 to prescribe two aspirins and a call in the morning, you may be on the hook for any amount above the reasonable fee for such a consultation. (Check this point with your insurer and avoid paying the doctor for the excess amount if the insurance contract doesn't permit him or her to collect it.) Remember that contracts with doctors are no different from contracts with anyone else. Negotiate, and don't be shy about complaining after the fact. When you're sick or in pain, you're in no condition for give-and-take.

• **Major medical** picks up where basic coverage leaves off. It covers expenses above the relatively low ceiling of basic coverage and kicks in when a major medical condition must be treated. Its coverage is broader and often includes a cap on **coinsurance** so that, after a certain point—often $2,000 to $3,000—all expenses are paid by the insurer. This insurance is frequently **direct billed** by the providers, because no one expects people to front thousands or tens of thousands while waiting for a claim to be turned around.

Few people can afford to buy indemnity-type coverage for themselves these days. Individuals and families who must provide their own health insurance and more and more employers are turning to **health maintenance organizations,** or HMOs. Patients in HMOs choose from a network of physicians, hospitals, and often pharmacies and laboratories, and pay only a small fee, perhaps $5 or $10, for each office visit. HMOs are by far the most economical form of medical insurance. But you get what you pay for. Patients have less choice of physicians and hospitals, and providers have an incentive to see as many patients as possible in a day, because they receive a flat fee per patient. And under many of these plans you are not allowed to see a specialist unless a primary care physician certifies that specialist care is appropriate.

Many employers offer a combination of HMOs and indemnity plans, sometimes called a **Preferred Provider Plan** or **PPO**. Under these plans you can either go to an out-of-network doctor, pay at the point of service (the doctor's office), and receive 70 or 75 percent

A PREMIUM ON PREMIUMS

More and more workers are being asked to pick up part of the cost of health-care premiums. If this is the case for you, see if your employer can arrange to have premiums taken out of your pretax income under an IRS-approved plan that your employer's benefits specialist or accountant should know about. The advantage of this is that your taxable income is reduced, and you save on income taxes.

If you and your spouse are employed and both employers offer health insurance, it might pay to drop the extra coverage—or it might not. Double coverage has some advantages: you may be able to submit the amounts you pay as coinsurance and in meeting deductibles on the first plan to the second plan. In the case of coinsurance, for example, if the first plan pays 80 percent, you can get back 80 percent of the remaining 20 percent—another 16 percent—from the second plan. Thus, your total coverage would be 96 percent instead of 80 percent. Whether or not this pays depends on your respective plans' deductibles, coinsurance caps, and, of course, the amount of your contribution toward premiums. If premiums are not an issue, there is no reason to leave the plan, except to save your employer money—perhaps a wise thing to do. When employers cover the worker but charge extra for spouses or dependents, it might pay to just drop the part you pay for.

Remember, though, that once you've dropped coverage for someone on an employer-sponsored plan, it may be difficult to get that person back on the plan if circumstances change. Insurers are generally allowed to check for **insurability** and reject or limit coverage for applicants who have a pre-existing or ongoing condition.

indemnification, or go within the network and get the full economic advantages of the HMO.

If you are looking for an HMO, you'll want to scan the respective plans' physician and hospital lists, see if patients must go to a central location or to doctors' offices in their areas, and keep an especially close eye on maternity benefits. When joining any health-care plan as an individual, be sure to learn as much about the plan as you can from the materials the company provides. Even more important, don't even consider a plan until you've spoken to someone who's in it and found out what they think of the available doctors, claim handling, and other details. And, of course, avoid plans if you learn that they forbid doctors from recommending anything less than 100 percent of the specialist care or other attention patients need.

LIFE INSURANCE

Life insurance policies come in many different forms. Companies are constantly trying to find an insurance product that sells best in a given niche of the market. Many policies are hybrids of the traditional basic types or add new features meant to make them more attractive. There are alternatives to life insurance policies, such as annuities, which a sophisticated investor can use in place of insurance. And a whole new wave in estate planning has developed around the use of life insurance, purchased late in life at high premiums, to provide assets to beneficiaries. The reason for this is that the proceeds of life insurance are tax-free to the recipient under federal law and are only charged against the decedent's (deceased person's) estate if the estate is higher than the current floor of $600,000.

The purpose of life insurance is not to provide a windfall to someone in the event of your death but to provide security for people who otherwise had been counting on your income for support. These people are designated by you as the **beneficiaries** of your life insurance policy. Some employers provide some life insurance to their employees, sometimes as part of a collective bargaining requirement. Different financial planners give different rules of thumb about how much insurance you need, but most speak in terms of three to five years' worth of income. Thus, if you make $45,000 a year, you should consider $150,000 to $250,000 worth of insurance. This **death benefit**, or amount of insurance payable on your death, would provide a cushion of several years for your family to readjust to the loss of your income. They could either pay off major debts (such as a mortgage) and put the remainder in an interest-bearing instrument for continuing expenses or just put the whole amount in a safe investment and continue as they had when your income was coming in.

The cost of life insurance is fundamentally based on the statistical likelihood of death within a certain period for people fitting certain criteria. The major criteria are gender (because life expectancies are different for men and women), age, weight for a given height, and whether or not you smoke. Obviously, the younger you are and the better shape you're in, the more likely you are to live longer, and the lower your premiums will be. For smokers the best way to save a bundle on premiums is to become ex-smokers and reapply after a year.

There are two basic kinds of life insurance policies: **term** life and **whole** life. The difference between them is like renting insurance and buying it. Term insurance is a contract, by its own terms automatically renewable for a set number of years. With term life you pay premiums for the term of the policy. When the term is over, that's the end of your relationship with your insurer. You may apply for a new policy—one rated for your new age and new health situation—but it will undoubtedly be costlier. And depending on your new circumstances, you may no longer be "insurable"; i.e., because of your health or age, the risk of your death could be too high for an insurer to bear.

Whole life, on the other hand, is a kind of investment. For most people, especially younger people, whole life premiums are more expensive than term life premiums. But as long as you keep current with your payments—which remain steady with whole life—you build up something called **cash value**. This cash value, after a certain number of years, is the amount that you could, if you wish, ask the insurance company to surrender to you if you want to terminate the policy. Eventually the cash value approaches the total amount of insurance you have bought, and indeed in some policies, such as **universal life** (a high-powered version of whole life), if you live to a certain age you actually "win" by getting an amount close to the death benefit, and the policy is automatically cancelled. (You can win with a whole life policy too, but ordinarily you have to live to be 100 to collect.)

The problem with whole life, besides its expense, is that the cash value is often substantially less than you would have if you had taken the amount of money you pay in premiums and invested in a certificate of deposit. The cash value in a universal policy depends on how well the insurance company manages its own investment portfolio or some other factor over which you have no control. In some cases, putting the money in the CD *and* paying term-life premiums could put you ahead of a whole life policy, especially with the group rates available for term policies.

On the other hand, many people do not have the discipline to do these things. Few people are tempted to cash in their insurance policies on a whim, but money in a CD or savings account is less sacrosanct. An insurance policy of this kind also takes care of both things for you. And more sophisticated policies, such as universal life, allow you to borrow against your cash value at a favorable rate, making the investment possibly more valuable than its straightforward return would indicate. Also, because term policies tend to get much more expensive as the years go by, the savings of youth may be less appreciated when paying high premiums at retirement age. And once that term contract is up, you have no financial benefit to show for maybe decades of premiums.

The main variations on term and whole life include:

- **universal life**, mentioned above, which also features flexibility in premium payment plans;
- **excess interest life**, which is like universal life and also allows use of income on the cash value to be applied to premiums;
- **variable life**, which permits the policyholder to participate in the investment of the cash value but does not guarantee the size of the death benefit; and
- **adjustable life**, more akin to term life but allows flexibility in shortening the term, the size of the death benefit, and premium payment plans after the policy is issued.

DISABILITY INSURANCE

Disability insurance is insurance that picks up where sick pay leaves off. It pays you a percentage of your salary for a certain period when you are unable to work as a result of a disability—a serious illness or injury.

Many experts maintain that disability insurance is more important than life insurance. Like life insurance, disability insurance policies offer many different types of benefits. It would be difficult to address all the important issues concerning disability insurance here, but there are certain points of which you should be aware.

In New York, New Jersey, Puerto Rico, and Rhode Island, workers are covered by disability insurance through their employers, who are required by law to provide temporary coverage. Employers in many other states voluntarily provide disability; to some extent, it takes pressure off them to continue extended sick pay. The period of disability covered by your employer's policy, however, may be as short as a month or two. Social Security also provides long-term disability coverage.

But some employers, and many other groups, offer participation in supplemental disability plans, which can also be purchased on an individual basis. The three main types of supplemental disability insurance are:

- **noncancellable**, which continues to protect you as long as you continue to pay premiums; benefits may increase with income;

- **guaranteed renewable**, which only guarantees the availability of coverage but not the premium amount; and

- **optionally renewable**, which is analogous to term insurance in the sense that each year you and the insurer consider a new contract with new terms.

As important as disability insurance is, keep in mind that almost all plans are based on the premise of your having a certain amount of savings socked away for a rainy day.

HOMEOWNERS AND RENTERS INSURANCE

One of the most important types of insurance you need is home-owners or renters insurance. There are two types of such insurance. **Liability** insurance indemnifies you for claims made by others against you for damage they sustain while on your property (or in your apartment) due to your negligence. This insurance can be extended to cover you for all personal liability, regardless of where it takes place, for your unintentional acts. The other type of insurance is **property** insurance, which covers your own loss of the contents of your home, and in the case of a homeowner, loss of the home itself, due to fire, theft, or other accident.

There are many kinds of homeowners policies, and the right kind for you depends on the kind of property you need to insure and, of course, your budget. Most mortgage lenders insist that you take out at least a basic **comprehensive** policy including liability and insurance for the structure on which the mortgage is held.

When choosing a policy, you will want to consider the following issues:

- Is loss to property indemnified at replacement value or actual market value with depreciation?

- Does the coverage on the main dwelling reflect a realistic valuation of the value of the house?

- Do you want extended coverage over things like burst pipes and structural failure?

Most policies give discounts for homes with fire alarms (which are mandatory in many places anyway) and other safety features, including proximity to a fire station and fire hydrants.

You should be aware that most homeowners policies exclude coverage for losses resulting from commercial use of the home or for professional or business activities and for personal liability arising out of extrahazardous activities such as flying or boating. Intentional activities are never covered. And keep in mind that most policies exclude coverage for damage caused by electrical wiring or plumbing installed by a unlicensed person.

RECORD KEEPING

To make a claim for property loss under your homeowners insurance, good record keeping is essential. You should have an inventory of basically all the personal property in your home, ideally with the amount you paid for it and the date and place of purchase. Photographs and videotapes are an excellent way to do this, especially for furnishings, interior decoration, and structural changes that would not be reflected in blueprints or surveys.

In addition to providing you with evidence of the value of your property, this exercise also gives you an idea of how much property insurance you need. And remember, just as the value of your home may change and should be reflected in your policy, so should the amount of coverage for personal effects as the years pass and you acquire more stuff. If some of that property is an art, coin, or antique collection, or some other kind of valuable, nonstandard property, you'll need to get a special rider.

AUTOMOBILE INSURANCE

The most compelling reason to buy automobile liability insurance is that in many states it's illegal to drive without it. The reason for this is that while you might not care whether you're covered in the event of an accident, the person in the other car does.

IN-HOME WORKERS

If you have a nanny or employ other workers in your home, such as a housekeeper, be sure to ask your broker to include riders for worker's compensation. You need it even for workers who don't live in. The rider covers your liability for injuries that employees sustain. Without it, you won't be covered. This coverage usually only costs a nominal sum above your regular premium. You are, of course, also legally responsible for these employees' unemployment and, in some states, disability insurance, plus Social Security, and all other withholding.

Car insurance is in many ways analogous to homeowners insurance. You can get both liability and property coverage—the latter known as **collision** coverage—with comprehensive policies providing both (as well as optional theft and vandalism coverage). Like homeowners insurance, if there is a lienholder on your car, you will be required to take out a property policy for protection of the lienholder's security interests. In both cases you must take a good look at the policy to see what is covered and what is excluded. And both types base your premium on an analysis of your riskiness as an insured and the value of the property involved.

On the other hand, there are important differences between car insurance and a homeowners policy. For one thing, there is also a distinct **medical** coverage, which you must have to cover injuries you and your passengers incur in an accident, up to a set limit per person. The liability coverage includes coverage for property damage (mainly the other car) and personal injury, also up to a certain amount with a total cap as well.

While many states require you to carry liability insurance, the amount you are required to cover is often quite small. If you have any assets at all, you will want to protect them from a judgment by getting the appropriate amount of insurance. Remember, there is such a thing as too much insurance: most of us don't need $5 million in liability insurance, as we're unlikely to ever incur liability on that scale.

NO-FAULT INSURANCE

Many states require drivers to participate in a no-fault insurance system. Under this system, some damage and some costs are automatically covered by the driver's own insurance, regardless of who is at fault. But keep in mind that this only concerns the relationship between you and the other driver. The insurance companies care very much who is at fault, and if an investigation reveals that it was you, expect a healthy increase in your premium— you're now a riskier driver to insure.

Another difference from homeowners insurance is that premiums for auto insurance are based on more complicated formulas. Insurers check your driving record going back several years and want to know how often you drive, how far, from where, and to where. They are especially interested in your "demographics": unmarried males under the age of thirty are notoriously bad risks, and their premiums tend to be sky-high.

When shopping for an auto policy, consider the following:

• Is there coverage for towing? (If you are a member of an auto club, this may be redundant.)

• Does the policy pay for replacement transportation if a damaged car is in the shop for an extended period? How much does it pay?

• Have you gotten discounts you are entitled to? Discounts are usually available for good students, cars with alarms, coverage of multiple vehicles on one policy, and many other things. Check with your agent.

MAKING CLAIMS

Crunch time for insurance is when you have claims to submit. A family with children and a medical indemnity plan may find the submission of claims to be an almost weekly occurrence. And indeed, medical claims are the easiest to make. You simply use the claim form provided by your insurance company or a reasonable copy (many medical establishments have a standard form on their computer), and give them all the information requested. If you find yourself making many claims, you can photocopy the form with the standard information (which remains the same each time) already written in.

On the other hand, years can go by between claims on your automobile and homeowners policies. Unlike medical policies, these claims are usually initiated by a call to your broker or insurance company (the latter usually provides a twenty-four-hour phone number to call in urgent claims). This call should be made as promptly as possible, or your rights to recover may be prejudiced. This enables the insurer to, in its judgment, promptly dispatch a **claims adjuster**, an investigator who reports to the insurer on the validity and extent of the claim.

In the case of home damage, you may proceed with emergency repairs, but it's a good idea to get in touch with your insurer as soon as possible before doing anything other than protecting safety and undamaged property.

The insurer will open a claim file, ask you various questions, and ask you to send documentation. In the case of an automobile claim involving an accident, the insurer will need the following:

- the time, date, and place of the accident;
- a general narrative description of what happened;
- the police or accident report;
- the name, driver's license number, and automobile registration number of other drivers involved;
- the insurance information for the other drivers involved;
- preliminary injury and damage information.

The insurance company and claim adjuster (often an outside contractor) will continue to ask for information as it develops. Do not fail to provide requested information. Your cooperation is required under the insurance policy; failure to assist in developing the claim can result in losing it.

If a liability claim is made against you because of an auto accident or an occurrence in your home, the insurer is obligated to follow up its claim investigation by providing legal counsel for your legal defense. This does not mean, however, that you cannot speak to your own lawyer for general advice or to work with the insurer's lawyer. This is obviously an expensive course to take, but in the case of a larger claim, it could be a healthy approach. You certainly don't need a lawyer to duplicate the work of the insurer's lawyer, but you might want to have someone reviewing the work.

CLAIMS PROBLEMS

Most insurers are professional and ethical, interested in handling your claim with a minimum of friction and providing you with the coverage for which you have paid. But you should be aware that once a claim is made, you and the insurer have different interests. You want to receive the largest indemnity check possible. The insurer wants to write the smallest check possible. Of course, the insurer will investigate the situation to see that you have held up your contractual obligations. The insurer is entitled to do that. Save yourself and your insurer a lot of trouble and keep good records of your communications with the insurer. Put as much in writing as you can.

Problems arise when some carriers decide that the economic cost of a claim is so high that they will take almost any route to avoid paying it. An insurer wrongfully denying a legitimate claim may be guilty of a tort, recognized in many states, of **bad-faith failure to indemnify**. In these states you can recover extra damages if you prove bad faith on the insurer's part. The purpose of this rule is to change the calculus that makes it worthwhile for the insurer to stonewall you and dare you to sue. Other states allow consumers to use the consumer fraud statutes for unfair claims practices. Certainly, if you are involved in a dispute involving unfair claims practices, communicate with your state's insurance commissioner and other consumer agencies.

Another area to watch is the behavior of the insurer's lawyer. Remember that liability insurance is litigation insurance—you are entitled to a full defense of claims against you. The insurer is not allowed to deny you a defense because it says that the claim against you would probably not be covered under its policy—for example, if your intentional conduct is part of the claim. In most states, as long as the claim against you *could* be covered under a reasonable reading of the policy, you are entitled to a defense. Thus, if the complaint against you includes both intentional *and* negligent conduct, the insurer must defend you as long as the negligence claim remains in the case. But take note: If the claim is successful, *and* the insurer was right in saying that you were not covered (i.e., in the case of intentional behavior), you must reimburse the insurer for legal expenses it incurred.

Because the insurer is paying for the lawyer, it has the prerogative of directing the actions of the lawyer. But the insurer's lawyer has a legal obligation of loyalty both to you and the insurer. Any time you have reason to believe that the lawyer is not looking out for you or that the lawyer is favoring the insurer's interests over yours, you should have independent counsel look into it.

For example, if a claim is made against you but you have a legitimate defense, the lawyer should not be eager to settle for some amount above its policy limit that leaves you holding the bag for the remainder. A legitimate settlement is one thing, but if you suspect the insurance company wants to cut its losses and avoid legal fees, sound the alarm. In the event that such behavior can be demonstrated to the court, the judge may order the insurer to pay for your separate counsel—someone of your own choice—as well. In such a case the company has forfeited its right to choose your lawyer by not acting in accordance with its fiduciary duty to you.

FRAUDULENT CLAIMS

Just as lying on your insurance application is a prescription for trouble, so is the filing of false, inflated, or otherwise fraudulent claims. The fact that insurers are big companies does not make it right or legal to steal from them. Such activity raises everyone's premiums. It also stands to land you in jail. More and more attorneys general, insurance commissioners, and insurance companies are coming down hard on insurance fraud. The upshot can be more than a denial of your claim. It can be a conviction for the felony of criminal fraud or similar charges, leading to stiff fines or perhaps jail time—for you and everyone involved in the fraud, including your spouse or other family members if they "helped out." It's not worth it.

CHAPTER THIRTEEN

The Consumer Minefield

Contracts in Context

A BOOK ADDRESSING ALL THE WAYS bad people are scheming to take your money away without delivering what you think you're getting would be considerably heftier than this one. But there are some fairly common situations to which you can apply the principles discussed elsewhere in the book.

ADVERTISEMENTS THAT HIT HOME

Chapter 5 discussed advertising in the sense most of us think of—stores or businesses taking out space in the paper or time on the radio or TV to lure you to what they have to offer. There are other kinds of advertisements besides store advertisements, however. Classified ads, mail and telephone solicitations, and other ways of reaching consumers are subject to the same rules as store advertisements. But in these contexts, the rules are somewhat harder to enforce. *Your* rule is this: Any contest or get-rich-quick scheme that requires you to part with money is probably a losing proposition. If it were so easy and quick, the pitchman wouldn't have to advertise it. Ask yourself if you've ever met anyone who achieved wealth by answering a classified ad for a product or service (as opposed to placing one!).

PYRAMID SCHEMES

It's worth familiarizing yourself with the concept of **pyramid schemes**. Ads for them may be found in the back of magazines, in classified ads, or on the community bulletin board at your supermarket or pizza restaurant. Or someone—maybe someone you know casually or even well—may contact you by mail or over the phone, promising you some huge return on your money and telling you of real people who made a bundle in the scheme.

That part is true, actually. Some did get a lot of money. But they did it illegally—by inducing people like you to pony up. The only way you could do the same is to con a large number of people to make the same mistake you did. The classic example is the ad that says, "Make money at home—send $5 and a self-addressed stamped envelope to learn the secret of wealth!" The envelope really does come back. The secret: Take out an ad offering to sell the secret of wealth for $5.

The courts have held many of these scams—and any promotion

PHARAOH OF FINANCE

Charles Ponzi offered jazz-age Bostonians a deal they couldn't resist: a 50 percent return in forty-five days, and 100 percent in ninety days. In 1920 the 38-year-old Ponzi claimed that he had a supply of fourteen-cent Spanish postal reply coupons that U.S. post offices were obliged to accept in return for sixty-four stamps. He generously offered investors the opportunity to participate in this windfall in return for a commission as well as consideration for his efforts (and those of a supposed team of agents) in procuring the stamps.

Ponzi raked in over $15 million in less than a year. His story was convincing because of the generous "returns" paid to his earliest investors—which were merely the receipts from the latest victims. As long as people down the line kept believing, he was able to deliver. Eventually, however, Ponzi's shady past and phony present became clear. Less than half of the money Ponzi collected was ever recovered, and his enterprise resulted in the failure of six banks. Ponzi gave his name to the Ponzi scheme, a classic mass **con game**, or "confidence game," a fraudulent scheme based on initially gaining the confidence and trust of the victim. Ponzi spent three and a half years in jail but avoided further imprisonment by—characteristically—jumping bail.

---

that promises an unrealistic return—to be false advertising. If they involve mail, they are postal violations. Some cases might involve violations of securities laws. Some of these scams are called "Ponzi schemes" (see "Pharaoh of Finance"), when the only returns are the funds of people newly recruited into the system. (By the way, multi-level distribution schemes, in which the consumer is paid for selling products and recruiting other distributors, pose risks similar to those of true Ponzi schemes.)

If you are contacted by mail regarding what seems like a fraudulent scheme, contact your local postmaster or the office of the U.S. Postal Service Inspector General. Otherwise, report such a pitch to your state or city's consumer protection office or state attorney general. Virtually all states now provide a way for shutting down these scams and recovering victims' money. The process may be long, however, and the longer it is, the less the chance that you'll see much, or any, of your money back.

DOOR-TO-DOOR SALES

Most people feel secure in their homes. Ironically, that feeling makes them especially vulnerable to door-to-door salespeople. That's particularly true of homebound people such as some elderly or persons with disabilities. You have few facts by which to judge a

---

SPECULATION

Speculation is not in itself fraudulent. Many fine fortunes have been made, and lost, by speculation, without anyone having a (legitimate) complaint. Speculation, however, is a game to be played only by someone who can afford to lose it. It's little more predictable than casino gambling or playing the horses. The best place for speculation is as part of a diversified investment portfolio. But there's no place for phony speculation schemes. One dependable red flag is that no legitimate speculative investment will ever promise or even strongly suggest a specific return to you.

---

door-to-door salesperson. There is no manager, no showroom, and no immediate way to assess the company that the salesperson represents (if there is one). Even if you have been contacted in advance by telephone and offered the opportunity for a "free in-home estimate" or "examination" or whatever, all you know is that the salesperson has a phone and, perhaps, a confederate. But once that sample case is sitting on your coffee table, who wants to be a rude host?

Unfortunately some door-to-door salespeople take advantage of this vulnerability. Thus, over the years the federal government and many states have passed laws regulating door-to-door sales.

If you do go through with a purchase, federal and state laws usually require such salespeople to provide you with the following details on your receipt:

- the seller's name and place of business;
- a description of the goods and services sold;
- the amount of money you paid or the value of any goods delivered to you;
- your cooling-off period rights (see below).

Also, if the salesperson makes the sale in Spanish or another language besides English, you may have the right to all the above details in that language.

THE COOLING-OFF PERIOD

What if your friendly visitor succeeded in closing the sale, but as soon as he or she went out the door, you got a sinking feeling—or perhaps a certain look from your spouse—that suggests maybe you don't need new drapes, vinyl windows, flower seeds, or encyclopedias just now after all? Federal law now requires a three-day cooling-off period for door-to-door sales. During that time you can cancel purchases you make from someone who both solicits and closes the sale at your home or even elsewhere, such as a hotel, that is not an established place of business.

You don't have to give any reason for changing your mind during the cooling-off period, and the three days don't start until you receive formal notice of your right to cancel. You can cancel almost any sale not made at a fixed place of business, including someone else's home. Federal law extends this cooling-off period to both credit and non-credit sales above a minimal amount. It also forbids the company to charge you a cancellation fee. The federal law will apply to most such cases, and many states have similar laws that fill in the gaps.

If you decide to cancel during the cooling-off period, state law will usually require the salesperson to refund your money, return any trade-in you made, and cancel and return the contract. The salesperson has ten business days to do this under federal law. You must make the goods available to be picked up during that period. Under federal law, if the salesperson waits longer than twenty calendar days, you may be allowed to keep the goods free.

DOOR-TO-DOOR HOME REPAIR SALES

This one is simple: If workers show up on your doorstep with "left-over" asphalt, shingles, or other material from a nearby job and offer you a sweet deal to fix your driveway, roof, or whatever, tell them to go somewhere else.

Make your home repairs when you're ready and only with contractors you know or who are recommended by an experienced friend. (See the section on home improvements below.) In any event, the last place on earth to make an important decision about home repair work is your front step, looking at four guys with shovels whom you've never seen before.

TIMESHARES

Timeshares are a period of time, maybe a week or so per year, that you can buy for a specific property (usually a residence at a resort), during which the right to use the property belongs to you. The idea is that you benefit by prepaying for a vacation place rather than renting it, as you otherwise might do. The profit that would have gone to the owner supposedly stays in your pocket.

One problem with timeshares is that the savings are often offset by expenses. If, like most people, you finance your timeshare purchase over time, the interest costs alone may eat away that supposed profit. Even if you pay cash, you lose the interest you could otherwise have earned on that money.

And unlike renters, who have the option of coming or not from season to season as a resort becomes more or less desirable, timeshare owners are generally locked in. In some cases they may be able to exchange their property, but that involves a formal exchange program and costs money. They usually cannot sell the property except at a substantial loss.

Furthermore, your timeshare contract will make you responsible to pay any increases in taxes, maintenance, or repairs. If you think any of these amounts are going to decrease, you're in for a big surprise.

EVEN STEVEN?

Timeshare sellers will often point out that, notwithstanding these problems, once you pay off the timeshare you will have "free" vacationing, so at some point you will break even with the cost of renting and eventually be in the black. But that break-even point, which takes in account all of your costs, including interest, may not come for ten to twenty years. Ask yourself whether you are prepared to vacation in the same place at the same time every year for the next decade so you can eventually save on your vacation expenses.

If you don't like the timeshare deal, you can always sell it. Well, maybe not "always." Maybe not ever. Practically speaking, many people who bought timeshares in the 1980s—when any investment involving real estate looked like a winner—have found themselves with white elephants on their hands. You may have to unload the timeshare for much less than you paid, if you can find a buyer at all. You may be stuck agreeing with the sponsors that they will take back the timeshare during the payment period and you will be off the hook for the rest of the term. You would get nothing back for what you've already paid in (which might be several times what you would have paid in rent) but you would have no further obligations.

PETS

Before you buy a pet, you have a right to know about the pet's health, family history or pedigree, training, and medical care, both normal and unusual. Many states even have specific "right to know" laws for pet purchasers. If your state doesn't, then general warranty laws apply.

If you buy a pet, and it turns out to be sick or injured, your recourse may depend on whether you bought the pet from a pet shop or a private owner. It also may depend on whether you had a written contract and what express and implied warranties exist under your state's laws. It also matters whether you bought this pet for a specific purpose, such as breeding it for competition. In general, it's best for you and the seller to sign a written agreement about your pet, which will clarify most of a new owner's questions.

One way of avoiding problems is to ask the seller for the name of the pet's veterinarian. Ask the vet for an opinion on the pet's health, which may alert you to potential problems before you complete the purchase.

If you have a problem with a pet purchase, many of the old standbys apply: Immediately notify the seller in writing, and keep a copy for yourself. Keep all contracts, papers, and even the original advertisement, if there was one. If you have not received a replacement or refund within thirty days, consider filing a small-claims lawsuit. Don't worry about becoming an expert on pet law. The judge will probably base a decision on the fairness of the case, not on technicalities.

HOME REPAIRS AND IMPROVEMENTS

There are a number of special legal protections for consumers who contract for home repairs or improvements. The Federal Trade Commission and federal truth-in-lending laws police this area. To a certain extent states regulate home repairs, too. Generally, as in any other contract, home-repair contractors may not mislead you in any way to get the job. Be aware of these techniques:

- promising a lower price for allowing your home to be used as a model or to advertise their work;

- promising better quality materials than they use (beware of bait-and-switch here as well);
- providing "free gifts" — find out when you will receive them or try to get a price reduction instead;
- not including delivery and installation costs in the price;
- starting work before you sign a contract, to intimidate you;
- claiming that your house is dangerous and needs repair;
- claiming that the contractor works for a government agency;
- offering you a rebate or referral fee if any of your friends agree to use the same contractor.

Protect yourself by getting several written estimates. Check into a contractor's track record with other customers before you sign a contract. That doesn't mean a friend with a cousin who does carpentry, by the way. All the goodwill in the world won't make that door close flush if it's not done right. Rather, your recommendations must come from people who have had work done in their own homes by the contractor. And don't let a book of photos sway you about the quality of a home contractor's work, because you're only going to see the contractor's "greatest hits."

Don't pay the full price in advance and certainly not in cash. Don't sign a completion certificate or receipt until the contractor finishes the work to your satisfaction, including cleanup. Hold back a portion of the price to cover the cost of a "punch list" of incomplete items.

Be sure the contract has all the details in writing. Too often a contract of this type will read "work as per agreement." Instead it should specify who will do the work and include a *detailed* description of the work, the materials to be used, and the start and completion dates. It also should contain all charges, including any finance charges if you are paying over a period of time. In addition, the contract should include the hourly rate on which the total cost is to be based. Be sure any guarantee is in writing (and that the company is well established and most likely will be in business long enough to honor the guarantee).

Be especially wary of any mortgage or security interest the contractor takes in your home, which means that you may lose your home if you don't meet the payments for the work. If the contractor takes a mortgage or security interest, federal law gives you three days to change your mind and cancel.

You should be aware that the contractor may be able to file a lien on your home even if the contract is silent on the point. That's because filing a lien is permitted under state law in the event of a dispute over payment. A **construction lien** or **mechanic's lien** is a claim, filed with a court or county clerk, on (or "against") property for satisfaction of a debt. It's subordinate to a mortgage, so it's not as serious a threat to your property, but it is a cloud on the title that might make it hard for you to sell the property. You can ask the contractor to waive the right to place a lien in the contract (the contractor might not agree) or withhold final payment until the contractor gives you a **release-of-lien** form that covers the work of subcontractors as well.

Consider having a lawyer look at the contract, especially if there's a security agreement. If problems do arise that threaten your rights to own your home, see a lawyer immediately. (For more on this topic, see chapter 11.)

APPLIANCE REPAIRS

Much of what chapter 9 discusses about car repairs also applies to home appliance repairs. You can best protect your rights by getting a written estimate before work begins. At least make sure you get an oral estimate telling how the repair shop will figure the total charge, including parts and labor. Also tell the repair shop to get your approval before beginning work. It will then be able to give you a better idea of how much the repair will cost.

When deciding whether to repair or replace an appliance, consider these points:

- the age of the appliance and its likely life span after this repair, compared with that of a new appliance;

- the operating costs and efficiency of the repaired appliance compared with a new appliance;

- the length of the warranty on the repair, compared with the warranty on a new appliance;

- the price of a new appliance compared with the cost of the repairs.

BUYING CLUBS

There are several different types of buying clubs. One of the more popular kinds is a compact disc (CD) or music club. It offers five or ten CDs or tapes to you for an initial nominal price. You might pay only a nickel or a dollar, plus postage and handling. In return you agree to buy a certain number of CDs or tapes at the regular club price over a period of time. The regular club price is much higher than the initial price and is often higher than normal retail store prices, especially with postage and handling. In fact, the average price including the introductory deal usually works out to your benefit. (Remember that there are costs involved in getting to a store, too.)

The potential problem with these clubs is that they automatically send you a CD or tape every month or so. Before shipping the item the club sends you a notice of the upcoming shipment. The only way to prevent the automatic shipment is to return the notice before the date it specifies. Book clubs operate on a similar basis. Other clubs, such as those that sell children's books or science books, don't send you any notice—they assume you want the whole library.

These clubs are not necessarily a bad deal. You may want to meet your additional obligation quickly and then resign your membership. Also, the clubs do offer many incentives to try to keep you as a member, which may be worthwhile to you. But if you forget to return the monthly notice, you will receive unwanted CDs or tapes, and you will be obligated to pay for them or return them, sometimes at your own expense. Most reputable organizations, however, such as the Book-of-the-Month Club, will send you a postage-paid mailing label to return unwanted materials easily and at no cost.

MERCHANDISE CLUBS

The idea behind merchandise clubs is that you pay a fee to qualify for discounts. The club presumably obtains these discounts because of its volume buying power. Before joining one, take a good look at what it promises. Will it limit you to certain manufacturers? Are catalogs easily accessible? Lists of shady clubs are often put out by the offices of state attorneys general and consumer protection agencies. Check with them first.

The better-known warehouse clubs can offer substantial savings even over a superstore discounter. Most accept only cash or a limited number of credit cards. It's strictly no-frills; most don't even bag your purchase. That's one way the discount is financed. But you have to know *exactly* what you want and hope the warehouse store has it. These stores will not special-order merchandise and may have only a few models of an appliance. You will get no sales help besides someone to take your money. If you're a novice purchaser for a complicated product such as a computer, it may be worth the few extra dollars when buying something so sophisticated, with so many optional features, to shop at a place where you can get some questions answered.

FUNERAL HOMES

No one wants to be a consumer of funeral home services, but unfortunately most of us do end up with this responsibility at some point. The Federal Trade Commission has established something called the **Funeral Practices Rule**, which has the effect of federal law, to ensure that consumers are not taken advantage of at this time. The Funeral Practices Rule requires mortuaries or funeral homes to give you prices and other information you request over the telephone. The intention is to prevent corrupt funeral home operators from requiring you to come to their showrooms, where they can prey on your weak emotional state.

Under the Funeral Practices Rule, when you visit a funeral home you must be given a written list with all the prices and services

THE TOP TEN CONSUMER PROBLEMS

The State of New Jersey's Office of Consumer Protection has published a list of the ten most troublesome consumer problems in that state. Unfortunately, these exist in every state. The New Jersey list also includes basic advice for handling each problem.

- Fly-by-night home-repair contractors (as discussed previously in this chapter).

- Telephone solicitations. Always ask the caller to send written information. Also, determine your total obligation before agreeing to anything. Don't give credit card information to strangers over the telephone.

- Furniture delivery delays. Do not accept "ASAP" (as soon as possible) as a delivery date in a sales contract. Get an exact date. If the merchandise doesn't show up by that date, you then have the right to cancel.

- Free vacation offers. An example is a postcard telling you about a "free vacation" you have won: just call a toll-free number and "confirm" your credit card number. Later, you learn the vacation is not as free as you thought. Play it safe—book your travel arrangements through a reliable agent or directly with travel carriers.

- Bait-and-switch tactics (see the section above on advertising).

- Mail-order rip-offs. When shopping by mail, you're always taking a risk. When the offer sounds too good to be true, it probably is.

- Work-at-home schemes. Usually aimed at young mothers and the disabled, these schemes promise to help you "earn money in your spare time." They'll ask you for $20 in "start-up" costs. What you'll get is information about how to rip someone else off the way they just cheated you.

- Detours around contract cooling-off periods (see the section above on door-to-door sales). Federal law only protects you if you sign the contract in your home or somewhere other than the normal place of business. Even at home, don't depend on a cooling-off period—think before you sign.

- Health spa memberships. Most complaints center on high-pressure sales tactics. A year's membership can cost quite a bundle. Make sure that you'll use it and that all understandings and assurances are in writing.

- Timeshare lures. People often buy timesharing vacations on impulse. Be sure you're ready to go to the same place during the same period of time for years to come. If the timesharing resort (or condominium or whatever) is not fully built, make sure all occupancy dates are in the contract and review these contracts with a lawyer. (High-pressure timeshare sales pitches have led to a federal law giving consumers some protections. If the property is located in another state, the federal **Interstate Land Sales Full Disclosure Act** gives you the right, in some circumstances, to get out of a timeshare contract.)

A listing of the top scams compiled by the Better Business Bureau of Mainland British Columbia (Canada) adds the following:

- Phony invoices that look authentic but are really solicitations;

- Advertisements offering "big money" overseas jobs, which are really selling nearly worthless listings;

- Look-alike postal notices asking for payment to release unsolicited merchandise held at a warehouse in the recipient's name;

- Offshore lotteries implying that you've won even before you buy your tickets;

- Loan brokers who charge hefty up-front fees but seldom deliver;

- Solicitations for "charities" that are really businesses;

- Solicitations for investments in third world countries.

offered, including the least expensive. You can keep this list. You have the right to choose any service offered as long as it does not violate state law. The funeral home must give you a copy of that state law. The funeral home must reveal any fees charged for outside items, such as flowers, and may not charge a handling fee for purchases of caskets from third parties. The home may not falsely state that embalming is required by state law, and it must give general information about embalming options. The Funeral Practices Rule also entitles you to an itemized list of all charges you incur. The general idea of the Funeral Practices Rule is that the funeral home must inform you of your options every step of the way.

You should also be aware that some funeral homes offer "free" estate planning or "trusts." It should be obvious that estate planning that's worth anything can't be free and that a funeral home is just about the last place you'd turn to for a good plan in any event. These are often imperfect or limited trusts that can complicate rather than simplify an estate and are usually just an attempt to sell preneed burial contracts that are often overpriced. In some states such promotions may constitute unauthorized practice of law.

TRAVEL

OVERBOOKING

Overbooking by hotels is a violation of your contract to rent a room—*if* you have paid in advance. Otherwise, the reservation is just a courtesy. Therefore, it's often worth it to pay for a hotel reservation by credit card when you make it. If you cancel within a couple of days before the reservation date, you probably will get a complete credit, depending on the credit card company's arrangement with the hotel. Also, many premium credit card companies guarantee their cardholders' hotel rooms through the evening if the rooms are reserved with the card. (Contact the credit card company if the hotel doesn't honor your reservation.)

If your room is unavailable even after you speak to the manager, you could have a contract claim. But it probably won't be worthwhile to pursue it legally because of the cost. Perhaps the best advice is to request firmly that the hotel arrange suitable alternate accommodations for you.

Airline overbooking is a little more complicated. Generally, even if you have paid in advance, you do not have a contract to go at a certain time. You only have a contract for a ticket for transport (or carriage) to a certain city. You do, however, have certain rights if you check in on time and have a confirmed reservation. Federal regulations require that if you get bumped against your wishes, the airline must give you a written statement describing your rights and explaining how the airline decides who gets on an oversold flight and who doesn't.

Travelers who don't get on the flight for which they have a confirmed reservation are often entitled to an on-the-spot payment as compensation. The amount depends on the price of the ticket and the length of the delay. There's no compensation if the airline can arrange to get you on another flight that is scheduled to arrive at your destination within one hour of your originally scheduled arrival time. If, however, the substitute transportation is scheduled to arrive more than one hour but less than two hours after your original time of arrival, the airline must pay you an amount equal to the one-way fare to your final destination, up to $200. You're entitled to up to $400 if your substitute transportation will not arrive within two hours (four hours for international flights).

These rules have exceptions and conditions. The U.S. Department of Transportation has published a pamphlet called *Fly-Rights* ($1.75), which contains a full discussion of this and other areas of airline law. It is available from the Superintendent of Documents, Order Department, U.S. Government Printing Office, P.O. Box 371954, Pittsburgh, PA 15025, (202)512-1800. The order number is 050-000-00513-5.

If you're just delayed, not bumped, ask the airline staff what services it will provide. Ask about meals, telephone calls, and overnight accommodations. You can complain to the U.S. Department of Transportation if you think an airline has abused you. But write to the airline first. In these competitive times for the travel industry, airlines are often responsive to consumer complaints.

CHARTER TOURS

When you sign up for a charter tour, your money often takes a twisting route to the tour operator. This leaves you vulnerable to many different stops that exist in between. The best approach is to pay by credit card. If you pay by check, the tour operator's brochure usually will specify the name of an escrow bank account where all payments eventually go. Make out your check to that account. Also, if possible, put the destination, dates, and other details on the face of the check, which should help the payment get to where it should go. That may expedite a refund if the tour is canceled or if the tour operator or travel agent goes out of business. Remember: *Your* contract is with the tour operator.

U.S. Department of Transportation regulations require that you be shown and sign an operator/participant contract, which describes your rights, before your payment is accepted. Demand it if it isn't offered to you.

Operators are permitted to carry large bonds rather than using escrow accounts, to reassure their customers. If an operator doesn't have an escrow account, ask for evidence of the bond and how you would be reimbursed in case of a default.

Often the travel agent will insist that the check be made out to the travel agency, because it is the policy of some agents to write a single check to the tour operator themselves. That's fine, but insist on a written guarantee from the tour operator and the agency, and make sure that the agency's check is made payable to the tour operator's escrow account. Reputable agents and operators should be willing to stand behind the tour.

You can also protect yourself by getting trip insurance. This guards you if you have to cancel the trip because of your illness or an illness in the immediate family. Various types of trip insurance, as well as message relaying and referrals to overseas legal and medical help, are also provided free by many premium credit cards.

CHAPTER FOURTEEN

The Consumer Superhighway

Consumer Rights in the Computer Age

WHILE ADVANCES IN TECHNOLOGY in recent years have moved so fast as to make new personal computer models obsolete as soon as they hit the market, the law . . . limps along. On the one hand, technology changes faster than the law can keep up with it. On the other hand, many in policymaking positions are reluctant to impose new regulatory restrictions in an era of development, international competition, and deregulation. Your solution, then, is to stay on your virtual toes, keep your data close to your vest, and don't let any technology you don't at least basically understand get control of your money.

AUTOMATIC TELLER MACHINES

Downtown, at the mall, at the superstore—everywhere—an automatic teller machine (ATM) is there, ready to give you cash in exchange for a swipe of your plastic and a few magic numbers. ATMs have become so prevalent that we forget that little more than a decade ago people had to decide how much cash they would need for the weekend before the end of banking hours on Friday or else had to hope to find a sympathetic grocery store where a check could be cashed. The convenience of ATMs, however, comes with a certain amount of expense and some exposure to risk as well.

Perhaps one of the most important unsung risks of ATM use is the havoc it can play with your checking balance. There was a time when transactions in a checking account revolved around the checkbook, where all the checks lived. Now you can withdraw money directly from your checking account (and even casually invade your savings!) and, if you're not careful, find yourself bouncing checks because you forget to enter these transactions in your checkbook. The trick, of course, is to save the ATM receipts and enter withdrawals in your check register as soon as possible—ideally, at least once a week.

Another approach might be to set up a savings account—not for savings but for spending. In other words, you might want to set aside an account into which you will make a budgeted monthly or bi-weekly deposit for withdrawals from your ATM. Then you don't have to worry about affecting your checking balance with your ATM use. It will also allow you to focus on your "spending money" or cash use without other transactions distracting you from monitoring this hard-to-capture spending. (Of course, keep your regular savings account for savings.)

Receipts, incidentally, should ideally be kept until you reconcile your account balance with the monthly bank statement. The idea is to ensure that the bank got as much of a deposit as you thought you put in and that it doesn't claim a larger withdrawal than you thought you made. Do this regularly and promptly, or you'll find yourself with a huge sheaf of these little slips and end up tossing them all. Bank computer errors are rare, but they have happened. Don't count on anyone else to catch them. But once you have done the reconciliation, there's no reason to keep the slips, which are hard to store and can become quite voluminous. The bank's confirming statement is good enough proof in case a dispute comes up later. If you're squeamish, however, you can keep the deposit receipts (see below) or retain all of them for three years at the most.

ATM FEES

When shopping for a place to open an account to which you want to gain access with an ATM, find out the different institutions' terms. This information should be available from bank personnel (not necessarily a teller, but certainly someone behind a desk) as well as in the mandatory disclosure forms provided with each new account. You can also get this information in pamphlets, arranged by subject, at the front of the lobby.

Any bank that charges you a fee simply for the privilege of having an ATM card should be someone else's bank. There's no reason to pay, either annually or even once, for this service today; anything less than basic ATM privileges with your account is simply not competitive. A small fee for replacing lost cards is not desirable but not necessarily unreasonable in itself. Remember that when you receive an ATM card from a bank, it comes with a disclosure form, like a credit card cardholder agreement, which is your formal contract with the issuer.

You should be able to find a bank that will allow you free (or very cheap—a quarter or so per transaction) use of its *own* ATMs for withdrawals and deposits. And, of course, the bank must have ATMs that are reasonably convenient for you. (If you live in a city, you'll find some ATM locations are closed for security reasons fairly early after sunset. Consider that when you're analyzing convenience.)

Very few banks will allow free ATM use even for their own customers beyond withdrawals and deposits. There are exceptions at some larger banks for larger customers, whose linked accounts maintain a minimum balance of $1,000 or more, depending on the bank. Be aware that most banks now require *minimum* balances for these privileges, not average balances. If your account sinks a nickel below that minimum for even one banking day, your privileges are shot for the month, possibly resulting in fees that you had not counted on paying!

Usually, however, each time you use the ATM for a balance update or an interim statement of account activity, you will incur a fee of up to a dollar, or more. Although interim accountings can be of some use, activities such as checking your balance are available from many banks by a twenty-four-hour computerized phone line—for free, from the privacy and warmth of your own home and usually toll-free if you're on the road.

Virtually all ATM cards are hooked into one or more ATM networks such as MAC, NYCE, Cirrus, etc. These consortiums allow their members to use ATM cards from other member banks for some or all transactions. This can be a tremendous convenience, obviously. Most people with an ATM card can rightly feel confident about getting access to their checking or savings accounts anywhere in the United States, or even internationally. But once you leave your home bank, you are subject to whatever per-transaction charge the consortium permits member banks to pass on, unless your bank "eats" it for you (that is, your bank will automatically deduct the fee from your account). These can be half a dollar, a dollar, or sometimes several dollars, particularly at resorts, airports, and casinos. As with so many other little charges, these can add up.

One way to reduce ATM fees, as discussed above, is to find a bank that allows free or very cheap ATM access to its own customers. That means that if you've racked up $20 or $30 in ATM fees from the machine in your office lobby, maybe you should factor that amount into your reckoning for whether it's worth opening an account at that bank. Numbers like that also suggest that you could try to estimate your cash needs with a little more long-term perspective. If you're going to the ATM every day—or more often—you're fooling yourself about how much cash you spend. You may say you can quit whenever you want, but this is not just an ATM-fee problem. It's a budgeting and cash-management problem that requires a little honest reflection on your part.

Remember, by the way, that using your ATM card at the gas station or grocery check-out lane is the same as using an outside-bank ATM, and you will be charged accordingly, whether you take back cash or not.

ATM DEPOSITS

You can make deposits at ATMs belonging to your bank or in your network. Those deposits are often credited a business day after you make them at your own bank's ATM or even later if it's at another bank within your network. Banks depend on the information you write on the ATM envelope plus the computerized information that goes along with the envelope. That's why many of these envelopes ask you to write your whole ATM card number on the envelope, in case the envelope and computerized transaction record don't match up exactly. You don't really have to put down your whole card number, but it isn't a bad idea.

Remember that your receipt of an ATM deposit transaction only reflects the information that you input on the ATM keypad. It does not prove that you deposited any amount, only that you were, at the time of the transaction, *stating* that you were depositing that amount. For this reason, some people never make substantial deposits of cash by ATM, and this is probably a good approach. Your checks should, besides being endorsed, also contain the notation "for deposit only" under the endorsement, ideally with the name of your bank and your account number as well. Be sure to confirm the amount actually posted to your account by your monthly statement or, if your bank has one, its computerized bank-by-phone system.

Do yourself a favor in terms of security, and at the same time show consideration for others who might want to use the machine: Fill out a withdrawal slip while still in your car, or complete an envelope off to the side, before inserting your card. (There's nothing wrong with taking a few extra envelopes from machines you use often so you can prepare them in advance.) It isn't fair to make others wait while you do your paperwork.

ATM SECURITY

The ready availability of cash through ATMs has obviously not escaped the notice of people who'd like to make your cash readily available to themselves. Most ATM security tips are self-evident:

- **Watch your back.** Be careful where and when you go to the ATM. If the ATM you're planning on using is in a risky neighborhood and that withdrawal can wait until tomorrow morning, perhaps it ought to. If someone seems to be hanging around the ATM with no business to do there, look for another machine. If you really need the cash tonight, it may be worth it to look for a supermarket or another indoor, secure location with an ATM.

- **Guard your PIN.** Your personal identification number (PIN) is the key that unlocks your ATM card. Short of your spouse or your mom, no one should know your PIN. Certainly don't write it down on the card or anywhere else if you can avoid it. There is absolutely no reason to ever give it to anyone over the telephone. If someone is watching you input your PIN a little too closely, hit the cancel button and finish the transaction later or elsewhere.

• **Don't leave a paper trail.** If you don't want to keep your ATM slips, leave them at the site only if there is a completely secure place to toss them—ideally, after you've torn them up. Otherwise, take them with you. It's no one's business how much money is in your account or, for that matter, that you have "insufficient funds for the requested transaction." And some receipts also contain your

BUYING A COMPUTER

Not only is the computer this book was written on obsolete by now, it was begun on a computer that became obsolete before the book was halfway finished. But obsolescence means different things to different people—computer users, manufacturers, and salespeople, for example. The fact that for a few thousand dollars you can buy a computer system many times more powerful than what NASA used to put men on the moon doesn't mean those guys didn't get to the moon.

This isn't the place to examine all of the issues involved in buying a computer. You have to bring yourself up to speed before plunking down the kind of money a computer system requires. But, as in buying a car, do not allow yourself to buy more than you need or conceivably will need in the foreseeable future. Each little $100 more for the next-generation feature adds up fast. Bring an expert with you if you can.

Also be realistic when choosing peripherals such as printers and monitors. If your main use of the computer is for word processing and you're not the game-playing type, maybe a minimum of multimedia equipment is appropriate. Don't rush to spend money on a color or laser printer if there's no realistic prospect of your needing what it provides.

Finally, check out the manufacturer's reputation for telephone support of its product as well as the hours of support operation and typical on-hold times.

account number and other numbers from which clever techno-thiefs can clone your card.

One last detail. If your ATM isn't the kind where you just swipe your card and take it back, don't forget to take it back after the transaction. But if you do forget, contact the exact branch or bank whose ATM you used as soon as they open. (Without your PIN, the card should not be usable by anyone else, so the delay should not cause a security breach.) Cards left in the machine are eventually pulled back in for retrieval in the morning. But some branches automatically dispose of them, or send them to hopelessly inscrutable central offices if they aren't claimed promptly. If the bank doesn't have your card, call the issuer (if different from the bank whose ATM you used) and have it canceled and replaced immediately.

COMPUTER SOFTWARE

Software is a bunch of magnetic "ones and zeros," or electronic signals, that takes your thousands of dollars' worth of plastic, metal, and glass—your personal computer, or hardware—and animates it into something that lets you "fly" an airplane, balance your checkbook, or manage your small business. Most personal computers sold today come with a bundle of software preloaded into the computer. In addition to an operating system, typically DOS (Disk Operating System) and Windows, or Macintosh, most consumer-targeted computer packages include basic financial, word processing, communications, and entertainment software.

But as your computing sophistication grows, you will inevitably want to add your own software. This book is not a shopping guide; you must familiarize yourself with the technical specifications and performance characteristics of different hardware and software combinations. There are, however, some important legal issues connected with buying and using software.

Remember that software is a commodity that costs money to produce and whose producers are as entitled to payment as the producers of cars, food, and shelter. The fact that there is no direct cost to the producer if someone makes an illegal copy of the software does not change this legal and moral fact. (There are indirect costs to unauthorized copying, starting with the lost revenue to the developer.) The fact that "everyone does it," of course, is also of no moral or legal consequence.

Illegally copying software is no more legitimate than copying videotapes, books, or musical recordings. For that matter, it is no more legitimate than stealing an apple—a costly apple—from the front of the grocer's store simply because you can, or cashing someone else's paycheck. Software piracy deprives the producer of the fruit of the producer's labor, something that any working person or anyone who owns property should understand. You should be no more ready to steal software than to steal anything else.

Software is legally usable only by people or businesses who purchase a **license**. That is simply permission to use the software, which is protected by copyright. Most software that you buy in the store and much of what comes with your computer (such as software on compact discs) comes with a **shrink-wrap license**. (The software already loaded into your computer is covered by licenses arranged with the company that preloaded it and to which you agree under a principle analogous to the shrink-wrap license.) Under this license system, the manufacturer regards you as agreeing to the terms of its

---

SHAREWARE AND FREEWARE

Besides software that you purchase, there are two other legitimate sources of sophisticated programming:

Shareware is protected by copyright, but the copyright holder permits free copying and distribution. The new user is usually requested, on the honor system, to remit a relatively small payment for costs and to register as a user.

Freeware is what it sounds like: free as the air. Programmers make it available through on-line bulletin boards and user groups. You may not have the right to copy it for others, however, because the programmer might want it to keep tabs on where it goes.

---

licensing agreement contained inside the package once you open the plastic shrink-wrap of the package.

We say "the manufacturer regards you," because the state of the law regarding shrink-wrap licenses is in flux. (A uniform state law that will clarify the rules is under development.) Some argue that it is a fundamental point of contract law that someone cannot agree to a contract whose terms are unknown, as is the case with the shrink-wrap license. Others say that by opening the package, you waive the right to be fully informed of the license, which in any event is non-negotiable if you want to use the software. More subtle forms of the shrink-wrap license have been developed and are in development, and they are coming closer to being universally recognized.

In any event, none of this means that the general principles about copying software are suspended in a shrink-wrap-licensing context—only that the fine details of enforcement and technicalities are still being debated in the courts, legislatures, and government agencies such as the U.S. Patent and Trademark Office and the Library of Congress (which supervises copyright).

Fundamentally, these are your obligations regarding the use of software you purchase:

- **You may not make copies for the use of others.** "Others" obviously includes your brother-in-law, your coworkers, and your friends. Does it include other computers you use? That depends. Some licenses are designed to apply to **networks**, a system of interconnected computers that is, in a sense, one computing system. Few consumers are buying software for networks, of course. Some lawyers who specialize in this field maintain that you are entitled to use software that you buy both on the computer you keep at your desk and your laptop, although certainly not the one at work if its use is for your employer's benefit. (The typical software piracy path is, of course, usually the other way—software legitimately purchased by businesses ends up on employees' home computers for their own use.) Presumably you are not using both of these at the same time, although it gets muddier if one is for your use and one is for the use of your high schooler or spouse.

Other legal experts—many of whom represent software developers—disagree and say each software license is for use on one machine, period. It wouldn't hurt to see what rights the license actually does grant you, of course, but the point is that many legal experts doubt the legality of some license limitations.

• **You have a right to make backup copies.** Even though your software comes on a disk or CD, most lawyers in this field agree, as do many software manufacturers, that you are entitled to make a backup copy of the software for protection in case the original disk is damaged or defective. (The copy on your computer's hard drive is always vulnerable to a crash or other system disaster, and software companies recognize this as well as anyone, especially because their software often causes the problem!) CDs, because of the huge amount of information they contain, are technologically not capable of being copied onto the less capacious floppy disks, although you

---

YOUR RIGHTS AS A SOFTWARE CONSUMER

Software may come on a little floppy disk—or ten of them—or a CD, but while it may transform your existence, it can also present as many performance problems and threats to your well-being as any large appliance. Avoid any software that does not include some degree of free telephone support, at least for a limited time. The developer's confidence in the product is ultimately reflected in the extent to which the developer stands behind it. Ideally this support should be accessible with a toll-free call during more than regular business hours. Practically speaking, however, this may be unobtainable. The world's largest software developer only provides support through its regular lines on the West Coast, although observers report that early problems with interminable holding times (which add insult to the injury of a toll call) have largely been relieved.

For more sophisticated users, help with popular programs is also obtainable on line, through company- and user-sponsored bulletin boards and forums, as well as by electronic mail.

---

can buy "writeable" CDs that work with special CD recorders that are now widely available. These can come in handy if you want to back up a multidisc program. (Note that some software manufacturers make copying harder by using specially manufactured disks that hold more data than the disks you can buy off the shelf.)

ON-LINE COMPUTING SERVICES

Many disk drives could be filled with the clichés that have been spun about the increasing influence of **on-line** services for your computer. These services, which include such major players as CompuServe, America Online, and Prodigy, offer consumers the opportunity to hook up their computers by modem to a network of computerized information, commerce, discourse, and leisure activities. On-line providers are also gateways to such resources as the Internet and the World Wide Web, as well as electronic mail, or E-mail. In these on-line worlds, you can casually, cheaply—and, if you wish, anonymously—communicate with people around the globe.

These services are still in the process of working out their pricing schemes. With the advent of software-giant Microsoft's own network, with access built in to the Windows 95 operating system, some of the more established services have cut prices in an effort to stay ahead of the curve. Another factor keeping prices of the established services down is the increasing availability of relatively cheap, flat-rate Internet-only services (i.e., no special forums, services, or other features for members).

With the traditional services, the two main factors you want to look for, in terms of affordability, is how many free on-line hours, or **connect time**, you get for your monthly fee (one or more plans might be offered), and what you pay for each additional hour after that. You have to have a good sense of how much time you will really spend on line. Many of the companies are flexible about allowing you to switch plans in the middle if your usage turns out to be more or less than expected. There is no reason to commit to any membership period, and any plan that requires it should be avoided.

There are also new, innovative companies that offer a flat fee for unlimited connect time to the Internet and sometimes to their own more limited members-only services. Note that their advertised fee is usually the lower of two fees; to get the **graphical interface** necessary to make full use of the World Wide Web's panoply of images and sounds, you have to pay slightly more. Because these companies offer unlimited connect time, the early experience with some is that their servers, or central dial-up lines, are clogged with users and their customer service lines are jammed. You might want to try one of these companies at first to avoid the pressure of having to pay more for more time on line as you learn your way around. Perhaps you'll have no problems. On the other hand, the better-established companies are somewhat more user-friendly—usually.

Indeed, more than money is at stake when deciding which service you should go with. Advocates of the services are positively passionate about the advantages of one over the other. Besides access to the Internet and the World Wide Web, which by definition cannot practically be censored by your provider, each service offers its own **forums**, which are electronic "meeting places" where people exchange ideas about issues, culture, each other, or whatever they wish. These are monitored for basic manners and vulgarity by many services, especially the more expensive ones. Each time you log in, you will be offered all kinds of on-line diversions, contests, and information—a truly stunning array.

But remember that the services that charge for connect time intend to keep you logged on for as long as possible. A fun treasure hunt that takes you throughout the network or the World Wide Web in search of prizes is not quite the same as filling out a *Reader's Digest* or Publishers Clearinghouse contest blank. With the latter, your time is your own. With the on-line contest, the more you play, the more you pay.

CAUTION ON LINE

Don't let your guard down when communicating with strangers on line. The major services usually require that your real name and address be available to them, although you are often able to choose a pseudonym for participation in forums. But even if you are relatively anonymous, there's no reason not to be a *mensch* ("good guy"). For one, if you're a "flamer"—someone who, as some people do on the road, think that their anonymity is a license to be a jerk—you might get booted out of a forum on one of the monitored services. But also, considering the sophistication of some computer-savvy people, your anonymity might not be as well protected as you think. Not by a long shot. So don't get the wrong people sore at you. You could even find yourself on the wrong end of a harassment lawsuit.

There are many on-line shopping opportunities, but don't get carried away. Besides using up connect time, they don't necessarily offer better deals than catalog or store shopping. The proprietors have the capacity to be uniquely untraceable, requiring only some way to put up a **Web site**, or an electronic "page" on the World Wide Web, to hawk their wares. The ethereal nature of these businesses make catalog shopping seem as stable and predictable as a day trip to the huge Macy's in New York.

Then there's the whole question of transmitting your credit card information over the wires. Although some services claim to use truly secure lines, most experts are skeptical that information like this can be kept secret from truly sophisticated hackers, or computer experts-cum-pests. (Some experts say that once your computer is hooked up to a modem and a phone line, *all* the data on your computer are fair game for anyone who knows where to find you.) The same goes for data sent by electronic mail. In the latter case, even if no one is snooping on the line, a typing error in your E-mail address can result in sensitive or confidential information hurling through cyberspace to someone who never heard of you until just now. Caution is the word.

ON-LINE SOFTWARE

Your computer needs programming that tells it how to connect to the on-line service. Most services provide free software that enables you to gain access to their systems. But remember, again, that their incentive is to keep you on line for as long as possible. While there isn't necessarily anything nefarious about the software your provider sends you or which comes prepackaged on your computer (see above), you may be better off in the long run with commercial software, which you then customize according to the instructions that come with it or that it walks you through when you load it.

For that matter, you might want to know what different providers are doing to enable their users to take maximum advantage of the services they offer. For example, one service provides its users with a program called "Information Manager" for use with forums, electronic mail, and the Internet. The program, while easy to use, is not terribly efficient. Thus, while composing messages for use in a forum and especially to respond to messages left for you, you must, for all practical purposes, remain on line. A company not affiliated with the service, however, makes software that basically vacuums up all the messages you would want to read or respond to in the forums you indicate and puts them on your hard drive. You then read them and respond if you want to, at your own pace, off line. The service has cooperated with the programmers and users of this software. But another popular service has not cooperated with users wishing to use different software. Issues like this are minor compared to the overall quality of the service. But as you sound out users of on-line services, also look for little things that might make some difference to you.

CONNECT CHARGES

Finally, make sure the amount of on-line time for which you are billed corresponds to your own records—either your software's local gauge (i.e., in your computer) of how much time you've spent on line, or your own egg timer. The same company that made it difficult for customers to use their own connect-time-saving software has also been cited for billing people for more time than they were actually connected. They added thirty-second increments to each connection made by customers to account for the time phone lines were occupied making the connection, even though the customers were getting no on-line benefit. There's no reason in cyberspace to put up with that.

■

And Let Slip the Dogs of Law

Breach of Contract and Remedies

A BREACH OF CONTRACT—also called a **default**—is one party's failure, without a legally valid excuse, to live up to any of his or her responsibilities under a contract. A breach can occur by:

- failure to perform as promised;
- making it impossible for the other party to perform;
- repudiation of the contract (announcing an intent not to perform).

FAILURE TO PERFORM

Someone has "failed to perform" who has not performed a material part of the contract by a reasonable (or agreed-upon) deadline. Suppose your friend promised to buy your Edsel for $1,000 and to pay you "sometime early next week." It would be a material breach for your friend never to pay you or to pay you six months later. If your friend paid you on Thursday of next week, however, it probably would not be a breach. You did not explicitly make time an essential part of the contract—the source of the phrase "time is of the essence."

A breach doesn't have to be so straightforward. Sometimes a party breaches by making performance impossible. Suppose you hire a cleaning service to clean your house on Sunday at a rate of $50 for the day. Early Sunday morning you go out for the day and lock the door behind you, neglecting to make arrangements to let the cleaning people into the house. You've breached by making performance impossible and would owe the money because the cleaning service was ready and able to clean your house and presumably turned down requests to clean for other clients.

A breach can also be **partial**. That happens when the contract has several parts, each of which can be treated as a separate contract. If one of those parts is breached, you could sue for damages, even though there isn't a total breach. An example of this would be a landowner hiring a contractor to perform a construction project within certain deadlines. These deadlines have already been missed, but overall the project is going well. As long as the delay (the breach) is not material, the owner can continue the contractual relationship but sue for whatever damages were suffered as a result of the delay (for example, canceled leases). On the other hand, if the delay is material—so damaging to the project that it seriously undermines its value—the breach strikes at the heart of the contract and is total. The owner may terminate it and pursue remedies against the builder while hiring someone else to finish the job.

Another kind of breach is a **repudiation**. Repudiation is a clear statement made by one party before performance is due that states by words, circumstances, or conduct that the party cannot or will not perform a material part of that party's contract obligations. Suppose that on the day before your friend was to pick up the Edsel you promised to sell her, you sent her a message that you had decided to sell the car to someone else or had sold it. That message or act would be a repudiation. In contrast, it's not repudiation if one party will not perform because of an honest disagreement over the contract's terms.

REMEDIES FOR BREACH OF CONTRACT

When someone breaches a contract with you, you are no longer obligated to keep your end of the bargain. You may proceed in several ways:

- urge the breaching party to reconsider the breach;
- if it's a contract with a merchant, get help from local, state, or federal consumer agencies;

- bring the breaching party to an agency for alternative dispute resolution;
- sue for damages or other remedies.

You may wonder what the point is of asking the breaching party to reconsider. One advantage is that it's cheap. Often the only cost is the price of a telephone call and a little pride. The breaching party may have breached the contract because of a misunderstanding. Perhaps the breaching party just needs a little more time. Or maybe you could renegotiate.

You may very well be able to come up with a solution that will leave both of you better off than if you went to court. If you do hire a lawyer, the first thing that lawyer is likely to do is try to persuade the breaching party to perform.

Starting with that offer to settle the matter, keep good records of all your communications with the other side. Once you see you're in for a struggle, make a file. Keep copies of any letters you send, and move all receipts, serial numbers, warranty cards, and the like to this file.

If you get nowhere with personal communications, the next step before getting courts or lawyers involved may be to go over the other side's head, so to speak.

If the dispute is between you and a merchant, you might want to contact the manufacturer of the product. If it involves a large chain of stores, contact the management of the chain. This goes for services, too.

Assuming you're still not getting satisfaction, try contacting a consumer protection agency, either in your city or state. The Federal Trade Commission is less likely to get involved in small disputes. If, however, the FTC believes that what happened to you has occurred to many people nationwide, it might be interested. The FTC's involvement carries a lot of weight. The same goes with your state attorney general or local consumer agency. Complaining to the Better Business Bureau or a consumer action hotline in the media may also push the other party to settle. Another resource is your local post office, where you can report shady business practices that took place through the mail.

OTHER SELF-HELP METHODS

STOPPING PAYMENT

If you're involved in a transaction where you paid by check, and the other person refuses to refund your money, you may call your bank and **stop payment** on that check. That prevents the bank from paying the check, assuming the check has not yet cleared your account. Remember, you're still liable for the purchase price until a court decides otherwise.

You may be sued by the seller for the amount in dispute, and unless you have a legal excuse not to pay, you'll end up writing another check. Also be aware that when you stop payment, you raise the stakes and diminish the chance of a settlement: merchants and contractors don't take kindly to this technique.

Note that stopping payment on a check is not the same as having insufficient funds to cover the check, which may carry criminal penalties. Stopping payment on a check is your legal right if you have a valid claim.

To do it, call your bank and give them the relevant information about the check. The bank will then send you a form to confirm your instructions in writing, which you must return within a certain number of days for the bank to honor your request for very long. If you don't provide all the information your bank requires, your stop-payment order might not be good. The bank's charge for this service will usually be $10 to $30 or even more.

Don't try to avoid the fee by reducing your bank balance so the check won't clear. The bank can't read your mind, so other checks you've written may not be paid, or the bank might even pay the check you don't want paid in an attempt to accommodate you. More important, you will have gone from exercising a legal right (stopping payment) to committing a legal wrong (passing a bad check).

Once you've provided information to the bank, you should inform the seller of your action. Calling and writing to explain why you stopped the check asserts your claim and may keep the seller from attempting to prosecute you. You also salvage a tiny bit of goodwill, which may help you eventually settle the matter, especially because you've helped the other side avoid the fee their own bank charges on returned or uncollectable checks.

If your bank has paid the check, you'll have to try to void the contract and get your money back in other ways discussed here.

CREDIT CARD PURCHASES

These days, of course, many purchases are made with credit cards. Then the **Fair Credit Billing Act** may protect you. Under the Act, charges for products that you rightfully refuse to accept on delivery or that aren't delivered according to an agreement are regarded by the law as billing errors that the card issuer must investigate. So are charges for something you didn't buy or charges by someone not authorized to use your account. Errors in arithmatic and failures to properly identify a charge are also errors. During the investigation you don't have to pay. The issuer may resolve the matter by granting you a permanent credit.

You may also avoid payment for shoddy or damaged goods or poor service if you refuse payment under state law and the merchant refuses to make an adjustment. In these cases, credit card issuers usually will intercede and investigate your claim. They often classify the charge as disputed and allow you to skip payment to them, without interest, during the investigation. If the merchant refuses to cooperate, or the card issuer confirms your version of the facts and agrees that you have been aggrieved, they will credit the amount of the purchase as appropriate.

GETTING OUT OF A CONTRACT

Sometimes you'll find yourself in a position where you have to breach a contract. Breaching a contract isn't always a bad thing to do, as long as you're ready to take your lumps. Sometimes the price you pay through a remedy for breach is less damaging than performing a contract that has become a big mistake.

SUING FOR A BREACH OF CONTRACT

There are times when self-help will only take you so far, after which you need to consider your legal options. The most common legal remedy for breach of contract is a **suit** for damages, usually **compensatory damages**. This is the amount of money it would take to put you in as good a position as if there had not been a breach of contract. The idea is to give you "the benefit of the bargain."

What's an example of compensatory damages? Imagine that you hired a contractor to paint your house for $500. This job could cost as much as $650, but you've negotiated a great deal. Now the contractor regrets agreeing to the $500 price and breaches. If you can prove all the facts just stated, you can recover $150, or whatever the difference is between $500 and what it ultimately cost you to have your house painted.

There are other kinds of contract damages. The most common ones are:

• **Consequential damages**, as discussed in the section on warranties. These may be available in a contract suit, depending on the language of the contract. (Usually contracts, especially warranties, are explicit in actually excluding these kinds of damages.)

• **Punitive damages**, available if the breaching party's behavior was offensive to the court. Punitive damages are virtually never recovered in a suit for breach of contract, but it may be possible to get punitive damages or some form of statutory damages (legal penalties) under a consumer fraud law or in a suit for fraud.

• **Liquidated damages**, an amount built in to the contract. Although one or both parties have effectively breached the contract, this term will stand, as long as it is a fair estimate of the damages. In contrast, the courts will not enforce a penalty clause, an amount of liquidated damages that is way out of line with the actual loss. Liquidated damages clauses are usually found in consumer contracts, if at all, as something available *against* the consumer, however, and not in the consumer's favor.

- **Nominal damages**, awarded when you win your case but you have not proved much of a loss. The court may award you a token amount.

There are other remedies in a contract suit beside damages. The main one is **specific performance**, a court order requiring the breaching party to perform as promised in the contract. Courts have historically been reluctant to award this because it is awkward to enforce, but that reluctance is ebbing. They will impose specific performance if no other remedy is available because of the contract's subject matter, such as real estate or a unique piece of personal property. It will almost never be applied to personal services contracts, however—that is, to force a party to render the promised service.

A court may also **rescind** (cancel) a contract that one party has breached. The court may then order the breaching party to pay the other side any expenses incurred; it could also order the return of goods sold. Or, the court could **reform** the contract. That involves rewriting the contract according to what the court concludes, based on evidence at trial, the parties actually intended. Although these have traditionally been rare remedies, they are being used increasingly under the provisions of many states' consumer fraud laws.

WHERE TO SUE

Most consumers will do best in **small claims court**, a special division of the courts set up in most jurisdictions. Small claims court hears cases in which the damages requested are below a set amount, usually a few thousand dollars. There are no juries. The procedures in small claims court are streamlined, with a minimum of paperwork—they're designed for the "do-it-yourselfer." Indeed, judges are particularly solicitous of consumers who are not represented by counsel in these courts. Be prepared, however, for a hard press by the judge and his or her staff—perhaps even in the courthouse hallways on the day of trial—on both parties to compromise.

Larger cases cannot be heard in small claims court. At this point you would be well advised to seek the advice of a lawyer. Do not try this at home: "real" court is not for amateurs. Procedural rules, knowledge of the law, and courtroom methods are much more complex than they seem on television. In these courtrooms the judges have busy dockets and no time to assist sincere but overwhelmed nonlawyers. But the legal training necessary to make the case is well within the competence of an experienced attorney, whom you can find through references from friends, family, or your local bar association.

REASONS NOT TO SUE

One reason not to sue, beside the obvious ones alluded to above, is even more obvious—you could lose. The contract defenses discussed at the beginning of this book are a two-way street. Any one of them may be asserted as a defense to your suit for breach, including the defense that there was never a contract at all.

It is also possible that you could be **countersued**. That means the person or company you're suing could sue you back, perhaps making a claim for back payments that it otherwise may have let go in light of your complaints. You might emerge from the courthouse not only without satisfaction but with a judgment debt to pay.

That judgment debt could include attorneys' fees, too, if your contract provides for that. You must consider all the contract terms discussed, such as choice of law and choice of forum, which affect your right to sue. Your suit may be made subject to instant dismissal, in which case you will have invested your time for nothing (and lost money—filing fees can range from $20 or so for small claims court, to hundreds of dollars to sue for larger amounts).

All in all, undertaking a lawsuit, especially in a court other than small claims, can be a very annoying, time-consuming, expensive, and disappointing process. Long ago, a successful corporate lawyer advised other attorneys to, above all, "discourage litigation." How much more does Abraham Lincoln's advice apply to the rest of us? You have to think hard about whether suing is worth it in terms of both economic and spiritual cost. Then think again.

THE CONSUMER FRAUD ACTS

In addition to your traditional private right to sue, laws prohibiting unfair and deceptive trade practices in consumer transactions have been enacted in every state. These laws are sometimes known as the "little FTC acts" because they establish state-law prohibitions and penalties for a wide range of unfair and deceptive trade practices similar to those monitored by the Federal Trade Commission. For your purposes, the main difference is that these laws, more commonly called **consumer fraud acts**, allow the consumer to act as a "private attorney general": While allowing state authorities to take action against violators, like their federal counterparts, these laws also give powerful tools to consumers harmed by unfair and deceptive trade practices.

The consumer fraud acts apply to almost all consumer sales transactions. They are both extremely flexible and very potent, often providing for **treble (triple) damages** when a violation is found. Generally requiring lower legal hurdles than traditional fraud remedies—for example, intent to deceive is usually not a requirement—these laws usually provide for both action by state agencies and recovery by private lawsuits. These laws are the ultimate legal reaction to caveat emptor. Their use involves numerous technicalities, and competent legal advice is almost certainly necessary to take advantage of them. Nonetheless, their basic elements can be briefly explained.

Unfair conduct is that which, although not necessarily illegal,

- offends public policy as established by statute, common law, or other means;
- is immoral, unethical, troublesome, or corrupt; and
- substantially injures consumers (or competitors or other businesspeople).

Deceptive conduct is behavior, usually a statement or other **representation** (behavior amounting to a representation), that may have caused you to act differently than you otherwise would have. The representation does not have to involve the product's qualities, but it might include any aspect that could be an important factor in deciding whether to buy the goods. An example would be stating that the engine on that Edsel has eight cylinders when it really has six. The quality may be fine, but the buyer may have been seeking a car with an eight-cylinder engine.

The unfair or deceptive act does *not* have to be intentional. In many states the seller does not even know about the deception. Rather, the court considers the effect that the seller's conduct might possibly have on the general public or the people to whom the seller advertised the product. It looks at the behavior in terms of what impression it would have had on a reasonable person.

To use an unfair and deceptive practices statute, you should make a written demand for relief before you sue. The law allows the seller one last chance to make good. If you must sue, many states require proof of injury before you may recover. Loss of money or property is enough to prove this. You should be able to show that the seller's actions actually caused the injury. For example, only if you were determined to buy the car no matter what the seller said, and the seller can prove this, would you have a hard time showing

---

ABILITY TO PAY

Keep in mind that every lawsuit is ultimately as good as the defendant's ability to pay. If the company you sue has gone through the bankruptcy process, your contract could legally be disavowed. If the company has ceased doing business or is under the protection of bankruptcy laws, your chances of recovering anything of value are small.

If you have a contract that is still in force with a troubled company, you may have to have the rest of your contract needs filled by another company if the one you have a contract with can't come through. Then you may have a damages claim against the first company. If the company is in bankruptcy, you may be contacted by the bankruptcy court, or you may need a lawyer's help to file your claim. If your claim isn't substantial, though, it's usually not worth the trouble.

---

that the seller's conduct caused you injury or loss. If you based your decision to buy on what the seller told you, or if you were coerced into buying something that you didn't really want, then you may be able to use the statute.

If you win, many states permit you to recover double or triple damages and attorneys' fees. The purpose of these harsh penalties is to discourage sellers from committing unfair or deceptive acts in the future, because the risk of being subject to the penalties is higher than the profit sellers stand to make by chicanery.

MORE ON REASONABLENESS

Earlier we discussed the **reasonable person**. There are two principles that extend that fictional person's capacities into the practical realm. One is the concept of the **reasonable observer**, a reasonable person who sets the standard of whether an action or statement would reasonably suggest, for example, an offer or an acceptance or a repudiation. This person is not an eagle-eyed expert but stands for common sense.

Closely related is the concept of **knew or should have known**. If parties to a contract are considered to know or be "on notice" of something—say, that their offer has been accepted—it is not enough to ask whether they actually knew it. If it were, we would have only their word as really reliable evidence that they knew or didn't know. The law will not allow parties who should have known something through the reasonable exercise of their senses and intelligence to fail to use them. Thus, it isn't enough to say, "I didn't know the Edsel I sold you had no engine." That's something that someone selling a car reasonably *should* know.

WHERE TO GET MORE INFORMATION

■

GENERAL INFORMATION

In most states, a state agency, often the attorney general, has an office of consumer affairs and protection. (In some states this office is under the authority of the secretary of state.) These offices are good starting points both for filing complaints and obtaining free literature on consumer protection. They appear in your telephone directory under the state government listings, or you can call any state government information number.

Also consider contacting federal agencies, such as the Federal Trade Commission, if you think you have been subjected to a deceptive practice. You can call the FTC's Bureau of Consumer Protection at (202) 326-2222, fax (202) 326-2050, TDD (202) 326-2502, or write Federal Trade Commission, Bureau of Consumer Protection, 6th and Pennsylvania Avenue, NW, Washington, DC 20580. The FTC's regional offices are listed below.

Suite 1000
1718 Peachtree Street, NW
Atlanta, GA 30367
(404) 347-4836
Fax: (404) 347-4725

Suite 810
101 Merrimac Street
Boston, MA 02114-4719
(617) 424-5960
Fax: (617) 424-5998

Suite 1860
55 East Monroe Street
Chicago, IL 60603
(312) 353-4423
Fax: (312) 353-4438

Suite 520-A
668 Euclid Avenue
Cleveland, OH 44114
(216) 522-4207
Fax: (216) 522-7239

Suite 500
100 N. Central Expressway
Dallas, TX 75201
(214) 767-5501
Fax: (214) 767-5519

Suite 1523
1961 Stout Street
Denver, CO 80294
(303) 844-2271
Fax: (303) 844-3599

Suite 13209
11000 Wilshire Blvd.
Los Angeles, CA 90024
(310) 235-4000
Fax: (310) 235-7976

Suite 570
901 Market Street
San Francisco, CA 94103
(415) 356-5270
Fax: (415) 356-5284

Suite 1300
150 William Street
New York, NY 10038
(212) 264-1207
Fax: (212) 264-0459

2806 Federal Building
915 Second Avenue
Seattle, WA 98174
(206) 220-6363
Fax: (206) 220-6366

Consumer problems involving the U.S. mail in any way can be brought to the attention of:

U.S. Postal Service
Consumer Complaints
900 Brentwood Road, NE
Washington, DC 20066-7203
(202) 636-1400

State and local bar associations often have lawyer referral services through which you may locate lawyers who can help you with consumer problems.

The local Better Business Bureau can be helpful. Some television and radio stations or newspapers have "action lines" that follow up on complaints. They often get results in exchange for being able to use your complaint on the air or in the paper.

PUBLICATIONS

State and local bar associations often publish free pamphlets and handbooks on legal problems.

The National Consumers League (NCL) publishes a variety of booklets and guides on several topics of importance to consumers. The NCL is a not-for-profit membership group conducting research, education, and advocacy on consumer issues. Call or write them at 1701 K Street, NW, Suite 1200, Washington DC 20006; (202) 835-3323, fax (202) 835-0747.

The *Consumer's Resource Handbook* can help you locate the proper source of help for many different consumer problems. It includes a directory of federal agencies. The handbook is available free of charge from the Consumer Information Center, P.O. Box 100, Pueblo, CO 81002; (719) 948-3334.

The federal government publishes many helpful brochures and handbooks for consumers on everything from credit to cars and from weight-loss programs to food products. Some are available for little or no charge from the Consumer Information Center at the address listed above. Contact them for a free catalog.

Others are available free from the FTC. For a list of publications, write the Federal Trade Commission, Public Reference Branch, Room 130, 6th Street and Pennsylvania Avenue NW, Washington, DC 20580; (202) 326-2222. Full text of almost all of these brochures and booklets is available at the FTC's Internet site: http://www.ftc.gov.

Here are some FTC titles, listed by topic.

AUTOMOBILES

Auto Service Contracts
Buying a Used Car (Spanish only)*
Car Ads: Low-Interest Loans and Other Offers
Car Financing Scams
A Consumer Guide to Vehicle Leasing
New Car Buying Guide (Spanish only)*
Renting a Car
Taking the Scare Out of Auto Repair
Vehicle Repossession†

BUYING/WORKING AT HOME

The Cooling-Off Rule†
Shopping by Phone and Mail†
Work-at-Home Schemes†

*See "Other FTC Publications" for English version   †Also in Spanish

*See "Other FTC Publications" for English version   †Also in Spanish

*See "Other FTC Publications" for English version   †Also in Spanish

Telemarketing Travel Fraud
Telephone Scams and Older Consumers

Some popular FTC publications, including English-language editions of several publications, are available only from the Consumer Information Center, Pueblo, CO 81009. Some are free; the rest have a nominal cost. They include:

Automobiles: *Buying a Used Car, New Car Buying Guide*

Buying at Home: *Cybershopping: Protecting Yourself*

Credit: *Choosing/Using Credit Cards, Fair Debt Collection, How to Dispute Credit Report Errors, Solving Credit Problems*

Services: *Funerals: A Consumer Guide, Online Scams: Road Hazards on the Information Superhighway, Viatical Settlements*

HOME OWNERSHIP/MORTGAGES

Nearly every state has federal information centers where information on federal services, programs, and regulations is available to consumers, including homeowners. Check the government pages of your local telephone directory for the office near you. The local library can also be a good source of helpful, free information.

For information on HUD programs, contact the federal Department of Housing and Urban Development, Library and Information Services, 451 Seventh Street, SW, Room 8141 Washington, DC 20410; (202) 708-1422. This information also may be available at some local HUD offices.

The federal government publishes many free or low-cost pamphlets on home ownership and home buying. Contact the Consumer Information Center and the FTC at the addresses above.

The Internal Revenue Service is an excellent source of information on tax questions relating to owning a home. Its national toll-free number is (800) 829-3676. Its tele-tax service has recorded tax information on 140 topics. You can find the toll-free phone number for your state by calling the IRS office in your area. Topics include the sale of a home, reporting gains from home sales, installment plans, and exclusion of gain for people aged 55 or older.

ABA GUIDE TO CONSUMER LAW

The IRS also publishes several free pamphlets dealing with common tax questions. These include: *Real Estate Taxes* (Publication 530), *Limits on Home Mortgage Interest Deductions* (Publication 936), and *Tax Information on Selling Your Home* (Publication 523).

TENANT ISSUES/LEASES

Many states and cities have departments of housing, departments of fair housing, or departments of human affairs, which can usually answer questions and accept complaints of discrimination and inadequate maintenance. You can also get information on local housing codes and code enforcement. Check government listings in the local telephone directory.

The U.S. Department of Housing and Urban Development has offices in many large cities and is involved in many landlord-tenant issues. HUD has regulations governing public housing, publicly subsidized housing, and fair housing. HUD can answer questions and accept complaints of housing discrimination.

Tenants may seek the assistance of the National Housing Institute, which provides information and referral to local tenant organizations. NHI is located at 439 Main Street, Orange, NJ 07050; (201) 678-3110.

INSURANCE

For information to help you understand state laws and insurance, contact Insurance Information Institute, 110 William Street, New York, NY 10038; (212) 669-9200.

The Insurance Information Institute has not only many useful pamphlets, but it also has state and regional counterparts.

AUTOMOBILES

Earlier in this chapter, the FTC section lists many free and low-cost publications on automobiles. The following list is a starting point for getting more details or registering various types of complaints.

The American Automobile Manufacturers Association (AAMA) publishes *Motor Vehicle Facts and Figures* annually. It also publishes a complete *Directory of Motor Vehicle Related Associations*. For details on how to obtain these publications, call (313) 872-4311, or write American Automobile Manufacturers Association, 7430 Second Avenue, Suite 300, Detroit, MI 48202.

The Automobile Importers of America is the foreign-car counterpart of the AAMA. For details, call (703) 416-1577 or write Automobile Importers of America, 1725 Jefferson Davis Highway, Arlington, VA 22202.

The National Automobile Dealers Association is a major trade association of U.S. automobile dealers. It publishes a number of brochures for consumers on topics such as automotive safety. For details, call (703) 821-7000 or (800) 252-6232, or write National Automobile Dealers Association, 8400 Westpark Drive, McLean, VA 22102.

The Recreational Vehicle Industry Association is a national trade association representing manufacturers of motor homes, travel trailers, truck campers, multiuse vehicles, and component-part suppliers. It publishes brochures offering hints for buyers, tips for campers, and safety and driving tips, among other topics. For details, call (703) 620-6003, or write Recreational Vehicle Industry Association, 1896 Preston White Drive, Reston, VA 20191.

The Rubber Manufacturers Association offers information on tires and other rubber products. For details, call (202) 682-4800 or (800) 325-5095, or write Rubber Manufacturers Association, 1400 K Street, NW, Washington, DC 20005.

For information and publications on using certified car technicians for repairs, contact Automotive Service Excellence, 13505 Dulles Technology Drive, Herndon, VA 22071-3413; (703) 713-3800.

You also can call the car manufacturers' headquarters or their regional offices directly. Ask your local dealer for details.

Every local Better Business Bureau has a hot line for automobile-related complaints, particularly regarding warranties. The BBB arranges arbitration hearings for participating manufacturers. Check your local telephone directory or write Council of Better Business Bureaus, Inc., 4200 Wilson Boulevard, Eighth Floor, Arlington, VA 22203; (703) 276-0100.

The National Highway Traffic Safety Administration (NHTSA) provides information on car recalls and defect investigations. You also can report safety-related defects. The NHTSA offers a toll-free auto safety hot line. In the District of Columbia, you can call this hot line at (202) 366-0123. In the continental United States, call the hot line at (800) 424-9393. Or write National Highway Traffic Safety Administration, 400 Seventh Street, SW, Washington, DC 20590.

The Center for Auto Safety provides information on automobile defects for various models of cars and may follow up on consumer complaints. Write Center for Auto Safety, Suite 410, 2001 S Street, NW, Washington, DC 20009 or call (202) 328-7700.

The United States Consumer Product Safety Commission is a federal agency that offers safety-related information on most, but not all, products available on the consumer market. In Maryland, call (301) 504-0580 and ask for the "Public Affairs Department." In the rest of the United States, call (800) 638-2772. Or you can write U.S. Consumer Product Safety Commission, Washington, DC 20207.

Other organizations that can help with automobile-related problems include the Consumer Federation of America, 1424 16th Street, NW, Suite 604, Washington, DC 20036; (202) 387-6121; National Safety Council, 1121 Springlake Drive, Itasca, IL 60130; (630) 285-1121; and the National Transportation Safety Board, 490 L'Enfant East, SW, Washington, DC 20594; (202) 382-6600.

For additional assistance with automobile-related problems or questions, you also can contact your state attorney general's offices or your state Department of Consumer Affairs. Some states have separate bureaus that handle only motor vehicle problems. Your state or local Department of Motor Vehicles may also be helpful. Check your local telephone directory.

CREDIT

PUBLICATIONS ON CREDIT

The National Institute for Consumer Education offers many free and low-cost publications on credit. Write them at 207 Rackham Building, Eastern Michigan University, Ypsilanti, MI 48197, call (313) 487-2292; or reach them at home page http://www.emich.edu/public/coe/nice/nice/html.

For information about credit cards, RAM Research Corp. issues a comprehensive monthly survey highlighting low-rate cards, no-annual-fee cards, gold cards, and secured cards. It is available from P.O. Box 1700, Frederick, MD 21702. Bankcard Holders of America (524 Branch Ave., Salem, VA 24153) offers useful but less inclusive reports on low-rate or no-fee cards, gold cards, rebate and frequent flier cards, and secured cards.

You can obtain various publications without charge from the Board of Governors of the Federal Reserve System, Publications Services, Mail Stop 138, 20 C Street, NW, Washington, DC 20551.

These publications include *Consumer Handbook of Credit Protection Laws,* a 44-page booklet that explains how to use the credit laws to shop for credit. It also tells you how to apply for credit, keep up your credit ratings, and complain about an unfair deal. Other publications include *Shop . . . The Card You Pick Can Save You Money; How to File a Consumer Complaint; When Your Home is on the Line: What You Should Know About Home Equity Lines of Credit.*

The Federal Trade Commission publishes many popular consumer credit publications in English and Spanish. See the section on FTC publications earlier in this chapter.

WHERE TO RESOLVE DISPUTES

What if you believe that you have been improperly treated by a credit grantor? Resolving the problem involves a sequence of four possible steps—each more aggressive than the last. Disputes can almost always be settled long before the third and fourth steps.

1. Check to be sure that you have the correct information regard-

ing your rights under the law and the credit grantor's obligation to you under the law. In addition to the information included in this book, this section provides other sources that you may wish to review.

2. If you are reasonably confident that your complaint is well-founded, contact the creditor by phone or, if the matter is quite serious, by letter. Be sure to give your name, address, account number, and a statement of your concern. If your initial contact is by telephone, get the name of the person with whom you talked. To compete effectively, most credit grantors wish to keep good customers by settling complaints fairly and quickly. Nonetheless, create a paper trail by keeping a written record or log of all of your contacts with the creditor.

3. If you are not satisfied with the settlement offered by the creditor, based on your study of your rights under the law, the next step is to contact any state or federal agency that regulates your creditor. It is best to write the appropriate agency and to supply a copy of the written record that you have maintained. By sending a copy of the letter to your creditor, you may focus attention on your complaint. While the regulatory agency may require some time to get to your problem, it will often be able to arrange a solution that will be satisfactory to you. A description of the various regulatory agencies that might be involved and their addresses are included in this section.

4. If the regulatory agency fails to satisfy you, you can hire your own attorney to pursue the matter. However, if you do not win, you are likely to be liable for your attorney's fees. In some cases that may be true even if you win.

The next part of this resource section relates to step three. It provides lists of the major federal laws and the agencies responsible for enforcing those laws. First, determine the federal act that applies to your complaint. Second, identify the type of credit grantor against whom you have a complaint. Then look up the address of the agency so you can write to make your complaint. If you need more help, call your local consumer protection office. You can find the telephone number in your local telephone directory under the listings for your local or state government.

The **Truth in Lending Act (TILA)** requires all credit grantors to provide you with the annual percentage rate (APR), costs and terms, and other relevant information on the credit sought and obtained. Typical credit grantors are banks, department stores, credit card issuers, finance companies, and oil companies.

The **Equal Credit Opportunity Act (ECOA)** prohibits discrimination against a credit applicant and debtor because of age (except for capacity to contract), sex, marital status, race, color, religion, national origin, receipt of public aid, or exercise of certain legal rights.

The **Fair Credit Reporting Act (FCRA)** establishes a procedure for correcting mistakes on your credit record and requires that the record be kept confidential.

The **Fair Credit Billing Act (FCBA)** establishes a procedure for promptly correcting errors on a credit account and prevents damage to your credit rating while you are settling a dispute.

The **Consumer Leasing Act (CLA)** requires disclosure of information that helps you compare the cost and terms of one lease with another. It also orders firms that offer leases to reveal facts that help you compare the cost and terms of leasing with those for buying on credit or with cash.

The **Fair Debt Collection Practices Act (FDCPA)** applies to people and firms that regularly collect debts for others. It prohibits them from performing abusive collection practices and allows consumers to dispute a debt and halt unreasonable collection activities.

WHERE TO FILE YOUR COMPLAINT

You should file complaints about consumer credit reporting agencies or debt collection agencies with the Federal Trade Commission. The same goes for complaints about violations of the **Truth-in-Lending Act** and other federal laws involving credit issued by retail stores, department stores, and small loan and finance companies and for credit-related complaints about oil companies, public utility companies, state credit unions, or travel and entertainment credit card companies. Contact the national or regional office of the FTC, as listed in the first part of this chapter.

If a financial institution has violated a federal law discussed in this book, the regulatory agency that oversees that category of institutions might be able to help you. The following information will help you decide which agency to contact.

- **National bank.** If the word "National" appears in the bank's name or the initials N.A. or N.T.S.A. appear after its name, write Comptroller of the Currency, Consumer Affairs Division, 250 E Street, SW, Washington, DC 20219; (202) 622-2000.

- **State-chartered bank** that is a member of the Federal Reserve System, FDIC insured. The bank will display two signs on the door of the bank or in the lobby. One will say "Member, Federal Reserve System." The other will state "Deposits Insured by the Federal Deposit Insurance Corporation." For complaints of violations, write Federal Reserve System, Division of Consumer and Community Affairs, 20th and Constitution Avenue, NW, Washington, DC 20551; (202) 452-3000.

For violations of state laws, write your state banking department. For the address and telephone number, consult the state government listings in your local telephone directory.

- **State-chartered bank**, insured by the Federal Deposit Insurance Corporation (FDIC) but *not* a member of the Federal Reserve System. The bank will display a very conspicuous sign that says "Deposits Insured by the Federal Deposit Insurance Corporation." However, there will not be a sign saying "Member, Federal Reserve System." Write Federal Deposit Insurance Corporation, Office of Bank Customer Affairs, 550 17th St., NW, Washington, DC 20429; (202) 393-8400.

The FDIC maintains a toll-free telephone hot line for consumers. It allows the public to ask questions or offer views and complaints about consumer protection or civil rights matters involving FDIC-supervised banks. These include about 8,700 state-chartered banks that are not members of the Federal Reserve System. The toll-free number is (800) 424-5488, Monday through Friday, from 9 A.M. to 4 P.M. eastern standard time. In the District of Columbia, the consumer information number is (202) 942-3100. The toll-free number also reaches a telecommunication device for the deaf (TDD), which can be reached in the Washington area by calling (202) 934-3342.

• **Federally chartered** or **federally insured savings and loan association.** The word "Federal" usually appears in the name of the savings and loan association. Write the Office of Thrift Supervision in your region. (If you choose the wrong region, your complaint will be forwarded to the appropriate office.)

Northeast Region
10 Exchange Place Centre
18th Floor
Jersey City, NJ 07302
(201) 413-1000

Southeast Region
1475 Peachtree Street, NE
Atlanta, GA 30309
(404) 888-0771

Central Region
Suite 1300
200 W. Madison
Chicago, IL 60606
(312) 917-5000

Midwest Region
Suite 600
122 W. John Carpenter Freeway
Irving, TX 75034-2010
(214) 281-2000

Western Region
P.O. Box 7165
1 Montgomery Street
San Francisco, CA 94120
(415) 616-1500

Federally chartered credit unions. The term "Federal credit union" appears in the name of the credit union. Write National Credit Union Administration, 1775 Duke Street, Alexandria, VA 22314-3428; (703) 518-6300.

State-chartered, federally insured credit unions. These will display a sign indicating that the NCUA (National Credit Union Administration) insures the deposits. Write your state agency that regulates credit unions or the Federal Trade Commission.

INDEX

acceleration clauses, 107, 137
acceptance, 18–27
  and assent, 18
  defined, 18
  and implied vs. express contract, 20
  mailbox rule of, 18
  silence and, 18–19
actions, 7
adhesion, contracts of, 38–42, 178
adjustable life insurance, 186
adjustable-rate loans, 164–65
adjustable-rate mortgages (ARMs), 164–65
adjusted balance, 130
ADR (alternative dispute resolution), 4, 45
adversary proceeding, 7
advertising, 57–61
  bait and switch, 60
  false or deceptive, 57–60
  of material aspects, 59
  for motor vehicles, 99, 108
  and palming off, 59
  price tags and, 60–61
  and solicitations, 207
  and trademark rights, 58
  and unfair competition, 58
  window signs and, 60–61
agency, 24
agents, 24–26
  defined, 24
  insurance, 176
  and principals, 25
  real estate, 141–44, 152–53
agreement, 11
  installment credit, 126
  listing, 145–47
  noninstallment credit, 127
  open-end credit, 126
  open thirty-day, 127
  preliminary, 38, 147
  revolving credit, 126
  security, 107
agreement to agree, 20
airline law, 209
alternative dispute resolution (ADR), 4, 45
amendments, to contracts, 40
amortization, 163
  negative, 167
apparent authority, 25
appliance repairs, 203–4

appraiser, home, 152
appreciation, of property value, 70
APRs (annual percentage rates):
  and consumer credit, 127–28
  and financing new car purchase, 103–6
arbitration, 4
  binding, 45
  and discovery, 47
arbitration clauses, 45–47
ARMs (adjustable-rate mortgages), 164–65
assent, 18
assignment of contractual rights, 26–27
ATMs (automatic teller machines), 211–17
  deposits with, 214–15
  and disclosure forms, 213
  fees for use of, 212–14
  and minimum balances, 213
  and PIN, 215–16
  security of, 215–17
attorney, in home sale, 152
attorney-approval rider, 147, 150, 151–53
attorney review period, 149
attorneys' fees, waiver of, 54
automobiles, see cars
average daily balance, 130

bad-faith failure to indemnify, 193
bait and switch, 60
balloon loans, 165–66
banks:
  and ATMs, 211–17
  information about, 249–50
  and stop payment orders, 228–29
beneficiaries, of insurance, 184
bequests, promised, 15
binding, insurance policies, 177
binding arbitration, 45
blue sky laws, 51
breach of contract, 225–35
  consumer fraud acts, 233–35
  failure to perform, 225–26
  partial, 226
  remedies for, 226–27, 228–29
  suing for, 230–32
bridge loans, 163
brokers:
  insurance, 176
  and leases, 72
builder, buying a home from, 148
business law, 8–9

tax deductibility of, 128
mortgagor, 168
multilevel distribution schemes, 197
Multiple Listing Service (MLS), 143, 152
mutuality of obligations, 21
mutual mistake, 34

National Foundation for Consumer Credit, 136
necessaries, for minors, 12
negative amortization, 167
net lease, 115
networks, computer, 219–20
no-fault insurance, 190
nominal damages, 231
noncancellable insurance, 187
noncompliance, material, 82
noninstallment credit agreement, 127
notary public, 16

offer, 16–27
    and acceptance, 18–27
    defined, 16
    in home purchase, 147–49
    and option, 17
offeree, 16
offeror, 16
on-line computer services, 221–24
on-line warranty support, 92–94
open-end credit agreement, 126
open-end lease, 115
open listings, 145
open thirty-day agreement, 127
option, 17
optionally renewable insurance, 187
option contracts, 17
optionee, 17
oral contracts, 13–16, 42
overbooking, of travel, 208–9
over-the-limit fees, 131

palming off, 59
parol evidence rule, 14
party to be charged, 15
performance:
    impossibility of, 35
    impracticability of, 35
    specific, 231
periodic tenancy, 74
personal property, 8
persons:
    corporations as, 9
    reasonable, 19, 235
pets, 201
PIN (personal identification number), 215–16
piracy, software, 219
PMI (Private Mortgage Insurance), 160, 172
points, on mortgage, 162

Ponzi schemes, 196, 197
PPO (preferred provider plan), 183–84
preliminary agreement, 38, 147
premiums, insurance, 175, 180–81, 183
prepayment penalty, 168
previous balance, 130
price, and value, 22, 90, 157–58
price tags and window signs, 60–61
principal, in loans, 127
principals, 25, 141
Private Mortgage Insurance (PMI), 160, 172
procedural law, 50
promises, 15, 23, 24
promissory notes, 169
property:
    appreciation/depreciation of, 70
    bequests of, 15
    equity in, 70, 115
    liens on, 55, 106–7, 140, 203
    personal, 8
    real, 8
    redemption of, 107
    re-let, 80
    repossession of, 106–8
    timeshares in, 199–201, 207
property insurance, 188
property law, 8
provisions, of contract, 10–13
public policy, and law, 29–30
punitive damages, 53, 230
purchase agreement, for new car, 102–3
purchase option, 119
pyramid schemes, 195–97

ratification, of contracts, 29
real estate:
    agents, 141–42, 143–44, 152–53
    closing, 170–72
    commissions on, 146
    condos and co-ops, 173–74
    disclosures about, 157
    elements of, 140
    information sources, 241
    Interstate Land Sales Full Disclosure Act, 207
    listing agreement for, 145–47
    RESPA, 170
    transactions in, 140–47
    see also home purchase; home sale
real property, 8
reasonable observer, 235
reasonable person, 19, 235
redemption, of property, 107
reform (rewriting) of contracts, 29, 231
registered trademarks, 58
regulatory consumer protection, 5–6
release-of-lien form, 203
re-let property, 80

INDEX

ABOUT THE AUTHOR

RONALD D. COLEMAN is a lawyer at Pitney, Hardin, Kipp & Szuch, a corporate law firm in Morristown, New Jersey. His work as a commercial litigator has centered on contract disputes in the areas of insurance coverage, consumer protection, and trade law. He is author of the *Princeton Review Prelaw Companion* (Random House), has contributed to the *ABA Journal,* and is a former contributing editor of *Student Lawyer* magazine. He has taught contract law as an adjunct law professor at Seton Hall University in Newark, New Jersey, and lectures for the New York branch of Jerusalem's Aish HaTorah College of Jewish Studies. A graduate of Princeton University and Northwestern University School of Law, he lives with his family in Clifton, New Jersey.